599.7442 Fergus, Charles.
F
         Swamp screamer.

$23.00

BAKER & TAYLOR

A Rough-Shooting Dog
The Wingless Crow
Shadow Catcher
The Upland Equation

SWAMP SCREAMER

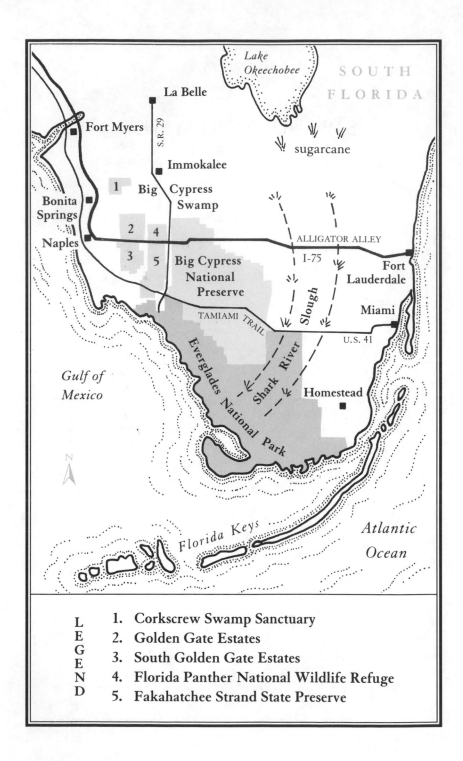

Charles Fergus

SWAMP SCREAMER

AT LARGE WITH THE FLORIDA PANTHER

NORTH POINT PRESS
Farrar, Straus and Giroux
New York

LIBRARY OF CONGRESS CATALOGING-IN-PUBLICATION DATA
Fergus, Charles.
Swamp screamer: at large with the Florida panther / Charles
Fergus. —1st ed.
p.   cm.
1. Florida panther.   2. Endangered species—Florida.   3. Wildlife
conservation—Florida.   I. Title.
QL737.C23F47   1996   599.74′428—dc20   95-6752   CIP

FOR

S. LEONARD RUBINSTEIN

CONTENTS

Let me give him one more name, and call him the Story Lion! Owing to his size, agility, alleged fierceness, and very wide geographical distribution, he is the storyteller's animal *par excellence*.

—American zoologist William T. Hornaday
discussing the many names of the puma,
in an article published in 1894

SWAMP SCREAMER

SWAMP SCREAMERS

A cool breeze sifted through the slash pines and made the palmettos rasp and rattle. We came to a mud hole, stopped, and knelt. The print was sharp and fresh: four toes fronting a three-lobed pad, three inches wide and three inches from the tip of the leading toe to the back of the pad. It was the track of a Florida panther, one of perhaps fifty living in the shrinking wild lands of South Florida, the last pumas east of the Mississippi.

I was with Deborah Jansen. Jansen is a biologist at Big Cypress National Preserve, which borders Everglades National Park to the west. That morning, she had flown and located her panthers. I knew essentially what she had done because I had accompanied her a few days earlier on a similar flight. She had donned coveralls and boots and strapped herself into the passenger seat of a single-engine Cessna. The craft had risen above the grassy, watery expanse of the 2,400-square-mile preserve; above the flat land with its cypress strands and hardwood hammocks, its wet marl prairies and dry pinelands, the snowflake dots that were egrets and herons and ibises, the woods roads and swamp-buggy scars fanning out from ramshackle hunting camps. The pilot had flown in lazy arcs, banking to one side and then to the other (it had made me sick to my stomach), letting Jansen scan the terrain with the antennae clamped to the left and right wing struts of the tan-and-brown Cessna. Through earphones, Jansen listened for radio signals from the transmitter collars worn by the three panthers she was monitoring. Detecting a signal, she began switching from one antenna to the other—left, right, left, right—and directing the pilot toward the stronger pulse. Soon the Cessna was describing a tight circle above a lithe tawny cat tucked away in the green landscape.

Without ever actually seeing him, Jansen had located panther number 42, a young male, in a remote part of the preserve known as Raccoon Point. On a map, she had fixed his position just north of the trail we were now easing along. The trail was slick with brown mud. It had recently been traversed by all-terrain vehicles; mingled with the marks of their knobby tires were the cloven, heart-shaped tracks of deer, the four-toed lineations of wild turkeys, the half-dollar imprints of bobcats, and, in mud hole after mud hole, the big rounded pug marks of the panther.

Number 42 was new to Raccoon Point. He was the forty-second wild panther in the state of Florida to be fitted with a radio collar. He had been born in Everglades National Park two years earlier. His father was also his brother. His father was alive, but their mother was dead. When she and the one other female panther in the Everglades died unexpectedly in the summer of 1991, the tiny population there had fallen apart. Driven to find others of his kind, 42 had done the improbable: headed west across Shark River Slough (the word, a regional term, is pronounced SLOO), a shallow, grassy watercourse five miles wide; traversed a busy highway; and, having traveled some sixty miles, homed in on the two female panthers, numbers 23 and 38, that Jansen had been monitoring for two years. In those years, neither female had mated (there had been no proximate males with whom to consort) or given birth to kittens.

The Everglades male had stayed with Number 38 for a week. Once, from the air, Jansen had spotted the two cats walking side by side through the sawgrass. Now, based on today's earlier radio-locations, she was sure that the male had left Number 38 and gotten with Number 23, whom Jansen calls Annie. The panthers, Jansen believed, were together in a hammock ("hammock" comes from a West Indian word meaning "shady place"), a slight rise of land supporting a jungle-like growth of shrubs and trees.

Jansen is a trim woman in her mid-forties, of medium height, with graying, sun-bleached hair and piercing pale-blue eyes. She had been generous to me, a visiting writer and a stranger, taking me along while she did her fieldwork and even letting me bunk on the screened-in porch of the small house she rents on the preserve. During our days together, I had discovered that Jansen does not waste words under normal circumstances; at Raccoon Point that evening she was practically silent. She shrugged off her backpack, got out some sections of metal tubing, and fitted them together into an antenna. The antenna was shaped like the letter H laid out flat, one foot by two feet in size, with a wooden handle projecting from the underside. Jansen plugged a wire from the antenna into a small receiver kept in her other hand. She adjusted a dial, raised the antenna above her head, and moved it slowly from side to side.

Chirp. Chirp. Chirp. Chirp. A high-pitched tone issued from the receiver. Jansen turned the antenna in smaller and smaller arcs. She looked like a priest or a shaman conducting a ritual in the woods. The chirping sound strengthened, faded, strengthened again. When the antenna finally stopped moving—the receiver chirping crisply—it pointed at a hammock a hundred yards away.

"Annie," Jansen whispered.

She changed the frequency setting while keeping the antenna directed toward the hammock.

Chirp. Chirp. Chirp. Chirp. The same strong, regular pulse.

"Forty-two," Jansen said. "They're together."

We sat behind a screen of brush and ate a picnic supper. We held off on the potato chips, afraid that the crunching might carry. The dusk deepened. Chuck-will's-widows fluttered after insects between the pines. A barred owl called in the distance, a hollow-voiced, ornate *Who cooks for you, who cooks for you-all?* Jansen checked both frequencies again. The signals remained strong. The breeze was in our faces, so probably the panthers had not smelled our scent; it seemed possible that they had heard us, despite our efforts to walk quietly. But if they knew that humans were close by, it had not made them move off.

In the distance, an oil pump thumped rhythmically. Oil exploration and production continue in the Big Cypress, just one of many compromises that led to the preserve's establishment in 1974. (A National Preserve is much like a National Park, except that certain activities not permitted in a park—oil extraction, logging, hunting, and the use of conveyances such as swamp buggies and all-terrain vehicles—may go on in a preserve.) To reach this place, Jansen and I had unlocked a gate, driven out the oil company's gravel road, parked at a wide spot, and hiked half a mile along the ATV trail. Now we sat in the gathering darkness, our eyes and ears straining toward the hammock. We waited. Quietly swatted a few mosquitoes.

Yowwwwwl! The cry was sharp and descending.

Yowwwwwwwwwl! Like a street cat's caterwaul, but throatier and much louder. The sound filled the glade. Which cat—male or female? Were they mating? I had read that few people, even seasoned cat hunters and wildlife biologists, had ever actually heard pumas caterwauling; some even doubted that pumas vocalized in this manner. Had I not known there were two such creatures close by, the sound might have terrified me. As it was, I wondered if I *should* feel terrified. Jansen obviously did not; she was grinning. We had not come specifically to hear panthers caterwauling. We had come to look for tracks and, just maybe, to glimpse a shadowy form at dusk. We had come so that Jansen, using the hand-held antenna, could confirm on the ground the tryst she had inferred from the air.

The yowling was visceral, uplifting, the sound of great beasts that—although collared, numbered, and kept under near-constant surveillance—still held some control over their lives.

The cat yowled again and again, maybe half a dozen times more, and fell silent.

Fireflies blinked across the pinelands. Stars brightened in the purple-black sky. Cabbage palms were spiky black hulks. The barred owl kept calling, farther off now but still distinct, its voice an intricate counterpoint to the dull mechanical throbbing of the oil pump. The air grew cool and damp; through it came the breeze, warm and wonderfully fragrant, soughing in the pines. To the east, a bank of clouds hung low over the horizon, reflecting an orangish glow: Miami. We heard no more yowls. After a while we packed the gear and picked our way out, following the trail between the pines.

The Florida panther is not really a panther. "Panther" is more properly a term for the leopard, *Panthera pardus*, a spotted cat living in Africa and Asia. The panther of Florida is actually a puma, a member of the species *Felis concolor*, whose Latin binomial means "cat of one color." In the Western United States, the puma is known as "cougar" (from the Portuguese *cuguardo*, an evolved form of a South American Indian word), "mountain lion," or just plain "lion." In the Northeast, where it is officially considered extinct, it is called "catamount" (for "cat of the mountain"), "panther," and its variant, "painter." The most broadly accepted name, puma, comes from the Quechua, a language of the Andes; apparently the word is not a descriptive term and is simply a name for the big cat. (The Incas of ancient Peru revered the puma. They thought that eclipses occurred when a puma tried to eat the sun. They depicted the animal in stone friezes, named important citizens after it, and kept pumas in underground labyrinths, feeding them on criminals and traitors.) Today, *Felis concolor* ranges throughout South America as far south as Patagonia. It inhabits Central America and much of Western North America from Texas to British Columbia. Before European settlement, its distribution in the New World was greater than that of any other wild mammal. (It may still be.) It preys on creatures as small as grasshoppers and as large as elk. It is the largest feline predator across much of its range (the jaguar of Central and South America is marginally larger), up to eight feet from its nose to the tip of its two- to three-foot tail, weighing seventy-five pounds (a small female) to 250 pounds (a large male).

Taxonomists have split the species into as many as thirty sub-species, or races, including the Texas puma (*Felis concolor stanleyana*, named for Stanley Young, a hunter once employed by the federal government to destroy pumas and other predators), the Yuma puma (*Felis concolor browni*, a rare taxon of Arizona), *hippolestes* ("horse killer"), *missoulensis, californica, oregonensis, azteca, costaricensis, patagonica, capricornensis*—too many subspecies for the concept to have much meaning. They are all the same animal, they could all interbreed, they live in jungles, grasslands, forests, and deserts, from sea level to seventeen thousand feet, in wildernesses and on the edges of cities, thirty variants of puma, thirty races, of which the Florida panther—*Felis concolor coryi*—is one.

It is called *coryi* because a man named Charles Cory shot one at the end of the nineteenth century and described the animal for science. Cory was curator of the Department of Ornithology at the Field Museum of Natural History in Chicago. He was also an avid sportsman, and in 1895 he went panther hunting in the Everglades along with four other men, including a local guide named John Davis. The party was equipped with horse-drawn wagons, tents, and dogs. It took them from the middle of February until the middle of April to kill their first panther, which the professor shot with a rifle after the dogs had brought it to bay against a cypress log. The panther, a female, measured seven feet from her nose to the tip of her tail. At first taxonomists thought the cat a wholly new species, but eventually they realized it was just another sort of puma.

In 1896, in his book *Hunting and Fishing in Florida*, Cory wrote:

> The Florida Panther is still not uncommon in the more unsettled portions of the State. It is somewhat smaller and more rufous in color than its Northern brethren, and its feet are smaller in proportion to the size of the animal. It is comparatively shy and is difficult to find on account of its habit of continually wandering about, rarely staying long in one place unless attracted there by an unusual abundance of food, such as in the vicinity of a hog camp or where deer are very plenty; but as a rule they move about a great deal, often traveling twenty miles or more in a night.

Three and a half centuries before Cory described the panther, Hernando de Soto, in an account of his expedition through Florida in 1539, observed that the Indians there guarded their mortuaries after dark to keep panthers from eating the dead. The Quaker naturalist William Bartram traveled through the Southeast in the late 1700s and wrote concerning panthers: "They are very large, strong, and fierce, and are too numerous, and are very mischievous." Bartram noted that the settlers also referred to the cats as "tygers." (Today there are Tiger Islands, Tiger Creeks, and Tiger Hammocks scattered across Florida.) Over the years other colloquial names grew up: swamp devil, swamp screamer, night crier, deer killer, white lion, swamp lion, tall grass creeper, and slough walker.

Because panthers preyed on livestock—and sometimes even on humans—the settlers were quick to kill them. Unlike wolves, panthers did not instinctively avoid steel traps and human scent.

Chased by dogs, they usually climbed into trees, making themselves easy targets. The settlers, and Indians in the settlers' pay, shot off the deer, the panthers' main foodstuff. Perhaps this sudden dearth of prey is the major reason that the number of cats quickly dwindled. An agricultural report published in 1854 in Mississippi noted, "The Panther is now rarely met with, except in dense and extensive swamps and canebrakes." In 1887 the state of Florida offered a five-dollar bounty for a panther scalp. Near Juno, Florida, in 1895, a female panther mauled two young men who had killed and begun skinning her kitten. (The men survived, considerably frayed about the edges, to tell the tale.) Around the turn of the century, in the sleepy settlement of Miami, a panther loped along after a woman bicyclist who was carrying a beefsteak in her basket. By the early 1900s, panthers were scarce in Tennessee, found only "in the impassable brakes and harricanes." In 1921, *A Biological Survey of Alabama* reported: "The cougar, or 'panther,' as this animal is usually called, doubtless in early times occupied the greater part of the State; it is now nearly, if not quite, exterminated." By the 1930s, many people assumed that Florida's panthers had vanished. (Though who could really tell? The swamps were still vast, despite assiduous efforts to drain them.) In 1935 a sport named David Newell brought to Florida two professional puma hunters from Arizona, along with their trail hounds. Newell and his friends camped in Big Cypress Swamp. Although the Audubon Society had written to Newell asking him not to exterminate the Florida panther, he nonetheless promptly killed three panthers the first two mornings out, all within four miles of camp. In five weeks the party shot eight altogether.

For years after Newell's hunt, panthers continued to be fair game in Florida, although so few were bagged or even seen that the state finally banned hunting them in 1958. Reports of sightings kept trickling in, and occasionally a panther would get hit by a car or be shot. Many authorities believed the subspecies had been essentially extinguished. By then, times had changed, and so had attitudes. In 1967 *Felis concolor coryi* became a charter member of the federal government's endangered species list. In 1973, Ronald Nowak, a biologist, and Roy McBride, a professional hunter from Texas, went looking for Florida panthers under the auspices of the World Wildlife Fund. McBride used his pack of hounds to tree a panther along Fisheating Creek, west of Lake Okeechobee in South Florida. The cat, a female, was tranquillized and examined briefly: found to be skinny, tick-infested, her teeth worn down to nubs, maybe nine or ten years old—elderly, as wild pumas go. In 1981 a young wildlife biologist for the Florida Game Commission, after checking out thousands of reports and searching for tracks across most of the state, succeeded in capturing a panther in a mucky part of South Florida known as Fakahatchee Strand. (Roy McBride, by now free-lancing for the Game Commission, had treed it with his hounds.) The biologist, Robert Christopher Belden, called the animal panther number 1, put a radio collar around its neck, and turned it loose.

Six days after we heard the panthers caterwauling, Deborah Jansen and I returned to Raccoon Point. It was midday. We drove in on the narrow oil company road, Jansen radioing ahead periodically to alert tankers that might be barreling toward us on the flat, graveled artery. We stopped at a turnout, and from a trailer hauled behind her truck, Jansen unloaded a Yamaha 350 Big Bear four-wheel-drive all-terrain vehicle. Jansen works for the National Park Service, which administers both Big Cypress National Preserve and the adjacent Everglades National Park; they provided the monstrous ATV, Jansen drove it, and I sat on the back holding on for dear life. We bumped across ditches and bucked through puddles. Mud splashed our clothes, branches scraped our arms and legs. Finally we parked and walked.

From the air Jansen had radio-located numbers 23 and 42 together in several places; now she wanted to check the sites on the ground. She unfolded a photo-based topographic map, a complex mosaic of tan, gray, and green. Similar maps covering her office wall were freckled with hundreds of brightly colored stick-on dots, each dot inked with a panther's number and a radio-location date. As we hiked through the knee-deep grass, Jansen periodically consulted the map. The sun glared down. A red-shouldered hawk keened from the top of a tree. Red-bellied woodpeckers chattered. Lizards darted around tree trunks. I kept an eye peeled for snakes: the preserve is home to diamondback and pygmy rattlers, water moccasins, and coral snakes. Finally Jansen stopped. She looked closely at the surrounding patches of palmetto, at the scattered wind-swaying pines, at the low growth of cypress. She assembled the antenna. Number 42, the Everglades male, had left Number 23 several days earlier and moved off by himself to the west of Raccoon Point. Jansen checked his frequency and, as expected, got no response. Then she tried Annie, Number 23.

The signal was not the usual musical chirping but a flat, loud THUMP THUMP THUMP. Jansen unplugged the antenna. Even without it the receiver continued to emit its harsh, steady tone.

Jansen motioned that we should move away, and we crept off for about a hundred yards.

"How close were we?" I whispered.

"Fifty yards. Maybe less. Did you see that big clump of palmetto? She must have been in it."

"She just lay there and let us walk right up to her?"

Jansen, who appeared quite unruffled, nodded. "She felt secure. Anyway, she's used to people."

Annie, Number 23, had been born in Everglades National Park five years earlier. Her mother, Number 15, had been captured and collared by another Park Service biologist, Oron Bass. Bass, whom everyone calls Sonny, had filled me in on what he referred to as Annie's "checkered career." When Annie was six months old, Bass had recaptured her mother by homing in on 15's collar signal and treeing her with hounds; he darted and anesthetized her, and also both of her kittens, which, fitted with their own radio collars, became panthers 22 and 23. When Annie's mother woke up, she wandered off with 22 but without 23. The biologists put 23 in a cage. A few days later they treed 15 and reunited the family. After a few months, the cats were treed again to make sure the kittens' collars were not becoming too tight. And again, amid the uproar, her mother left 23 behind. Annie (as in Little Orphan Annie) was judged too young to survive on her own. She spent a year in a rare-animal breeding compound in North Florida. There, in a fifteen-acre pen, she taught herself to hunt and kill: rabbits, hogs, and finally fawn deer. When the biologists thought her ready, she was let go in the Everglades. She wandered west into Shark River Slough. It was summer, Florida's rainy season. The water level rose in the slough, marooning Annie on a hammock, where she stayed for thirteen days, until the biologists fetched her. The following spring, released in the park again, she began prowling around: south into the mangroves on the salt-water fringe of Florida Bay, east almost to Florida City, west to Big Pine Key, near where she was born. In May she struck off westward across Shark River Slough, and this time she made it across, showing that the slough was not the absolute barrier many observers had supposed it to be. Number 23 then said goodbye to Everglades National Park and turned north into Big Cypress National Preserve. Still moving northward, she negotiated busy U.S. Route 41, the Tamiami Trail. (The name is a concatenation of "Tampa to Miami.") Finally she seemed to settle in, in the area of Big Cypress Swamp known as Raccoon Point, where it became Deborah Jansen's task to monitor her.

Jansen and I sloshed through tea-colored water, shattering the reflections of stunted cypress trees. Big Cypress Swamp is so named not because the trees are big but because the swamp is extensive. The cypresses were bare now in February; in the next few weeks they would start sending forth their feathery needles, and the swamp would become lush and green. Clinging to the rough bark and the branches of the trees were vines, ferns, and air plants. Among the air plants were spiky pineapple-like ones called bromeliads, bristly bundles six feet high, from some of which protruded long, tapering flowers like fingers dipped in red paint. A dozen ibises—white birds with neon-red legs and faces —erupted from the slough, squawking and splashing up water that caught the brilliance of the sun. High overhead a wood stork crossed the firmament, its labored flight and bent-at-the-waist posture giving it a primitive, almost saurian, aspect. The afternoon sky was a deep, cloudless blue. The water was warm where the sun beat down on it; in the shade of the cypresses it felt chilly on my calves and feet.

We reached dry land. Our shoes squelched, and grasses hissed against our legs. Palmettos rocked and rustled in the wind, their polished leaves reflecting the sunlight. Back into the water again, through another band of cypresses, their trunks flaring broadly where they met the water, their scaly, lichen-flecked bark lit golden by the lowering sun.

We came to another hammock, a rise of land about fifty yards across. Jansen was fairly certain that the cats had spent a day there together. The hammock, a few inches higher than the surrounding swamp, gave root to a mix of temperate and tropical plants, familiar species like red maple, willow, and elderberry growing alongside mahogany, wild tamarind, gumbo-limbo, poisonwood, and strangler fig. Trunks slanted, vines dangled, branches merged. Where the sun reached in, ferns and briars choked the ground. In the middle of this riot of vegetation was a clearing, like a small room, roofed over by the trees. Scratch marks furrowed the dusty soil; perhaps they had been left by the panthers making love.

Jansen searched about and found a skull. It had a long snout, faintly splayed tusks, and heavy flattened molars; it was the skull of a feral hog. In its dome, a neat round hole showed where a tooth had penetrated. The flesh had been picked clean and the brain scoured from its chamber. Jansen placed the skull, along with a few bones and a stinking flap of brown hide, into a plastic bag. She put the bag in her backpack. "At least he wasn't a total lout," she said, humor expanding her tone. "At least he took her out to dinner before he laid her."

2

THE HOT GARDENS
OF THE SUN

The pitch of the engines changed as the airliner began its descent. A murmur rose from the passengers, families headed for Disney World, white-haired tour members, college students anticipating languor in the Florida sun. Closing my book, I looked out at the land coming up: roads like children's mazes, pale against the green; crop fields, power lines, the jade grid of citrus, the straight lines of human artifice broken by a swath of pine woods and marsh following a river's broad meander. On the way down, the jet threaded between billowing clouds. Resolution sharpened: shopping centers, trailer villages, red-tiled roofs, cul-de-sacs; swimming pools, tennis courts, power-boats scratching white wakes across sun-winking lakes, orange trees speckled with fruit. The plane touched down and taxied to a stop. Outside, the baggage attendants wore shorts and T-shirts. (It had been 20 degrees and flurrying when I boarded back home.) Stepping from the aircraft, entering the covered walkway to the terminal, I smelled and felt it: plants and humus and humidity, the cloying hothouse atmosphere of the American subtropics.

Not long after, I was fiddling with the controls of a rental car, shutting off the air conditioning, pressing the button to lower a window, catching the sultry ozone perfume of a rain shower, thunder muttering in the distance, sun shafts angling down between heaped-up roseate clouds, palm fronds waving, egrets and herons haunting the water-filled roadside ditch, the car skimming along smoothly (no frost-buckled pavement here)—heading south, steady at 60, heading for panther country.

I have always been attracted to pumas, albeit in a fairly abstract way. Although I have hiked and camped in puma country all over the American West, I have never spotted one. I have read accounts of pumas in the writings of early explorers, hunters, and naturalists. The puma strikes me as a singularly graceful animal, the ultimate solitary predator. People claim that they see pumas in Pennsylvania, where I live—although the state wildlife commission tells them they are seeing ghosts, that the animal has not existed in the state since the 1800s. (At one time pumas were common in Pennsylvania. Courthouse records in my home county, Centre, show that one local hunter bagged sixty-four of them between 1820 and 1845; during that same period, some six hundred were slain in Centre County alone, with who knows how many killed statewide.)

If pumas did not still exist in Pennsylvania—and I myself had never seen one—they certainly did in Florida. Every so often I would read in a newspaper or a magazine about Florida panthers being killed on the highways, the race threatened by inbreeding or the erosion of their habitat, or a parcel of land set aside for them. My wife's parents had retired to Florida; once we took a trip with them to Everglades National Park, where the visitors' center was buzzing because moments earlier several people had watched a panther cross the road.

What was it about Florida's panther that intrigued me? It lived in a place that was part of my country—and yet seemed foreign. The panther was one form of wildlife that Floridians were actively trying to protect. It had become a symbolic creature, occupying the point of collision between people and money and nature in a state that was growing by leaps and bounds. If the panther vanished (and it looked as if it might do so, within my lifetime and maybe even within the next few years), it would take with it a powerful reason for preserving the remaining wild lands of Florida, the places that could recall for people the natural allure that had drawn so many of them to that exotic, fecund peninsula in the first place.

In 1867, at the age of twenty-nine, John Muir walked all the way from Kentucky to Florida, the fabled "land of flowers." He averaged twenty-five miles a day. He carried a compass, comb, brush, towel, soap, a change of underclothing, a small New Testament, a copy of *Paradise Lost*, and a plant press, which made many Southerners assume he was an herb doctor. He worried about alligators, bands of unreconstructed Confederate guerrillas, and "robber negroes." The journal he kept makes no mention of panthers. He ate a lot of bread, often carrying a loaf and snacking as he hiked. He put up at inns, bought lodging at farmers' homes, and, where settlement was sparse, slept in the woods, where he was tormented by mosquitoes.

Muir noted: "Florida is so watery and vine-tied that pathless wanderings are not easily possible in any direction."

"It is impossible to write the dimmest picture of plant grandeur so redundant, unfathomable."

"I am now in the hot gardens of the sun, where the palm meets the pine, longed and prayed for and often visited in dreams."

Botanizing his way southward, Muir ended up at Cedar Key on the Gulf Coast, delirious with malaria. Revived, he took ship for California, never again to return to Florida, where, he wrote, he had frequently found himself "overwhelmed by the vastness and unapproachableness of the great guarded sea of sunny plants."

As it had been for Muir, Florida was for me an enticing place that could also turn and bite. I did not worry about Confederate guerrillas, although drug traffickers were somewhat on my mind. (A friend of a friend, a bird-watcher, was sitting in his car outside a tavern in rural Florida, taking notes on the day's sightings, when a man stepped out of the bushes, apparently mistook him for a narcotics agent jotting down license-plate numbers, and put a bullet through his shoulder.) Florida—natural Florida, or what was left of it—was lush and provocative. I once watched a cardinal in a Florida swamp, and it was no longer just a pretty flash of color and song but a fearsome predator in its own right. It landed on a log next to where I was sitting, furiously crushed a black beetle between its orange mandibles, discarded with a shake of its head the beetle's jet wing sheaths and spiny legs, swallowed, defecated, and flew off. Surely I could have seen the same thing in the woods back home, but in Florida, in that green seethe of vegetation, the red bird's otherness was magnified.

I often felt disquieted in Florida, although less by the vastness or unapproachableness of the vegetation than by how harshly the hand of man had treated the land. At times I might as well have been in the suburbs of Philadelphia, surrounded as I was by highways, fast-food restaurants, shopping malls, condominiums, and motels. So much of Florida had been fenced off and paved over and built upon that it was hard to find untrammeled country; when I did find it, it was usually in a park or a preserve.

Newly arrived in Florida, tooling along in my rental car, I felt like a statistic: one of 44 million tourists who descend on the state each year. More than 14 million people live permanently in Florida, making it the fourth most populous state. An average of 2,400 new residents arrive daily, while 1,400 depart (move away, keel over on the fairway, die of gunshot wounds and in car wrecks). Both coasts are strung with cities, and roads crisscross the interior. Every hour, it is said, almost 20 acres of land are cleared in Florida. Every day, 450 acres. Every year, 164,000 acres. Conservationists aver that natural Florida is disappearing at twice the rate of the Brazilian rain forest. To date, people have converted about half of Florida into cities, towns, and agricultural land.

Usually I flew into Orlando, a burgeoning city in the center of the state. South of Orlando, suburbs and retirement villages checkerboard the Lake Wales Ridge, the sandy, unprepossessing (at roughly two hundred feet above sea level) north-south spine of central Florida. On much of the Lake Wales Ridge, orange and grapefruit groves are as unremitting as Illinois cornfields. Farther south, the citrus gives way to cattle ranching. The land is flat. The most striking vertical features are the clouds: pure white, cantaloupe, bruise-blue, maroon, lemon, straw, the colors intensifying and waning in the shifting light. Egrets perch on the backs of flop-eared cattle. Tall grasses wave in the warm wind. The prairies suggest a great savanna, dotted with clumps of palmetto and cabbage palm, in the distance a meandering line of trees that signals a slow-moving watercourse. (John Muir: "No stream that I crossed to-day appeared to have the least idea where it was going.")

Lake Okeechobee is a prominent enough landform to appear on the state silhouette decorating the Florida automobile license plate; it looks like a bullet hole, just below waist level. After the Great Lakes, Okeechobee is the largest lake in the lower forty-eight states. "Okeechobee" means "big water" in the language of the Seminole Indians. Big, but not deep. In places, it is said, one can walk out into the lake beyond sight of land, and stand with one's head above water. In the summer the lake swells and deepens as thunderclouds track in daily from the oceans surrounding the Florida peninsula, dumping rain on the lake itself and on the land whose streams and rivers drain into it. Sixty inches of rain fall on South Florida each year. Okeechobee leaks its waters southward through a broad, shallow flow: Shark River Slough, which curves around to the southwest into the Gulf of Mexico. The land tilts seaward at approximately two inches per mile. Before humans changed things, the water took nearly a year to travel the eighty or so miles from Okeechobee to the ocean. On its way, it nurtured the sawgrass plains, prairies, and cypress swamps of the Everglades and the Big Cypress, which together constitute the largest fresh-water marsh in the world.

In 1905 the newly elected governor of Florida, a man named Napoleon Bonaparte Broward, began making good on a campaign promise to drain the Everglades and open the land for development. Since then, an ever-expanding system of canals and dikes has altered the flow of water. Twice in the 1940s hurricanes slung Lake Okeechobee out of its bed and sent it surging across the land (as, no doubt, it had done periodically throughout time), drowning people by the hundreds. To control the lake, the U.S. Army Corps of Engineers ringed it with an earthen dike. Today, no water leaves Okeechobee except by human intention. Gauges and computers monitor the movement of the water. It is sluiced into the ocean when flooding seems imminent. At other times, it trickles down the canals to irrigate tomatoes, squash, cucumbers, wax beans, green beans (when you buy fresh vegetables in the dead of winter, they probably come from Florida). It slakes the thirst of the sun-coast cities: Miami, Fort Lauderdale, West Palm Beach. Any water that is left is shunted to the Everglades. Usually it is not enough. For decades the Glades have been drying out, the sloughs shrinking, dry-land plants taking over the marsh, the region's renowned wading birds—the formerly immense flocks of herons, egrets, ibises, spoonbills, and wood storks—dwindling to a tithe of their number.

The land just south of Okeechobee is given over to sugar cane. The plants grow in a monotonous jungle of tall green stalks. Clewiston, home of the corporate headquarters of U.S. Sugar, bills itself as "the sweetest town in America." In the fields that stretch for miles south of Clewiston, buses disgorge lean men with colored kerchiefs tied around their heads; most of the workers are from the Caribbean, and their skin is as dark as the muck soil. They cut the cane with long knives that flash in the sun. After the harvest, the plants' leaves are burned, and clouds of mustard-colored smoke drift across the land. The growing of sugar cane has consumed the topsoil, whose depth has dwindled from feet to inches. In Florida, the sugar industry is known as "Big Sugar." It is subsidized to the hilt by the state and federal governments. (Sugar cane is grown much more easily and economically in places farther south, such as Cuba.) Fertilizer runoff and wastes from sugar-processing plants pollute Lake Okeechobee and the Everglades; scientists believe that fallout from the cane smoke is bathing South Florida with mercury, which destroys brain cells and can be passed from mother to offspring in the womb. In the last few years, at least three Florida panthers have turned up dead, with alarmingly high levels of mercury in their bodies.

South and west of the cane lie more big ranches. Up until the late 1940s, this area was still unfenced—open range. Today you can drive along a back road and see the same ranch's NO TRESPASSING signs for ten miles. A family named Lykes is said to be the state's largest private landowner, with 277,000 acres, amounting to three-quarters of one county. It is common knowledge that panthers live on Lykes land, but the family will not let biologists enter and study them. The ranchlands are an empty country, stark and beautiful, the prairie interspersed with pine woods and cypress swamps. Few tourists see this part of the Sunshine State. On one of my trips I encountered a bird-watcher from Scotland out improving his life list in the lonely scrublands north of La Belle. In

Scots parlance, South Florida was "mamba country": miles and miles of bugger-all, miles and miles of nothing.

La Belle, population 8,000, is the seat of Hendry County; it is named for one (or more) of the daughters—Laura, Lee, and Belle—of pioneer Captain Francis Hendry. Each year the town hosts a Swamp Cabbage Festival in honor of the Florida state tree, the cabbage palm. From the local telephone directory: "Much of the citizenry of Florida, including La Belle, initially came from the defeated South in our own Civil War. The make up of our area was then heavily peopled by adventurers, escapees from the Georgia chain gang, hunters and trappers." Today La Belle has businesses where you can arrange to have your crops pollinated by honeybees, and where you can buy queen bees, brown cakes of beeswax, and twelve pounds of honey (orange blossom or palmetto) in a gallon jar. The courthouse, a yellow brick edifice with a bell tower, is shaded by ancient live oaks. Trailer slums edge the town. Mexican farmworkers, in sweat-stained cowboy hats and shirts open to the navel, shop in the local U Save grocery. One day in the U Save I bought some tangerines and tangelos. I got the bags mixed up before I reached the checkout. The cashier could not tell the fruit apart, and arbitrarily decided they were all tangelos. Behind me in line a smiling heavyset woman with curly blond hair told me, "You shouldn't of bought all that citrus, you could come out to my house and get it for nothin'. Ah hate citrus. My husband brings it home from work and it just sets. Lived here all my life, and I've never liked it. Where you from, honey?"

"Pennsylvania."

"No, I mean hereabouts in La Belle."

"Well, I live in Pennsylvania. I'm just passing through."

"*Pennsylvania?* My Lord. I was there once. Here in La Belle, I was seein' this boy from Pennsylvania. One day he said, 'I'd like to borrow your car and drive home.' When he said 'home,' it turned out he meant Pennsylvania! They arrested him up there, but they wouldn't send my car back. It was ninety degrees when I got on the plane in Tampa, and when I landed in Pittsburgh there was three foot of snow on the ground. I always said I'd do like Marilyn Monroe and run naked in the snow if I ever saw any. So I peeled off my clothes right there at the airport, and that's just what I did!" She laughed loudly. Other customers standing in line smiled. "The judge told me that if I ever came back to Pennsylvania again, I should try to keep my clothes on."

I was so nonplussed by this exchange that I failed to ask if she had ever seen a panther.

From La Belle, two-lane Florida Route 29 arrows south to Immokalee, a small town that nevertheless manages to string itself out, its long main street lined with warehouses, agricultural supply stores, and tractor dealerships. Pickup trucks have American flag decals in their rear windows, with the message "These colors don't run." On Sunday mornings the radio plays Latino music. Immokalee has a tortilla takeout, a Spanish-American market, and a reputation for knife fights on Saturday night. The Hispanics work in the crop and vegetable fields, on the ranches, or in the expanding citrus industry, which many conservationists identify as the single largest threat to the Florida panther. Following a series of damaging freezes in the 1980s in central Florida, corporations began moving their groves southward. Big processing plants that turn oranges into juice concentrate stand beside the highway; grackles peck at insects among the fruit heaped in open-bed trailers. In the four counties around Immokalee, which contain the best remaining panther habitat in South Florida, more than half the private land now being used by panthers—most of it pine woods and unimproved range—has received state permits for conversion to citriculture.

South of Immokalee the land becomes less hospitable to farming, lower and wetter, the prairie interrupted more frequently by sloughs and swamps. Airboats and swamp buggies sit parked in people's yards, like snowmobiles up North. The road perches on a barrow of spoil; the ditch that contributed the fill, on the road's east side, brims with dark water.

On the berm, yellow signs flash past:

ENTERING PANTHER HABITAT
LESS THAN 30 REMAINING
PLEASE DRIVE CAREFULLY, NIGHT SPEED LIMIT 45
PANTHER CROSSING NEXT 3 MILES

More panthers are killed by cars and trucks on Route 29 than by any other cause. Traveling the road, I always held to the speed limit, especially at night, although others whipped past like I was standing still. I had this worrisome vision: I would be driving along, relaxed, listening out the window to the frogs and toads shrilling, smelling the myriad rich scents of the swamp—when a tan, long-tailed cat would materialize in the headlights as it sprang onto the road in front of the car.

Two centuries ago the Florida panther lived throughout the South. To the west it merged with another subspecies, the Texas puma, *Felis concolor stanleyana*, which yet haunts the dry rimrock of the Lone Star State. To the northwest—in what is now Arkansas and Missouri—it interbred with the Rocky Mountain puma, *Felis concolor hippolestes*, now withdrawn into the fastnesses of the Rockies and seemingly in no danger of extinction anytime soon. To the north, the panther blended with the Eastern mountain lion, *Felis concolor couguar*, a race whose last confirmed member was killed in New York's Adirondack range in the winter of 1908.

It is not that the pumas of the Southeast were pushed ever southward until they all ended up in Florida. Panthers in eastern Texas, Louisiana, Mississippi, Alabama, Georgia, South Carolina, Tennessee, Arkansas, and Missouri were eradicated when settlers transformed the land from swamps and woods into towns and farms. Ecologists suggest that a peak population of 1,360 panthers may have inhabited Florida alone, before European settlement. The panthers living in Florida today—the current estimate is fifty adults and half again as many kittens—descend from animals that inhabited a terrain so forbidding and inaccessible that people were unable or disinclined to wipe them out.

The Florida panther is considered one of the rarest mammals in the world. In Florida, if convicted of deliberately killing a panther, you are adjudged a felon and can be jailed for five years. Under the federal Endangered Species Act, not only is it a crime to kill a panther but it is unlawful to destroy panther habitat. The laws notwithstanding, people still shoot panthers on occasion and wreck their habitat at a terrific rate.

Conservationists call the panther a "flagship species," meaning that its presence affords at least some protection to other less glamorous creatures sharing its realm. People argue over how best to help the panther. They file lawsuits concerning the panther. A panther is one thing to a field biologist, and another thing to a bureaucrat, a deer hunter, an animal-rights activist, a rancher, a suburbanite, and a corporate head who suspects the beasts are skulking on land scheduled to become an orange grove or a waste incinerator site or an office complex. (Some Floridians love panthers to the point of emulating them. One man, Jim McMullen, soaked himself in puma urine and ate the leftovers at panther kills. After months of sneaking about in the swamps—a quest that is detailed in his book, *Cry of the Panther*, published in 1984— McMullen claimed to have achieved "affinity" with the panther when he looked one in the eye.)

In Florida in 1982, schoolchildren picked the panther as the state animal, rejecting the alligator and the manatee. To most of the general public, the panther constitutes a type of "charismatic megafauna," a phrase coined to describe the larger and more romantic forms of endangered wildlife. The grizzly bear, peregrine falcon, whooping crane, red wolf—even the nude-headed, carrion-eating California condor—are all charismatic megafauna. The Ozark big-eared bat and New Mexican ridge-nosed rattlesnake and Houston toad and Kretschmarr Cave mold beetle and desert pupfish and white wartyback pearly mussel (let alone the hundreds of endangered plants) inspire less devotion. The Endangered Species Act does not play favorites. In theory, it extends as much protection to the blue-tailed mole skink (a threatened lizardlike denizen of the sandy uplands of central Florida) as it does to the panther. In practical terms, however, the panther gets the attention, while the "creepy-crawlies" (as some biologists refer to skinks and other obscure or unpopular creatures) must languish. In 1990, over half the $100 million spent on endangered life forms by state and federal governments went toward saving only eleven species (the panther included)—less than 2 percent of those on the endangered species list.

The official line is that panthers inhabit only southernmost Florida. Yet people report them from Okefenokee Swamp on the Georgia line. From the pine forests of the northern Panhandle. The brakes along the Suwannee River. The undeveloped Big Bend country south of Tallahassee. The Ocala National Forest north of Orlando. Up and down the St. Johns River, flowing through its largely undeveloped corridor from Orlando north to Jacksonville. Maybe these are alien pumas. The Florida Game Commission licenses over one thousand pumas owned by private citizens and menageries, and undoubtedly some of these cats escape or are turned loose. (Then there are the unlicensed pumas, such as the one, of an indeterminate race, which game wardens rescued from a cage in a Miami junkyard. The cat was to have been sacrificed in a ceremony of the Santeria religion, a Cuban cult that blends animistic African beliefs with Roman Catholicism.) All over Florida, people see panthers: ambling across roads in broad daylight, drinking from highway culverts, loping across golf courses, popping their heads up in vegetable gardens. Here is a typical account, filed in 1989, recording a sighting made by a ten-year-old girl in a partially developed housing subdivision in Highlands County, Florida:

> The child was playing in the small mowed back yard of the house adjacent to dense flatwoods. She was retrieving a ball that had rolled to within a few inches of the lawn. As she bent to pick up the ball, she found herself looking into the face of a panther lying in the tall grass and brush, apparently not more than 2 to 3 ft. away. The cat got up, walked away a short distance, then turned around to look at the child, who ran to the house to tell her mother.

Despite the great volume of reports, flesh-and-blood panthers almost never show up anywhere outside South Florida—roughly from Lake Okeechobee southward. Usually they are found after their radio collars go into a "mortality mode," a speeded-up dirge of chirps that commences two hours after the transmitters have ceased all movement. Panthers inhabit the considerable public land in South Florida (much of it low, wet, and less productive of prey than the drier, more-fertile private lands to the north), including Big Cypress National Preserve, Fakahatchee Strand State Preserve, and the Florida Panther National Wildlife Refuge. With the exception of one aging male, no longer do they live in Everglades National Park. They hunt for deer and hogs on sprawling landscam ghost towns, where roads grid the swamp, street signs go to rust, and houses cannot be found. They range through the

52,000 acres of the Big Cypress Seminole Indian Reservation and the 267,000 acres of the adjoining Miccosukee Indian Reservation. They slip through the suburbs of Naples and Fort Myers, fast-growing cities pinching in on South Florida from the west. They go north into the excellent but insecure habitat on the private cattle ranches of Hendry, Glades, Charlotte, and De Soto Counties.

When I first visited Florida, I drove around the state talking to people about panthers. Of necessity, much of my time was spent in cities and towns. When I found good country—when I got out from behind the windshield and out of the air conditioning and entered what was left of the real Florida—I met strange and lovely things.

Thigh-deep in Fakahatchee Strand, surrounded by bird chatter and cypress knees and epiphytic orchids and strap ferns, I watched an alligator slip off a log and swim straight toward me, leaving a trail of bubbles on the olive-colored water. (My guide assured me, correctly as it turned out, that the reptile was only seeking the safety of deep water between itself and us.) Camped in the pine woods, safely behind mosquito netting, I listened to the winged hordes raising their bloodthirsty song and remembered the miseries of Muir. One night I was jerked awake, my scalp tingling, by an owl screaming in a tree above my tent. I was startled by snakes, hectored by horseflies, and sliced by cutgrass. I broke out in a rash from poison ivy. One of my toenails developed a fungal infection and fell off. I dodged a hurricane. I shivered in the January rain in North Florida and sweltered in the August sun in South Florida. Mold grew on my toothbrush. The pages of my notebooks wrinkled in the damp. I saw anole lizards and sand skinks and pig frogs and gopher tortoises. I watched bald eagles and caracaras and limpkins and burrowing owls and swallow-tailed kites that, soaring against the perfect blue sky, looked like bandleaders decked out in white tuxedos. Riding in an airplane with a wildlife biologist, I saw a panther padding across a prairie, like a long tawny fish in a sea of grass.

3

WIRING THEM UP

Robert Christopher Belden, the biologist who collared the first Florida panther, is a quiet, reserved man in his late forties. He goes by the nickname Chris. He is slender, of medium height, his eyes alert and brown as tannin water. His beard—long, black, and crinkly—contrasts with the formality of his drab uniform shirt bearing the epaulets and sleeve patches of the Florida Game Commission. One afternoon I met with Belden at his home, west of Gainesville in northern Florida. The dwelling was a neat, new-looking, board-and-batten two-story that Belden called his "mountain house," a style common in his native Tennessee. The house stood by itself in a grove of maples and pines, near a shallow, collapsed-in pit—an old phosphate mine now being reclaimed by the woods. Belden and I sat on a porch swing. The breeze whispered through the bottle-brush tips of the pines, a sibilance I would hear all over Florida.

In 1976, when Belden was a twenty-nine-year-old biologist not long out of graduate school, the Florida Game Commission assigned him the task of organizing and running a Florida Panther Record Clearinghouse. Floridians were urged to contact him whenever they saw panthers or found their tracks. "People reported tracks that had been made by dogs, bobcats, otters, alligators, and raccoons," said Belden. "They sent in pictures of house cats. They found panthers, dead on the road, that, when I got there, turned out to be deer, foxes, and, one time, a brindled pit bull terrier swollen up like a fifty-five gallon drum." And every once in a while someone reported a panther that turned out to be a panther.

By 1980 Belden had investigated more than a thousand reports statewide. All the verifiable records—tracks, and four actual panthers (three killed by cars, one shot by a turkey hunter who claimed the cat had attacked him)—came from South Florida. It was in South Florida that Ronald Nowak and Roy McBride, working for the World Wildlife Fund, had captured and briefly examined the decrepit female panther in 1973.

"We had gotten several reliable reports of cats in Fakahatchee Strand," Belden told me. "When we went there, we pretty quickly found tracks and scrapes." (A "scrape" is a mark in the soil made by a panther to delineate its personal territory.) Said Belden, "I proposed that the Game Commission try to capture some panthers, put radio collars on them, and study them, as had been done with pumas out West." The Game Commission agreed to the proposal. They engaged Roy McBride, of Alpine, Texas, former federal animal-control agent, fount of knowledge about predators the world over, killer of pumas and cheetahs and jaguars and leopards, hunter for hire. In February 1981 McBride loosed his cat-wise hounds on the old logging roads of Fakahatchee Strand. On the morning of the fourth day of hunting they encountered hot scent and, after a brief chase, were howling and leaping at the base of a tree.

McBride contacted Belden by radio. In an article, "It Was the Hunt of a Lifetime," which Belden later prepared for *Florida Wildlife* magazine, he wrote: "I had been studying panther sign in this South Florida swamp for four years but had never seen a panther in the wild. It sounded like I would soon get the chance."

Belden and his assistants started driving down the nearest logging road. They had gone a quarter of a mile over the rugged thoroughfare—choked by briars and brush, and rutted from years of swamp buggy use—when their truck bottomed out in a mud hole so deep that the front bumper rested on one side and the back bumper rested on the other. The biologists jumped out of the truck, loaded themselves down with capture equipment, and ran down the logging road. Every few hundred yards Belden would stop and use his antenna to find a radio signal from the transmitter collars worn by McBride's hounds. When the signal grew strong, and seemed to come from a point off to the side of the logging road, Belden and his colleagues waded into the swamp. They shouldered their way through thick-growing trees smothered with ferns and air plants. They sloshed through knee-deep water. They encountered concertina tangles of greenbriar and walls of under-brush so dense that they had to throw their weight against the vegetation to force a passage.

Finally, at 10:30 in the morning, an hour and a half after the panther had treed, the biologists heard the hounds barking. Hur-rying ahead, they spotted the dogs. Belden lifted up his eyes. "There," he wrote in his article for *Florida Wildlife*, "about fifteen feet up in a water oak was the first live Florida panther that I had ever seen. He looked huge!"

The biologists gathered beneath the tree. Belden and McBride estimated the weight of the cat at a hundred pounds, and Belden drew a suitable drug dose into a dart syringe. To McBride, prac-ticed in riflery, went the task of shooting the dart. He made a direct hit, on the panther's rump. After seven minutes the panther's mouth was hanging open slightly and his eyes were flickering. He stretched out on a limb. Since it was his research project, Belden felt duty-bound to be the one to scale the tree. He started climbing. He got about ten feet up and noticed that the top of the tree was dead and appeared to be weak. He hesitated. He tied a rope around the trunk and let it down to his assistants, thinking they might be able to shake the panther out. Just then McBride yelled, "He's coming down, you better get out of there!" Belden had started down the trunk when McBride yelled again. By now the panther was losing his balance. He was hanging above Belden's head by his front claws, which were slipping. Belden let go and saw the ground rushing up.

"I don't remember who hit the ground first, me or the panther," Belden told me. "The cat went stumbling off, and Roy ran him down and caught him by the tail. I grabbed him by the hind foot. He fell over, and I gave him another dose of the drug, and he passed out."

The panther, a male, weighed 120 pounds. He was six feet ten inches long. McBride checked the wear on the panther's teeth and pronounced him ten years old: another ancient cat. The panther had short grayish-tan fur. He had a coppery ridge running along his back, with an odd whorl of fur, like a cowlick, between his shoulders. His tail was thick like any puma's tail, but with one difference, something that Belden had noted on the road-killed panthers he had examined: the tip of the tail had a crook in it, like the last joint of a stiffened finger bent sharply to one side.

Thus began a stimulating, draining, embittering, and ultimately uplifting chapter of Chris Belden's life. He caught panther number 2 in 1981 and six more the next year. His photograph appeared in newspapers and magazines. He found himself in demand at wildlife conferences. The fact that pumas still existed east of the Mississippi astonished and captivated many people. The panther as a concept ("Save the panther!") began gaining momentum. Biologists and conservationists now estimated the number of panthers in Florida at anything from twelve to three hundred—even the larger figure a dangerously small one as animal populations go.

Belden's collared panthers all lived in and around Fakahatchee Strand, in Collier County in southwestern Florida. A strand is a long, linear forest occupying a swampy, troughlike depression where, over the centuries, soil has collected. Fakahatchee Strand is twenty miles long and five miles wide, running north-to-south. It is thickly grown with cypress, water oak, pop ash, red maple, and gumbo-limbo trees. The largest stand of royal palm trees in North America occurs in Fakahatchee Strand. There are plants thriving in the Fakahatchee that grow nowhere else on the continent but are common on islands in the Caribbean. (Perhaps hurricanes deposit the plants' seeds in the strand.) In summer the Fakahatchee fills up with water two to three feet deep; in winter the water goes down and in some places dries up altogether. "Fakahatchee" comes from the language of the Miccosukee, one of two remaining Indian tribes of Florida. It means forked river, although the forks the Indians were describing are not easy to identify. In the last century an Anglo-American traveler bestowed on Fakahatchee Strand the unoriginal cognomen "The Impenetrable Swamp." In the 1940s a lumber company used steam-powered dredges to penetrate it, heaping up the mucky soil into a network of raised tramways upon which railroad tracks were laid. The loggers took the virgin cypress—trees seven hundred years old and up to twenty-five feet in girth—and sold their water-resistant wood for house siding, pickle barrels, stadium seats, and the hulls of PT boats. After the loggers had gone, a land company bought Fakahatchee Strand, tried to drain it, broke it up into parcels, and sold it sight unseen to Northerners looking for their little piece of paradise, their five-acre ranchette in the Florida sun. Today, a few hunting camps dot Fakahatchee Strand, but most of it is owned by the state of Florida, the old tram roads gated off, the interior designated a preserve.

"I was living up in Gainesville at the time," Belden told me. "My wife and I had two young daughters. I would spend a week at home with them, then go south and try to monitor the cats we had collared—try to figure out where they lived, what they hunted, what they ate, how they interacted with each other." Just keeping track of the cats proved more difficult than anyone had imagined. "I had this red Ford pickup truck. In its bed was a telescoping mast that could raise an antenna twenty feet into the air. For sixteen hours a day I would drive the roads around Fak-ahatchee Strand and Big Cypress, and every mile I would stop, climb into the bed of the truck, crank up the antenna, and swivel it 360 degrees, trying to pick up a radio signal. Then I'd crank the antenna down, drive on another mile, stop, and do it again." Ninety-nine times out of one hundred, Belden would fail to detect a signal. "It took us six months to figure out we couldn't track them from the ground. When we started flying, we could locate all the cats nearly every day. That's when we discovered how mobile they are. It was nothing for one to move twenty miles in a night."

Sometimes, after fixing on a panther from the air, Belden would take a hand-held antenna and walk in on the animal. "I would never see one," he recalled. The panthers would see him, however. "They would hold still and let me pass, then sneak away. Or they might circle around behind me—not to attack me, but to avoid me. One time I walked in on a cat at night. He was lying in a little hammock just off a busy highway. I thought maybe he'd been hit by a car." Accompanied by Sonny Bass, the biologist from Everglades National Park, Belden insinuated himself into a tangle of stems, trunks, and vines. "I had this little two-cell flash-light that you had to jiggle every so often to get it to work. When we got close, I laid the antenna on the ground and still got a real strong beep. The cat had to be within ten or fifteen feet. I jiggled the light and played it all around. We couldn't see a thing. We didn't know if the cat was alive or dead. That got to me all of a sudden. I said to Sonny, 'If he's dead now, he'll still be dead tomorrow,' and we got out of there. The next day we flew, and the cat had moved a mile and a half. He hadn't been hurt at all."

Now that Belden had eight cats wearing collars, he started building a picture of the panther population. It appeared to be a stable but an aging one; most of the cats captured were from six to twelve years old. (The life expectancy of a puma in the wild is thought to be twelve years, or perhaps a few years more.) Panthers were dying on highways at an alarming rate: four deaths documented in a year and a half. Radio-location data showed that panthers tended to cross the roads at certain key points. In the heat of summer, Belden found, panthers traveled at night and holed up during the day; in winter, they sometimes moved about in daylight as well. They did not hesitate to swim across waterways; once, from the air, Belden spotted the head of a panther as it paddled across a marsh. The cats seemed unbothered by manmade racket such as rock quarrying, oil pumping, and highway traffic. They favored the dense cover of cypress strands and forests. They homed in on wildfires and often hung around the burned areas for weeks, perhaps attracted by the deer coming to feed on the succulent grasses and sprouts that pushed up after a burning.

One day in 1983, McBride's hounds ran a panther up a live oak in Fakahatchee Strand. This was to be a recapturing of panther number 3, a smallish female, to renew the batteries in her radio collar. According to Belden's records, the cat weighed seventy pounds. He prepared a dart with the same dose of the tranquillizer that he had used to sedate the animal the previous January. Because the dart rifle had been malfunctioning, the capture team elected to use a different tranquillizing gun, a pistol activated by compressed gas. A technician climbed partway up the tree, aimed the handgun, and shot from beneath the cat.

"Instead of hitting a muscle," Belden said, "the dart struck the femoral artery, on the back of the hind leg. It delivered the dose all at once. The cat was dead before she hit the ground." He paused. I found myself wondering how many times he had had to tell the story, how he had reduced and rationalized what had happened on that day. Belden had not written a magazine article about the event, although I sensed that this particular hunt, even more than the initial successful one, was for him "the hunt of a lifetime."

Belden spoke softly in his mellifluous Tennessee drawl. "I carried her out of the swamp. At that point I felt like I was carrying the whole subspecies on my shoulders. If the panther went extinct, it would be my fault. For all we knew, those eight cats were all that was left, and I had just killed one."

It is not particularly unusual for a wild animal to die after being sedated. But while another biologist might have sympathized with Belden's situation, the public and the press did not. An editorial in the *Miami Herald* labeled the panther's death "an outrage." The newspaper concluded that the panthers "should be left alone indefinitely. Let them breed and perhaps replenish their numbers, or let them live out their lives free, and wild, and in peace. Now is not the time to wire them up." Reacting to the outcry, Belden's superiors within the Florida Game Commission ordered him not to anesthetize any more cats. They quickly agreed to the appointment, by the governor of Florida, of an independent advisory committee that included scientists, academicians, and conservationists. The committee reviewed Belden's procedures and findings and pronounced them sound and of great value. Within two weeks the capture team was back in the field.

By accidentally killing the panther, Belden had riled up environmentalists and animal lovers. Presently he got himself into water that was several degrees warmer. Based on his radio-telemetry data, Belden thought that the hunting activities of humans might be harming Florida's panthers. He had found that huge expanses of public land, including most of Big Cypress National Preserve, appeared to be barren of panthers; this land was also heavily hunted for deer, hogs, and turkeys. He pointed out, at public meetings and to the press, that if hunters began killing fewer deer, the number of panthers might rise in response.

Belden's employer, the Florida Game Commission, exists to serve as much as to regulate the state's hunters and is acutely sensitive to pressure from them. The hunters did not like Belden's suggestions of shorter hunting seasons and fewer acres open to hunting. The Game Commission would do nothing to alienate them. Frustrated, and profoundly disturbed by the death of panther number 3, Belden resigned as chief biologist on the project.

He told me, "This is an area of my life that I've built a little wall around." He stared out at the woods. The porch swing had stopped gliding. "After I left South Florida, I went into a deep depression," he said. "My marriage almost fell apart. Then finally I read *The Power of Positive Thinking* by Norman Vincent Peale. And I realized that all of those things had happened for a purpose. The people, the events, the panther, were all instruments directing my life. I received Jesus Christ at that time. That's the one good thing that came out of it." In Belden's office in Gainesville, amid the usual biologist's bric-a-brac of skulls, maps, and plaster casts of tracks, I had noticed a stack of pamphlets with the message: "Do You Know for Certain That You Have Eternal Life and That You Will Go to Heaven When You Die?"

"People talk about the 'vortex of extinction,' " Belden continued. "The panther is in the vortex, all right. It's in the middle, or maybe way down at the bottom of it. I think that what we're doing, really, is documenting the tail end of the extinction process. We could go out next year, and all the cats could be gone."

Unless, I thought, Floridians follow through with genuine measures to assure the animal's survival; unless, perhaps, they even redefine what is meant by "Florida panther." Over the next few years I would see Chris Belden shed the last traces of his depression, think positively, and take what I interpreted to be the first concrete steps toward bringing back the panther in Florida.

4

BIT PLAYERS AND DRAGONS

In 1834, in northern Mississippi, Mrs. Mariam Forrest, accompanied by her sister, rode ten miles to call on their nearest neighbors. Returning home at dusk, she carried a gift from the neighbors, a basketful of newly hatched chicks whose peeping filled the woods. Just before the women reached their cabin, a panther leaped from the brush. Its front claws tore into Mrs. Forrest's side and neck. Its hind claws scored her horse's rump. The plunging of the horse threw the panther off, but not before it had raked the clothes from Mrs. Forrest's back. Her screams brought her family running, and the panther fled. (Mrs. Forrest is said to have steadfastly held on to the chicks.) After her wounds were treated and she was put to bed, her son Bedford, thirteen years old, announced, "I am going to trail that panther and kill him if he stays on the earth." He called the dogs and took his rifle and set off on the panther's trail. He slogged through canebrakes and briar patches. He cut a limber grapevine and tied one end of it around the neck of an old hound: when the other dogs were out of hearing, the old dog followed their scent. Finally the pack barked treed. At break of day, the young Forrest spied the panther up a large oak, flattened against a limb. He shot the cat through the heart and was home with its hide by nine o'clock. (Nathan Bedford Forrest would later achieve fame as a general of Confederate cavalry and, after the Civil War ended, the first president, or Grand Cyclops, of the Ku Klux Klan.)

For years, people derided pumas as "cowardly" because they fled from hounds—a puma will generally run from even a single dog, an animal it could swiftly subdue—and only rarely showed aggression to humans, even those who menaced them. John James Audubon called the puma "the most cowardly of any species of its size belonging to the genus." C. Hart Merriam, director of the Bureau of Biological Survey (later to become the U.S. Fish and Wildlife Service), characterized the puma as "the most cowardly of beasts." Theodore Roosevelt—who in his writings once described the puma as the "lord of stealthy murder"—seemed a bit put out when, in one instance, a mother puma fled from the hunting hounds, leaving her kittens to be destroyed by the pack. Jim Bob Tinsley, an experienced puma hunter, wrote in 1987 in his book *The Puma: Legendary Lion of the Americas*: "The puma does display extreme caution in the presence of man and his dogs at times. Some observers consider this [to be] intelligence rather than cowardice." John Seidensticker is a biologist who studied pumas in Idaho during the 1970s. In a recent article in *Smithsonian*, he contends that the circumspect demeanor of pumas around dogs "may be a survival tactic that had its genesis in the lions' role as bit players in the Pleistocene—social subordinates of many of the truly ferocious big carnivores then occupying center stage."

The Pleistocene Epoch began a million and a half years ago and lasted until perhaps ten thousand years in the past. It is sometimes called the Age of Mammals. The variety of mammalian species living during the period is staggering. In North America alone were all the mammals we have today plus various sorts of wild horses, asses, zebras, ground sloths, tapirs, llamas, capybaras, and camels; there were five kinds of elephants, and beavers the size of black bears. Today's gray wolf abounded, as did the larger and more formidable dire wolf, now extinct. Several species of burly hyena-like dogs thrived during the Pleistocene. There was a dhole dog of the genus *Cuon*, whose closest relatives live in Asia, hunt in packs, and are fierce enough to drive tigers off kills. Also our present-day wolverine, which takes guff from nobody and nothing, and an even bigger and presumably more adamant variety known to paleontologists as "the voracious flesh-eater." Black bears and grizzly bears played third and second fiddle, respectively, to the now-extinct short-faced bear, probably the most powerful predator in America.

Pleistocene cats ranged from smallish ones, such as the bobcat and lynx, up to great predators larger than today's lions and tigers. The saber-tooth, *Smilodon*, was as big as a lion; it may have stabbed its prey with its long upper canines, or used them to tear open carcasses. (A fossil has been found of a dire-wolf skull skewered by a broken-off *Smilodon* saber.) Two sorts of cheetah loped across the plains of North America, both of them as large as or larger than the puma. The long-toothed scimitar cat was robust enough to subsist mainly on mastodon calves. The jaguar, *Panthera onca*, left its bones as far north as Nebraska and Oregon. (In Florida, Pleistocene jaguar fossils greatly outnumber puma fossils from the same period.) The American lion—half again as big as the modern African species—inhabited Europe, Africa, and Asia, as well as North and South America, giving it perhaps the greatest range of any land mammal ever.

A trove of Pleistocene fossils has turned up at Rancho La Brea, a site just off Wilshire Boulevard in what is now downtown Los Angeles. There, pools of tar would ooze up from the ground and become covered with dust and rainwater; when animals came to drink, they mired in the tar. The struggling creatures drew in predators and scavengers, who in turn got stuck. Artists' conceptions of these death traps usually feature a troop of animals flailing their limbs and gnashing their outsize teeth (*Smilodon* is a clear favorite), but actually, according to one leading paleontologist, "an average of only one animal entrapped per year over the 30,000 year span . . . is more than sufficient to account for the enormous number of bones recovered." Fossilized pumas from the La Brea site have canine teeth slightly smaller than those of today's pumas, and bodies slightly larger; otherwise, their skeletons are the same.

Until recently, pumas had to deal with grizzly bears and packs of gray wolves, both of which were likely to dominate them, just as pumas lord it over coyotes and bobcats. Now, however, the puma finds itself at the top of the food chain (humans, at least for the most part, excepted). The grizzly bear is gone from the Rocky Mountains, aside from a few remote parts of Wyoming and Montana. Wolves have been hounded out of forty-six of the lower forty-eight states. (Biologists are reintroducing the red wolf, *Canis rufus*, to North Carolina and the gray wolf, *Canis lupus*, to Yellowstone National Park.) The puma still must contend with the jaguar in Central and South America, but perhaps the two do not meet each other very often; jaguars prefer hot lowland habitats, while pumas favor more open forests in the foothills and the mountains. The jaguar is heavier than the puma and more thickly muscled; the claws of the puma are larger and longer than those of the jaguar. Observers disagree as to which is the superior animal. Some claim that a puma, with its mobility and speed, will outfight a jaguar. Yet one Venezuelan scientist found evidence of an encounter between a jaguar and a puma, where all that remained of the puma were its feet.

The story of Bedford Forrest, who tracked down and killed the panther that had attacked his mother, is said to have inspired and shaped another Mississippian, Ben V. Lilly, born in 1856 and destined to become the foremost hunter of pumas that the continent has ever known. According to Lilly's biographer, J. Frank Dobie, "In Ben Lilly's mind, all panthers were dragons."

Ben Lilly's life and habits were the stuff of legend. At the time when Lilly was living in Mississippi, one observer wrote: "A man couldn't get through any of the woods without a compass in one hand and a cane ax in the other to blaze every foot of the way." Yet Ben Lilly could enter a swamp in the middle of the night, stick his knife in a tree, come out, and the next night reenter the swamp from any direction and go straight to the tree and recover the knife. He always said, "The mosquitoes just go *ping* against my hide, but they can't make a dent." He stood five feet nine inches, and weighed 180 pounds; barrel-chested, broad-shouldered, narrow-hipped, sinewy—"like a panther," Dobie noted. Lilly cut down bee trees and sold the honey; he logged, hunted for the market, and traded cattle; he did not care for farming; he might suddenly leave his family to go hunting and return days or months or a year later. Lilly was accustomed to wearing four shirts at a time, and kept cycling through them, letting rain clean off the outermost garment. He wore a beard, saying he never saw an adult man with an unwhiskered chin until he was almost grown. According to Dobie, Lilly weeded out unsuitable hounds from his hunting pack by bludgeoning them to death. When his dogs closed with a bear, he might kill the quarry with a knife; knowing that an animal will turn and bite at the place where it feels pain, he would reach over the bear and stab it in the far side, pull the knife back out, wait, and stab again. A skilled blacksmith, he made his own knives, tempering them in panther oil.

In 1906, the U.S. National Museum of Natural History, an arm of the Smithsonian Institution, hired Lilly to collect ivory-billed woodpeckers (the species is now extinct) in the Louisiana swamps. At about the same time, Lilly sent to the National Museum the skin and skull of an adult male puma he had killed in Concordia Parish, Louisiana. This creature would briefly be considered the type, or first, specimen of yet another puma subspecies, *Felis concolor arundivaga*, the canebrake puma. (It was later lumped in with the Florida panther.) In 1911, at the age of fifty-five, disheartened by the paucity of large predators left in the South, Lilly abandoned his ancestral home for good. He moved West and embarked on a career of killing pumas and bears for bounty payments in Arizona and New Mexico. On occasion, the Bureau of Biological Survey would send him to a difficult region to kill a particularly elusive and destructive predator. From 1912 to 1927, it is said, Lilly never came out of the mountains. When hunting, he wore shoes that weighed six pounds apiece, double-soled as they were with automobile tire tread, their heels plated with steel. Shod in these brogans, and carrying a rifle, dog chains, a knife, and a fifty-pound pack, he would clamber through the mountains all day. When Lilly got on a puma trail, he would stick to it until he killed the cat, or rain washed the scent away, or his dogs lost it. When hunting, he might go for days without sleeping. He would rope himself behind one of his hounds and follow a trail all night. If, however, his dogs treed a puma on a Saturday night, they would have to guard it until Monday, because Ben Lilly would not pull a trigger on the Sabbath.

Lilly is believed to have destroyed more than a thousand bears and pumas in his lifetime, most of them in the Southwest. If he killed one puma for every two weeks of hunting, Lilly figured he was doing well. In 1914, in one week he slew nine pumas and three bears. "I have killed the largest and best tribes of animals," he once wrote in a letter. He was a keen observer of the natural habits of his prey. "If you follow a lion for four or five days and don't get some education, you had better go back to plowing," he wrote. "Few people have worked out the roving habits of mountain lions. By the time a family is grown, their mother has shown them a lot of country. The young male strikes out earlier for himself than the young female, and he goes farther. Some females go a long way, but adult males are generally the farthest rovers." Lilly knew all about scrapes, which he called "lion markers." He believed that a grown puma would kill approximately two deer-size animals every ten days, which is pretty close to what modern biologists have found. In cooking, Lilly's choice of frying fat was puma. He ate puma steaks and puma jerky. He especially favored puma neck meat, believing that it imparted extra strength. He slept on the ground, in all seasons and weathers. Once, a big puma passed within twelve feet of where Lilly was sleeping; the cat sniffed at some of his mate's meat hanging in a tree, and passed on. In the morning, Lilly woke and examined the tracks. "Of course Mr. Lilly," wrote Dobie, "followed and killed."

Dobie's book *The Ben Lilly Legend* reproduces a manuscript written by Lilly in his later years, which relates stories about panthers attacking humans. "At the time of attacks on people in the South," Lilly noted, "settlers were scattered, and the panther had not yet learned to fear man." Because much land had been cleared, and the game decimated by the pioneer families, "panthers were often so short of food that they even ate scraps of meat and gnawed on bones thrown away from cabins in the woods."

Lilly wrote:

A squad of Negro men were clearing swamp land north of Vicksburg. They noticed a panther slipping around in the woods and warned two white men, brothers, who lived in a cabin nearby. Not long afterwards while one of [the brothers] was chopping wood about a hundred yards away from the cabin, he heard the other one scream. He had left him covered up in bed, shaking with a chill. He rushed to the cabin and as he went through the door was leaped upon by a panther. He had his ax but could not use it effectively. The panther escaped; it had killed the sick brother, and the second one was so badly wounded that he died.

Lilly told of a panther who leaped from a leaning tree onto an Indian out hunting deer in West Carroll Parish, Louisiana. The panther killed the man instantly "and then rolled him over and sucked blood from his throat."

In 1888 a trapper living in Hickory Grove, Mississippi, informed Lilly of a panther that had attacked two boys, eleven and fourteen years of age, out chopping wood near their home. A young man working nearby heard the commotion, picked up a billet used to rive boards, and clubbed the panther over the head, killing it. "It was not a large one. That night both boys died from their wounds, and they were buried in the same grave."

At a railroad station near Lake Charles, Louisiana, from which he occasionally shipped panther hides to the U.S. Biological Survey in Washington, Lilly met an old man who related several instances of panthers killing settlers around his home in southeastern Texas. It seems a man had built a cabin and was clearing land to farm; one evening he went to a neighbor's house, leaving his wife at home, chopping off cane and briars and burning them. The woman had left her baby playing on the ground while she worked. Her back was to the infant when it gave a loud squall; the woman turned in time to see a panther bound over the fence carrying the child in its jaws. At that moment a second baby in the house began to cry. The woman, fearing for its safety as well, rushed to it, gathered it in her arms, and ran back into the yard to follow the panther. Suddenly the same cat, or another one, perhaps attracted by the baby's crying, leaped from the brush and ran at the woman; she raced back into the house and slammed the door. When her husband returned, he found his wife holding the bar to the door and screaming, and the panther reared up with its paws on the entry. The man got a gun, but hesitated to shoot for fear the bullet would go through the door and hit his wife. The panther ran off into the woods. The next morning all the men in the vicinity arrived with their dogs. They hunted steadily for two weeks, killing eleven panthers but never finding the child who had been seized.

One wonders about the veracity of puma tales, especially those concerning attacks on humans. No doubt some of the stories have been embroidered upon. It seems equally certain that others are true. Theodore Roosevelt, as well as being the twenty-sixth President of the United States, was a lifelong naturalist, a part-time rancher, and an inveterate big-game hunter who once killed a puma with a knife. In 1885 he wrote:

When the continent was first settled, and for long afterward, the cougar was quite as dangerous an antagonist as the African or Indian leopard, and would even attack men unprovoked. An instance of this occurred in the annals of my father's family. Early in the present century one of my ancestral relatives, a Georgian, moved down to the wild and almost unknown country bordering on Florida. His plantation was surrounded by jungles in which all kinds of beasts swarmed. One of his negroes had a sweetheart on another plantation, and in visiting her, instead of going by the road he took a short cut through the swamps, heedless of the wild beasts, and armed only with a long knife, for he was a man of colossal strength, and of fierce determined temper. One night he started to return late, expecting to reach the plantation in time for his daily task on the morrow. But he never reached home, and it was thought he had run away. However, when search was made for him his body was found in the path through the swamp, all gashed and torn, and but a few steps from him the body of a cougar, stabbed and cut in many places.

It has long been supposed that panthers have a special taste for pregnant women. In the late 1890s in north-central Florida near the Oklawaha River, a young woman, heavy with child, was walking back to her cabin after visiting her parents, who lived nearby. Close behind her she heard a panther scream. Believing that the cat was following her, and reasoning that it might stop and inspect any article she left along the trail, the woman began shedding her clothes. Each time she dropped a garment she would hear the panther snarl as it ripped the item to shreds. By the time she got home, she was naked. The panther circled the cabin until the woman's husband arrived, then faded into the woods.

The next several stories are drawn from *DeVane's Early Florida History*.

In 1870, near the town of Arcadia, seven men went out hunting to replenish their lard stores. Since they were going strictly after hogs, they did not bother to take guns: their dogs would grab the hogs and hold them, and the animals' throats could then be slit with a knife. As the men rode across the prairie, the dogs jumped a panther, which dashed into a hammock and climbed a tree. After looking the panther over, the men decided they now needed a rifle, and one of the party galloped off. Just then the dogs discovered a second panther in the hammock. This one put its back against a stump and began dismantling the dogs. Dogs being extremely valuable animals in pioneer days—for hunting, for guarding, and for working livestock—the men were dismayed. One of them, Thomas Albritton, waded into the melee and "with sledge hammer fist blows," reported Mr. DeVane, stunned the panther. He then took out his pocketknife and cut the animal's throat. When the rifle arrived, it was turned on the panther in the tree. The men beheaded the cats so that they could claim the bounty payment and repaired to the Albritton household for a celebratory feast of "vegetables from the cow-penned garden, grated corn pone, potato pone, cassava pone, buttermilk and curd, homemade rice and red-eye gravy, corn syrup and honey."

Tom Ephram Williams, from around Tampa, crept onto a tree island in a swamp one evening, hoping to intercept a flock of turkeys coming to roost. Feeling drowsy, he took a nap. He woke and found he was being covered with leaves. Opening one eye, he determined that a panther was doing the covering. Williams lay like a stone. When the panther finished, it sauntered off. Williams brushed off the leaves, picked up his gun, and, wrote DeVane, "went home saying he wasn't turkey-hungry at all."

In 1858 a settler was splitting and squaring logs for the puncheon floor of his cabin, along Oak Creek in the prairie east of Sarasota. His daughter, age twelve, was washing dishes on a table in the yard while her younger brother played beneath it. A panther came from the woods and caught the boy by the foot. The daughter grabbed the boy and pulled him away from the panther, which then turned on her. The fracas brought the mother, father, and two dogs running, whereupon the panther let go of the girl and ran into the crawl space beneath the puncheon floor. The man grabbed the adz he had been using that morning, raised a puncheon which had not been nailed fast, and smote the cat, "the only panther," declared DeVane, "ever known to be killed before or since with a foot adz."

In 1991, Paul Beier, of the Department of Forestry and Resource Management at the University of California at Berkeley, published a paper summarizing puma attacks on humans in North America from 1890 to 1990. Beier had collected accounts from wildlife agencies and biologists in twelve Western states and two Canadian provinces; searched through government files and the scientific literature; and scoured newspapers and magazines, particularly *Outdoor Life*, which had long encouraged readers' letters on the topic. (The enraged puma charging the stalwart hunter remains a staple subject for that periodical's cover.) Beier defined "attack" as a case in which a wild puma bit, clawed, or knocked down a human being. He excluded maulings by captive pumas and incidents in which a person—usually a hunter—deliberately approached or harassed a puma. He also recorded "near-attacks," when a puma advanced toward a person at close range without making contact, or crouched beside a trail as if to pounce.

Beier believed that he had found all fatal attacks since 1890 and all nonfatal attacks since 1970. For the entire one hundred years, he could document only ten people killed and forty-eight injured by pumas. However, from 1970 to 1990 there were thirty-one nonfatal and five fatal attacks (plus four more fatal ones since Beier's study ended), more fatalities than in the preceding eight decades. Thirty-eight percent of all verifiable assaults took place on richly forested Vancouver Island, British Columbia. (The island has always had many deer and pumas, with excellent puma habitat only a few miles from the center of Vancouver, a city of half a million people.)

Beier discovered that two-thirds of the victims were children less than sixteen years old, most of them age five to nine. (It is well known that captive pumas see children as potential prey. The Florida Game Commission occasionally keeps puma in pens— panthers being rehabilitated after an injury or Western cats brought into the state for experimental release. I was told by a biologist that when a small child comes near a caged panther, the cat will instantly prick its ears forward, stare fixedly, and crouch in preparation for springing. This response, immediate and apparently instinctive, is so terrifying to children that the biologist quit taking his kids to see the cats.) In his study of puma attacks, Beier found that one-third of the children were alone at the time, almost half were in groups of children, and the rest were accompanied by adults. Of seventeen adult victims, eleven were alone when set upon.

In what Beier termed "the three most intrusive cases," a puma crashed through the window of an isolated cabin in British Columbia to attack a telephone lineman; another seized a two-year-old boy in the garage of his home in Lewis, Colorado, a village of 200; and a third grabbed a six-year-old boy in a residential neighborhood in Hinton, Alberta. (None of the three attacks proved fatal.) Two people were snatched from their tents in Big Bend National Park in Texas (they, too, escaped death). In another instance, a puma leaped on a boy as he rode past on a bicycle.

Wrote Beier: "Most victims (24 of 32 for which data exist) did not see the cougar before being clawed or bitten; thus, no preventive action was taken." In Olema, Washington, in 1924, tracks in the snow showed where a thirteen-year-old boy had tried to outrun a puma for about one hundred yards before being hauled down and killed. In only one case, in Vancouver in 1966, did an intended victim escape by running—a sixteen-year-old boy who fled after meeting a puma at twenty-five feet. "The cougar was gaining ground rapidly when the boy's boot fell off and the cougar attacked and ate [it]. This story was supported by the presence of boot fragments in the stomach of the cougar when it was shot an hour later."

When attacked by a puma, a person who "played dead" continued to be bitten and mauled, whereas one who fought back—with bare hands, a stick, a knife, a rock—usually repelled his or her assailant. Shouts intimidated the attacking puma and also drew other humans to drive the cat off. In 1970 in Kootenay National Park, British Columbia, a puma knocked down a fifty-year-old woman hiker, scratching her arm. "As she fell," wrote Beier, "she set up her backpack as a shield, faced the cougar and (in her words) 'began talking to her the way you would if you were trying to soothe a dog or cat.' " The woman kept cajoling the puma for what she believed to be half an hour, until some other hikers came along; one of the hikers shrilled on a whistle, and the puma ran off. (In Kansas, in 1871, a man being circled by a puma grabbed a couple of buffalo bones that were lying in the grass, whacked the bones savagely together, and jumped up and down, bellowing desperately. The puma turned and ran.) In 1990, a twenty-eight-year-old woman in Boulder, Colorado, stood her ground and shouted at two pumas as they approached. When they got close, she climbed a tree. The pumas climbed after her, one of them clawing her leg. The woman kicked one of the pumas and smacked the other with a stick. The cats jumped out of the tree and departed.

Of the pumas who launched attacks, little concrete information is known, even though most, wrote Beier, "were promptly shot and killed." Several were reported as "starved" and "emaciated" by newspapers quoting conservation officers, but when examined, the cats turned out to be of normal size and weight. In one incident, a rabid puma caused the only double fatality ever reported from a puma attack, in Morgan Hill, California, in 1909; both of the victims—a child and a woman who defended herself with a hatpin—died of rabies and not from direct physical trauma. A puma who attacked a boy and a girl in British Columbia in 1916 had cataracts. In Big Bend National Park in 1987, a yearling puma set upon and bit a woman; perhaps the cat was feeling testy, having been chased, treed, drugged, and collared by wildlife biologists four months earlier.

Another story comes from Texas, courtesy of Roy McBride. In West Texas, where McBride lives, pumas are perpetual targets. McBride has been hunting pumas for over thirty years; he hires himself out to sheep ranchers and kills pumas that prey on the flocks. He also earned a Master of Science degree at Sul Ross State University ("about the size of a high school," he told me) in his home town of Alpine. His thesis, "The Status and Ecology of the Mountain Lion (*Felis concolor stanleyana*) of the Texas-Mexico Border," includes an appendix headed "Unusual Behavior of Individual Lions," which includes this incident:

While hunting in the Christmas Mountains in February 1961, McBride discovered that four traps were missing from the head of a canyon. Tying his mule, he hiked down the arroyo looking for drag marks from the traps. (A puma trap is usually attached to a short length of chain and a two-pronged iron drag. When the animal moves about, the drag gets caught in the brush; the vegetation's flexibility can act to keep the beast from jerking out of the trap.)

McBride had an Airedale trap dog with him, but because poison baits for coyotes had been scattered in the vicinity, the dog was muzzled. McBride soon found three of the traps tangled together; then he came upon the fourth "with the toe of a large lion remaining in the trap." He picked up the trap (presumably discarding the toe) and began to roll the chain around it, preparing to carry it back up the canyon. The Airedale was nosing around in a rock pile at the base of the canyon wall. A movement caught McBride's eye, and he realized that "a large tom lion was galloping toward me in pursuit of the dog. The dog ran past me, and I could tell by the lion's eyes that his attention [had become] fixed on me." McBride drew a .22 pistol, shot at the lion, and, to his surprise, hit the onrushing cat in the head. It fell at McBride's feet with blood running out of one ear. Supposing it to be dead, McBride bent and picked up the trap again. Suddenly the cat sprang to its feet and lunged at him. McBride backpedaled around a boulder, threw the trap at the lion, and tried to shoot again, but his pistol was empty. Wrote McBride: "The temperature was below freezing and my hands were so numb that I couldn't get them between my leggings and into my pocket where I had a few shells. My dog would [attack] the lion from behind, but because of the muzzle, she couldn't catch it. However, when it would pause to try to catch the dog, I would gain ground. I finally managed to get my pistol reloaded and shot the lion again." McBride believed that "the lion had just gotten out of the trap as I arrived and no doubt felt he was still trapped and cornered." He added, "I have crawled into narrow caves with them many times with their displaying no more aggression than growling."

Since Beier published his study, a puma has killed an eighteen-year-old jogger near Idaho Springs, Colorado. In 1991, in a housing development near Vancouver, a puma walked up to a group of preschool children having lunch on a riverbank. It licked a boy's face, and when a teacher tried to pull the cat away, it mauled her and also the boy and a girl. A five-year-old child was killed on an Indian reservation in Montana. A bicyclist was attacked in

California. In 1994 a female puma dragged down a forty-year-old woman jogging in a state park in the Sierra foothills north of Sacramento. (The puma was hunted down and killed. Sympathetic Californians donated money to a regional zoo that had promised to care for the puma's cubs, as well as to a trust fund set up for the dead woman's children.) A puma killed a woman strolling in a state park near San Diego in 1994. In British Columbia, a grouse hunter walking down a forest road came face to face with a puma. The cat made no move to leave the trail. Reaching for a stone to throw at the cat, the man detected movement off to one side: a second puma was stalking him. He shot it, then turned and killed the first cat as it charged, too. John Seidensticker, commenting on the incident in his *Smithsonian* article, wrote: "When the hunter broke off eye contact and bent down, he had suddenly become prey."

Seidensticker had his own close call. In 1972, while working on a field study of pumas in Idaho, he radio-tracked an adult female through a stand of trees. At one point Seidensticker glanced up and there stood the puma, "looking right at me around a skinny lodgepole [pine] about sixty feet away. The cat hissed and laid her ears back. Then, holding her head low, she started moving toward me." With the cat thirty feet away, Seidensticker turned aside to break off a thick limb sticking up beside him. In that moment, the cat advanced to within twenty feet. "Taking shaky aim," Seidensticker wrote, "I threw my stick and hit her on the shoulder. After a moment's hesitation, she jumped and disappeared in the alders."

I looked up Seidensticker in Washington, D.C., where he is now curator of mammals at the National Zoo. A large, shambling man, bearded and balding, he lives with his wife and daughter in a rundown neighborhood within walking distance of the zoo. The place is a far cry from the Idaho wilderness where he studied pumas, and from the Montana ranch where he grew up. We sat on his back porch looking out over his yard, which he had transformed into a miniature wildlife preserve: plantings, rocks, and a small pond, used by rabbits, birds, snakes, turtles, toads. (Other back yards in the vicinity had overturned trash cans and rusting automobiles propped up on concrete blocks.) After his stint in Idaho and before coming to Washington, Seidensticker studied tigers and leopards in Nepal. In Bangladesh, Indonesia, and Sri Lanka, he helped wildlife agencies design parks to protect endangered animals. One of the resulting preserves is in the Sundarbans Delta of Bangladesh, where the Ganges, Brahmaputra, and Meghna Rivers drain into the Bay of Bengal. In the Sundarbans, Seidensticker told me, tigers are known as "forest policemen," and they kill more than three hundred people a year. "Everyone there can tell you about a relative or a friend killed and eaten by a tiger," he said. When I expressed horror at that situation, Seidensticker shrugged. "It all depends on what you're prepared to accept as a risk. When you leave here, you'll get in your car and drive home. There's a risk that you will be killed in an accident. Most of us accept that risk. Cars are a part of life. In the Sundarbans, tigers are a part of life."

I asked Seidensticker if he felt that people in the United States were willing to accept the hazard of being attacked by a puma in the wild. "I'm amazed at the change in attitudes toward lions in the West," he said. Pumas are now classified as game animals in most Western states; hunters are permitted to kill a limited number of the cats each year, but the pumas no longer are harassed year-round and greeted with bullets whenever they show up at human settlements. Most residents of what Seidensticker referred to as the "new West" were, he said, becoming accustomed to the quiet resurgence of *Felis concolor*. Most wanted to learn how to reduce the risks of running afoul of the cats. A puma that killed a person would still be hounded and quickly put to death, but so far the increase in attacks on humans, said Seidensticker, had not aroused the age-old enmity that had formerly caused people to kill every puma they could.

In Florida, people are probing deeper and deeper into panther habitat, both to build homes and to enjoy the natural beauty of the Sunshine State. Many Floridians seem to view the panther as an integral part of nature. They are comfortable, even enthusiastic, about living in a place where they have a chance, however slim, of seeing a panther. Many believe that a panther will leave them alone if they leave it alone. They believe that panthers and people can coexist.

In fact, they *do* coexist. A biologist for the Florida Game Commission, whose home is in a subdivision east of Naples, once radio-tracked a panther passing through a slough a quarter-mile from his back door. On another day, the biologist held up an antenna in the parking lot of his office, in the industrial fringe of Naples, and listened in on a collared panther as it slipped past garages, shopping centers, and restaurants, crossing roads (one imagines the cat crouching at the curb, looking both ways), threading its way through the tattered forest among thousands of oblivious Floridians, not one of whom called to report a panther that day.

5

THE VORTEX

By the early 1990s, there was no longer any doubt: the Florida panther, although not yet extinct, was on a fast track to oblivion. As orange groves were planted, as suburbs expanded, as highways pushed across prairies and through swamps, the panthers' living space dwindled. From the radio-telemetry studies that had been going on for almost a decade, biologists could document that, in many instances, fathers were breeding with daughters, brothers with sisters, mothers with sons.

The typical Florida panther had deformed vertebrae in its tail, causing a ninety-degree kink near the tip. It had a whorl of fur, like a cowlick, in the middle of its back. Odd characteristics, but not necessarily life-threatening ones. More unsettling was the fact that nearly every male panther had only one testicle descended into the scrotum. Veterinary analysis—which had gone on in tandem with the field biology—showed that the males had a high percentage of defective sperm. Most panther kittens had heart murmurs caused by leaky cardiac valves. (Fewer adults seemed to have the murmurs. Had they outgrown them? Or did a kitten with a murmur stand a poorer chance of growing up?) It seemed probable that inbreeding had reached such a critical level that it was causing these potentially lethal defects to emerge. What other hidden consequences might it be having? Lowered fecundity? Stunted growth? Less resistance to parasites, disease, environmental toxins?

The U.S. Fish and Wildlife Service, an arm of the Department of the Interior, is charged with protecting threatened and endangered species in the United States. In 1990 the Fish and Wildlife Service hired Ulysses S. Seal to organize two workshops on the Florida panther. Seal, a retired endocrinologist from the University of Minnesota, is one of the world's most powerful and persuasive proponents of captive breeding to help preserve endangered animals. He and several like-minded colleagues had devised a procedure called the "Species Survival Plan," useful in assessing the health and genetic diversity of a creature and developing recommendations for its continuance. Seal had helped wildlife agencies around the world write survival plans for more than one hundred endangered animals, including the Asian elephant, the white rhino, the Puerto Rican parrot, the red wolf, the black-footed ferret, the orangutan, and the tiger.

The two panther workshops brought together geneticists, specialists in animal reproduction and populations, field biologists, veterinarians, and state and federal officials. The scientists reviewed findings gleaned from field studies, population surveys, and gene analyses. They reduced those findings to numbers. They fed the numbers into a computer program with the rather dire name of VORTEX, developed by one of Seal's associates and designed to forecast the future of a species. VORTEX was not encouraging: even without a catastrophe like a disease epidemic, the probability that the Florida panther would die out within the next quarter century was 85 percent. The mean time to extinction was twenty years. According to VORTEX, chance events such as roadkills, deaths from disease, fluctuation in the sex ratio of offspring, and random gene transmission would combine to create a reproductive vortex in which the population would grow ever smaller, adults would have more trouble finding mates, inbreeding would intensify, genetic diversity would be lost—until the panther vanished.

Soon after the workshops, the Fish and Wildlife Service issued a proposal: Capture a limited number of Florida panthers—kittens mostly—and breed a separate population. A zoo population, held in isolation, would be a hedge against some malady destroying the entire subspecies. In captivity, breeding-age panthers could be paired with unrelated animals (or at least with distant relatives) rather than with siblings and parents. Captive-bred offspring could go back into the wild to boost natural populations or to establish new ones. Captive breeding had been tried on a host of wild animals, with varying degrees of success. In North America, it had helped the red wolf, black-footed ferret, whooping crane, peregrine falcon, and California condor. (Captive breeding was not without its difficulties. Conservationists had found it far easier to breed endangered birds than mammals; grazers than predators. With each generation born in captivity, the chances increased that the animals' instincts had been dulled. Mothers might no longer teach their young to hunt, or to fear humans or other predators, or to avoid dangers from snakes, porcupines, and the like. Breeding behaviors were sometimes lost. In the case of the whooping crane, a species of wading bird, one biologist had to "mate" with a crane that had become so habituated to humans that she ignored male cranes. The biologist slept in a pen with the female crane, leaped and danced with her in feigned courtship, and artificially inseminated her with whooping crane sperm. She laid fertile eggs.)

Critics of captive breeding pointed out that no one had ever successfully reintroduced large feline predators into the wild. And suppose the panthers did breed a surplus? The limited South Florida habitat already appeared to be full: young panthers were not establishing territories, were not being "recruited into the population," as the wildlife biologists put it. Where would the zoo-raised cats go? Where in all the Southeastern United States would there be room for a population of large, free-roaming carnivores?

In June 1990 I attended a meeting explaining the plan to breed Florida panthers in captivity. It was held at a Fish and Wildlife Service building in Arlington, Virginia. Bureaucrats, journalists, and members of environmental and animal-protection groups sat at a large table and around the perimeter of the room. The people were well dressed, convivial, and orderly. An official of the Fish and Wildlife Service convened the meeting and listed several hopeful signs that recently had appeared for the panther. A wealthy man, a New York paper manufacturer, had offered space to house captive panthers at White Oak Plantation, an isolated tract on the Florida–Georgia border that included a five-hundred-acre conservation center and a breeding facility for endangered animals. Reproductive physiologists were forging ahead with new techniques to help panthers reproduce, including artificial insemination and in vitro fertilization, even a protocol for freezing and preserving eggs and sperm taken from panthers killed on the highway. If successful, the procedure would allow scientists to produce off-spring from animals long since dead. (Methods of this sort had rarely been applied to wild animals, even to beasts with simpler reproductive systems and less complicated mating behaviors than the panther. No one knew when the techniques would be ready, or if they would ultimately work. The only thing that seemed clear was that pumas would breed in captivity: they did it all the time in zoos and menageries.)

The Florida Game Commission had identified target animals for capturing; they would keep a Florida Panther Stud Book aimed at achieving ideal pairings. The goal would be a colony of 130 panthers and offspring by the year 2000, 500 by 2010. Some biologists felt that panthers could be removed from the wild in ways that would not disrupt the natural population. The only adults to be captured would be ones that were not reproducing (for instance, young males with no room to establish territories of their own, or females who had never conceived and whose infertility might be reversed through surgery or artificial breeding). Mostly, though, kittens would be taken. If a female's kittens were re-moved, she would quickly recycle—go into estrus and breed again. Or one or two kittens could be plucked from a litter. Field studies had shown that half the kittens died in the wild before reaching six months of age. A single kitten receiving the sole attention of its mother might stand a better chance of surviving.

The Fish and Wildlife Service representative sat down; another speaker took his place. It was a hot, muggy afternoon, sunlight streaming in through the windows, and the air conditioning was not equal to the task. I watched people stifling yawns, rubbing their faces. Phrases like "multiagency approach," "viability anal-ysis," and "maximizing genetic diversity," many of them deliv-ered in a relaxed Southern inflection, began slipping through my brain. I thought about panthers in cages, test-tube kittens, orange groves obliterating pine forests, and suburbs blanketing the land. I considered the incongruity of drowsy bipeds in a glass-and-brick building planning the future of four-legged predators inhabiting swamps and forests a thousand miles away.

I found myself wondering: What are the panthers doing now?

. . .

Midafternoon, the temperature well above ninety. The blue sky is pillared with pink-tinted clouds. In the somnolent pine flat-woods, nothing much is stirring.

A faint breeze touches the saw palmettos. The palmetto leaves look like big fans, green starbursts a foot across, with dozens of radiating blades each ending in a point. The palmettos grow five and six feet tall. They crowd together so densely that nothing larger than a rabbit can enter without scraping the stalks together. When the breeze reaches them, the leaves sway gently, ticking and scratching against one another. The hundreds of leaves mesh together, their shiny surfaces reflecting the sun's glare.

Inside, the light is dimmer and the air twenty degrees cooler. At the center of the thicket, in a faint depression in the bare earth, a panther lies on his side. He is a young male barely two years old. His eyes are closed. His facial muscles twitch, his whiskers erecting and then lying down again. He lifts a forepaw and scratches the fur behind an ear. His head comes up slightly, eyes opening to slits, ears pricking and pointing in unison. The sound, from the thicket's edge thirty feet away, is of no significance, a mouse or a lizard scuttling past.

The panther stretches. He licks his paw, then uses it to smooth some disheveled fur on the side of his head. He settles again, tucking the paw against his chest.

For the next six hours the panther slips in and out of sleep. He listens to birds calling, insects droning, and thunder rumbling. Shadows lengthen in the pines. The light within the palmetto thicket dwindles. Finally the panther wakens fully. He gives his fur a thorough grooming, brushing and licking away twigs, dirt, and shards of leaves. He pays particular attention to a scabbed-over wound on one shoulder and an angry scar on a forelimb, fight-inflicted. He rises, lifting his haunches and stretching out his front paws: curved, needle-sharp claws extrude momentarily from their protective sheaths, then draw back in. Crouching, the panther slips down the narrow runway beneath the overarching stalks. At the edge of the thicket he stops. Narrow-mouthed toads bleat from a rain pond. A chuck-will's-widow chants. A night-flying beetle clatters past. The panther sniffs at the breeze and detects pine resin, dry grass, the slightly fermented mustiness of cow manure, and, like an off-color thread running through a tapestry, the faint but penetrating stench of carrion. It comes from a small hog, his kill of two days past. He fed on it once, eating all but the snout, hooves, and heavier bones. Then he sought out the palmetto thicket and rested.

Now he emerges into the evening. It is dark. The only light comes from fireflies, from stars peering between the clouds, and from pinkish-orange lightning flickering within the clouds. A few big raindrops smack against the palmetto fronds.

He pads off through the wire grass beneath the slash pines. On a game trail he stops and moves his bowels, then paws leaves and dirt over the mound. He sets off again, walking on his big cushioned toes, covering the ground silently, steadily. The pines give way to prairie. A cow, catching the panther's scent, lows anxiously, her calf shuffling at her side. He pays them no attention. (Cows are big, rambunctious. Deer are easier, and they abound.)

His face is short and Roman-nosed, his skull rounded. His lower jaw is equipped with strong muscles anchored to bone ridges at the top and back of his skull. His jawbones are stout. His lower jaw works only up and down—not in a side-to-side motion like that of a grazing animal. The panther's neck is slender. His cylindrical tail is carried behind him, curving down almost to the ground and turning up gradually to near the level of his hips. It has a black tip. Its sinuous arc is interrupted by a right-angled crook two inches from the tip.

The panther's body is long, his thighs solid. His forelegs are thickly muscled, his shoulders huge—well suited to their function of grabbing and holding prey. His short stiff fur is the unobtrusive grayish tan of a dead palmetto frond. His fur is darkest on his back, shading to pearly gray on his belly. His nose is a pink triangle, its apex pointing down. His ears, pale gray on the inside, are black on the outside; his eyes are surrounded by black, and vertical black marks adorn his muzzle. The facial markings have a purpose: should the panther confront a rival—his ears laid back, his mouth open in a snarl—the markings will accentuate the threatening expression and may help to defuse a full-scale fight.

The panther stops and stares. His eyes, greenish-yellow, are directed forward in his skull. They see stereoscopically, letting the panther judge distances with precision. They are large, to capture light, their round pupils now completely dilated. A light image entering the panther's eye passes through the retina, where it is absorbed, stimulating vision cells. If very dim, the image may not be detectable on its first passage. Behind the retina lies a mirrorlike layer, the tapetum, that accentuates the image and bounces it back, flashing it to the receptor cells a second time, twice as bright as the first.

The panther is hunting and moving, hunting and moving. His head shifts from side to side. His nose samples the breeze. He walks into a rain shower, the drops sluicing down his sides and dripping off his belly. A loud thunderclap makes him pause. Picking his way through the dripping grass, he passes out of the band of rain. He follows the edge of a cypress strand, the kind of brushy fringe to which, he has learned, plant-eaters are attracted. His eyes catch movement. Instantly he stops and sinks to a crouch.

The doe feeds on a low-growing buttonbush. Her fawn nuzzles her for milk, but she sidesteps him and continues to browse. The fawn is white-spotted, long-legged, nimble. The panther focuses on the doe, the bigger meal. He advances slowly, a few feet, stops, waits, and watches; a few feet more. He places a clump of palmettos between himself and the deer. He creeps closer. He is fifty yards away—quivering, lowering himself to the preparatory crouch—when the freshening downdraft of the thunderhead picks up his scent and carries it forward. Moments later the deer are bounding away, a pair of white tails flagging through the woods.

The panther straightens, licks some mud off a paw, and resumes his steady gait.

For the next two miles he does not actively hunt. He leaps across a barbed-wire fence and pads along a dusty road. In the weeds at the road's edge he hears a rustling: a cotton rat, which he kills with a slap of his paw. He bolts the rat, a five-ounce morsel that does little to fill his stomach. He crosses a patch of prairie, comes to another fence, and clears it with a bound. Two steps farther on, he finds himself on a hard slick surface that still holds the heat of the sun. He crosses the pavement, jumps another fence. Behind him and to one side, a small noise presents itself, gathers, and becomes a loud roaring. A beam of light cuts through the darkness. The panther pays scant attention to this irrelevant phenomenon as it whines and pounds on past, receding into the night.

He nears a building with a light affixed to a pole, where a dog growls and barks. He turns aside, makes a beeline across a pasture, and enters more pine woods. He comes to a bottleneck, a faint rise of land between two arms of a swamp. Here, shrubs grow thick. Following a trail, feeling the way with his whiskers, he proceeds cautiously into the blackness. He draws back his lips, flares his nostrils, and gulps in great volumes of air. Amid the myriad odors—deer, raccoon, bobcat, opossum—he smells it, a pungency at once tantalizing and terrifying: the scent of another panther.

The young panther draws back a few paces. To the cat who left this scent—a large, solid male three years his senior—the young panther almost lost his life. A week ago, the young panther had come upon the male in the company of a female. Before he could react, the older male swarmed all over him. The younger cat almost went down, but managed to set himself, deliver a blow with his paw, turn and run. In the brief exchange he had lost part of one ear, the muscle of his left forepaw had been laid bare, and his shoulder had been punctured by an inch-long canine tooth.

The young male edges closer to the scent. It permeates a scraped-together pile of leaves at the end of a bare, linear patch of ground. From the way in which the scrape points, he determines the male's direction of travel. Exploring further, the panther picks up a second, fainter scent: a female, not in estrus.

The panther plants both his hind feet next to the scrape left by the older male. He pushes his feet backward. The six-inch stroke mounds up its own small pile of debris. The young panther crouches and urinates on the pile. He turns, sniffs at it experimentally, and checks the older male's scrape again. He turns and leaves the crossing on an opposite heading. He goes south, away from his mother's home range, which he vacated almost a year ago. In a few days he will encounter a string of scrapes left by another dominant male. He will linger between the territories of the two reigning males until one of them dies: a car, disease, infection, a fight. Or he will keep on roving, floating across the land, risking his neck crossing roads and encountering surly male panthers, until (if he lives that long) he finds a space where no male holds sway and female panthers reside.

•   •   •

Now he is padding through the woods. Starlight bathes the
ground. The pines are vertical black bars. He smells fresh deer
droppings, and slows. He creeps along in silence. He catches the
sweet-sour scent of a deer. His left front paw halts and his right
paw lines up beside it, and he crouches slowly, as if all the air
were leaking out of him. His body is tense and ready. He hears a
tearing sound; teeth grinding at vegetation; then more tearing.

The deer's scent fills his senses. Flattened to the ground, he
inches forward. He sees the deer's shape broken into pieces by the
intervening stems of grass. The deer is moving as it feeds, coming
closer. A buck, with antlers in velvet. The deer wags its white
tail, a movement of habit. It sniffs the air; it samples with its ears.

The deer lowers its head to tear at a clump of grass. It is this
movement, this lowering of the shield of wariness, that triggers
the attack. The panther's hind legs propel him forward, he hits
the ground with his forepaws, his hind legs plant and uncoil again,
and as he reaches out in his final lunge at the buck, the deer has
time enough only to lift its head.

The panther seizes the buck, and the force of his attack bowls
the prey over. The panther sinks his teeth into the back of the
buck's neck near the head. The buck thumps onto the ground with
the cat astride him, hind claws hooked in the deer's flanks. The
panther's canine teeth, wedge-shaped and replete with pressure-
sensitive nerves, slice through the muscle layers in the deer's neck.
Biting swiftly, the panther probes with his canines for the space
between two vertebrae; finding it, he clamps down hard, severing
the spine.

The panther holds the deer down, its kicking becoming weaker
and more spasmodic, until finally it is dead.

The panther lies panting, his heart racing. He opens his jaws,
stands, and licks at blood on the deer's neck. His jaws grip the
deer across its brisket, and although the deer weighs almost as
much as he does, the panther lifts it a foot off the ground and
carries it, legs dangling and neck swaying, for a hundred yards.
He stashes it under a low-growing oak, walks off a short distance,
and flops down beneath another shrub.

An hour passes, during which the panther growls a bobcat off
the carcass. The eastern sky begins to pale. Birds call: mocking-

birds with their falsetto speechifying, jays wheedling, bobwhites, cardinals, doves. Finally the panther gets to his feet. With teeth and claws he opens the deer's belly. He draws out intestines, bladder, and paunch and nudges them aside. He eats the liver and the heart. Then the short ribs. Then the hindquarters, starting from the interior of the flanks. The sharp-edged teeth in the sides of his jaws shear off the still-warm flesh. Rough protuberances on his tongue scrape the meat from the bones.

When he finishes eating, he paws a few sticks and leaves onto the carcass. The sun angles in through the cabbage palms and the slash pines. The calling of the birds has subsided. The air is beginning to shimmer. The panther leaves his kill. He walks, his belly distended and swaying, until he finds a palmetto thicket. Crouching, he threads his way in.

6

NUMBER 46

The three biologists stood in water to mid-thigh. One of the men held an H-shaped antenna at his side. They stood bent forward at the waist, staring down at a hummock in the swamp, a patch of dry ground the size of a manhole cover. The biologists traded quiet remarks. Swamp birds shrieked in the foggy distance. Black water pooled at the bases of the gnarled cypress trees. On the patch of elevated ground, grass blades and ferns that had been crushed down were now slowly springing back up: a black bear had vacated the prominence about half a minute earlier.

One of the biologists was Dave Maehr. After Chris Belden resigned as project leader on the panther research effort (or had been taken off the project; it depended on whom you asked), and after Belden's successor (a man named John Roboski) elected to quit, Maehr was given the job. In his late thirties, Maehr is erect and fit, with chiseled features and blue eyes. Often when I saw him he was unshaven, perhaps having gotten up at some ungodly hour to preside over a panther capture (they are done early, before the heat of the day comes on) or to collar a bear caught in a snare set. Often he was grumpy, although on this particular morning in the swamp he seemed in a conciliatory mood. He had invited me to look for bears, because he was not allowed to invite me to look for panthers. Maehr had attached radio collars to several dozen black bears and professed to enjoy studying them more than the panthers, because people do not get as emotional about black bears. (At least not yet: there is a move afoot to classify the Florida black bear as an endangered subspecies.)

"Hey, look at this," Maehr said, pointing at some sheared-off green stems. "She's been eating pickerelweed." He located some wet greenish droppings and used sticks to tweezer them into a plastic bag. I stood in the chilly water with my arms crossed, not bothering to take notes. I myself was grumpy that morning. A year earlier I had written to the Florida Game Commission asking permission to watch as a panther was captured. Right now a crew was out trying to catch panthers, and here I was in South Florida, and it seemed to make sense that I join them. The day before, I had telephoned the Game Commission's chief of research in Tallahassee. In a maddeningly sweet Southern accent, he had assured me that there was a long list of people waiting to witness a capture, and that I had not risen to the top of the list.

The mobile radio carried by one of the biologists hummed and spoke: a dispatcher relayed the message that a panther had been treed in Big Cypress National Preserve.

Maehr and his colleagues turned and began splashing through the murky water. I followed, hoping for the best. After a few minutes we clambered onto a rise of land—an old tram road. We turned south and trotted along an overgrown trail. Blackberry canes tore at our clothes. Traffic hummed in the distance. In about ten minutes we reached the highway, Florida Route 84, known as Alligator Alley, which slices across the state from Fort Lauderdale on the east coast to Naples on the west. It bisects some excellent panther habitat, and for years panthers have been getting mowed down on the road. Now engineers are turning two-lane Alligator Alley into four-lane Interstate 75. In the process, they are punctuating the roadbed with twenty-three low, broad concrete tunnels, said to cost a million dollars each. The tunnels are situated at key crossings where high numbers of panthers historically have been killed. They will let panthers and other wildlife pass safely beneath the pavement, and will help restore the gradual north-to-south seeping of surface water upon which Big Cypress Swamp and the entire South Florida ecosystem depend.

We scaled a chain-link fence next to one of the wildlife underpasses and clambered over the guardrail. People whizzing by in automobiles looked at us askance. The two other biologists jumped into their truck (green, with a door emblem showing a bass, a buck, and, in yellow, the pendent outline of Florida), did a U-turn across the grass median strip, and raced off. Maehr and I got into his truck. It was his duty to be on hand when the panther was darted. I had ridden with him, leaving my car at his office in Naples, twenty miles away. He could not very well leave me stranded on Alligator Alley.

He frowned, exhaled loudly, and turned to stare at me.

"Tell them I wouldn't get out of the truck," I said, meaning it.

Maehr's eyes narrowed. He allowed the corners of his mouth to twitch upward slightly. Then he started the truck and put it in gear. On the radio he contacted another biologist, who had accompanied the houndsman that morning; in the background, the dogs could be heard barking excitedly. The biologist gave directions and told Maehr that the cat was an uncollared male.

"No collar?" Maehr asked quickly. No collar, confirmed the reply. "Well," Maehr rumbled at me, "this really *is* your lucky day."

We exited from Alligator Alley, drove a short distance, and entered the preserve through a locked gate. For several miles the gravel road was like a tunnel through the forest. Then it opened to the light. We passed a dilapidated hunting camp. We drove across a weedy field with a rickety corral. A rangy, roan-colored, long-horned cow stood gawking at us. We bumped down a narrow dirt track, fronds of cabbage palm whacking against the windshield. We stopped behind a green Ford Bronco. The veterinarians—three women—were taking their equipment out of the Bronco and loading it into backpacks. Now we could hear the dogs barking for real, somewhere off beyond the hammock, an open grove of live oaks festooned with Spanish moss.

We stepped through the hammock, redolent of cow manure and the tang of fallen wild oranges. The air felt cool. Fog touched the slick green leaves of the tall oaks, whose limbs curved and twisted like tentacles. Air plants covered the massive branches. Spanish moss hung down like patriarchs' beards. Beyond the hammock lay mucky ground thickly grown with water oaks, pop ash, and black gum trees, their trunks and branches decorated with ferns, vines, and more air plants. The houndsman's white Stetson could be discerned between the gnarled trunks. His dogs yipped and barked. A photographer from *National Geographic* (I had met him a few days before; no doubt he had risen meteorically to the top of the Game Commission's list) sent film whining through a motor-driven Nikon. The veterinarians and biologists crept closer.

Suddenly there was the panther. He stood on a limb twenty feet up, supple and lanky, with big paws and prizefighter shoulders. He was not snarling. He appeared to be quite calm, even curious, his haunches high and his head low, looking down at the dogs and the people gathering below. Then I saw the tip of his tail, which shook like a palsied hand.

One of the biologists donned a yellow climbing harness, secured a coil of dirty nylon rope to his belt, and laced on a pair of leather gaiters with down-pointing steel spikes. People spoke in subdued tones. Maehr assembled a rifle with a long barrel and a telescopic sight.

The houndsman—the Texan Roy McBride—gazed up at the panther and said he would weigh ninety pounds. To me, the cat appeared heavier than that. The veterinarian in charge, a vigorous, capable-looking woman in muddy black high-top basketball shoes and a Game Commission uniform (green trousers, tan shirt), drew the anesthetic into a dart syringe.

People with machetes cleared away brush from beneath the tree. They unfolded a net. "Want the crash bag?" someone asked. (The crash bag is a large compartmented nylon cushion that can be quickly filled with inflated plastic garbage bags.) Maehr shook his head. "He's low enough, we've got enough people." McBride came over and asked me to hold his hounds, which were now on leash. McBride appeared to be in his fifties. He was tall and clean-shaven, with a handsome, pinkly weathered face. In addition to his cowboy hat, he wore a canvas coat with rust-colored stains on one shoulder, blue jeans, and black rubber slip-on boots. He went to where Maehr was standing and took the rifle, which was operated with compressed gas, like a pellet or a BB gun. McBride opened the bolt and loaded the dart. He rested the gun against a tree, settled the buttstock into his shoulder, and peered through the sight.

The panther stood on the limb with its back toward me. A sudden *thwack*, and the dart was dangling from the cat's hind flank. He flinched and changed positions on the limb. He whipped his hawser of a tail. His mouth hung open, and his tongue panted.

The dart, with its red cloth packing, looked like some kind of brilliant swamp flower against his gray-tan coat.

For the next ten minutes the panther stood on the limb looking down. People waited with their faces turned up. Then the panther's head began to sag. He stretched out along the limb and wrapped his forepaws around it. The biologist with the climbing harness reached his hands high on the trunk, dug a spike into the bark, and stepped up. He repeated the movement with his other foot. Soon he had gained the branch on which the panther rested. The biologist slowly reached out and patted the cat's head. No response. He unhooked the cat's hind legs and gave his rump a gentle shove. (Dislodging a panther from a tree entails a certain risk. Once, a struggling panther sank its claws into a climbing biologist's posterior; they ripped loose when the cat fell.) The panther swung around to the bottom of the limb, still holding on with his great, knotted forelimbs; dangling there, he tried unsuccessfully to hook a hind leg back up. Beneath him, people held the net taut. The climbing biologist pried at the panther's front paws. Someone yelled "Here he comes!" and the cat was plummeting down, smacking into the net, bumping it against the ground. People threw the margins of the net over the panther, who flopped and kicked weakly beneath it. McBride came and got his dogs; talking softly to them, he led them over and let them smell their supine quarry.

The head veterinarian, Melody Roelke, ran her hand along the cat's flank. "He's gonna need some more drugs. This is a big boy. Say one hundred, one-ten?" Maehr and another biologist finished lashing the cat's paws together. They ran a hook through the cording and hoisted the panther beneath a scale. One hundred sixteen pounds. Around Roelke's neck hung a stethoscope, a necklace of drug vials, and a small tape recorder, into which she spoke: "Run time is fourteen minutes, eight seconds. The cat is still struggling and I'm giving him ketamine." She injected another syringe.

When the panther had gone limp, Maehr bear-hugged him over to a blue tarpaulin spread on the ground. Above the tarp a line ran between two trees; from it hung bags of intravenous solution, and two canvas medical kits unfolded to expose thermometers, pipettes, stethoscopes, vials, scissors, and scalpels.

Maehr stretched out a tape measure, bending it for the tail's right-angle kink. "Tail, sixty-seven centimeters."

Someone said, "Might be Nineteen and Twelve's kid from a couple of years ago."

"Total length, 225.5 centimeters."

"Maybe he's Thirty's brother."

While Maehr checked the panther's exterior, the veterinarians concerned themselves with the cat's insides. Already they had inserted needles and tubes to drip saline solution into the panther's bloodstream, to keep him hydrated. The biologists—four of them, all males—seemed ill at ease working with the veterinarians, who were all females. Both groups would act with careful politeness to each other, then snap.

"Heart rate, 180."

"Could you give me some *room?*"

"Looks like he's in pretty good shape."

"Been fighting. Look at those scars and nicks."

"Wait a minute, *I'm not done here.*"

"Low-grade systolic heart murmur."

"Neck, 43.5 centimeters."

"He has only one testicle."

"No feces are available."

With a socket wrench Maehr bolted a collar around the panther's neck. The collar was a broad band of cream-colored leather, its electronic components housed in a small rectangular container sealed by epoxy. Number 46: the forty-sixth Florida panther collared in eleven years.

The houndsman, McBride, pried open the panther's mouth, inspected the wear on his teeth, and guessed the cat's age at twenty-six months. I was surprised by how few teeth the cat had in its sturdy, foreshortened jaws, and how large they were, especially the shearing teeth, or carnassials, on the sides of the mandibles. (A puma has thirty teeth, sixteen above and fourteen below. A canid—a coyote or a wolf, for instance, with its much longer muzzle—has forty-two teeth.) "Damn," McBride drawled, pushing back his Stetson and exposing a band of pale forehead. "It'd help so much to cut a toe offa this cat, we could track him so much better. What do you say, Melody?"

Roelke smiled at the jest. She was busy, and she and her two assistants would stay that way for nearly two more hours. They drew blood samples. They snipped hair and plucked a whisker, to be checked for mercury levels. They injected vitamins and a deworming compound. They vaccinated for rabies and feline distemper. With cotton swabs they obtained mucus from the cat's nostrils. From his flanks they cut away patches of skin, little circles the diameter of a pencil eraser, and sutured the wounds shut. They pressed me into service plucking ectoparasites (ticks) off the cat's ears and the back of his neck and head. (The ticks were saved in a pill bottle.) Finally the veterinarians inserted a probe into the panther's rectum, sent a jolt of electricity to his prostate, and collected his semen in a test tube held over the end of his penis. With each electroejaculation, the unconscious panther spread his paws, his claws unsheathing, his entire body quivering.

A red portable generator blathered in the hammock; from it, an orange extension cord snaked over the ground to power a microscope's light. The veterinarians peered through the microscope at slides of the panther's sperm. Roelke opened a cooler and got out a block of dry ice. She took a piece of plywood studded with dozens of nails and pressed it into the ice, making a grid of holes. Using a pipette, she transferred drops of the panther's semen into the holes, where they froze instantly. She collected the little pellets and placed them in an insulated vessel.

When the veterinarians were finally finished, Maehr asked me and one other man to carry the cat a short distance off into the pop-ash thicket. I held the panther under his shoulders, and the other man took the hind end. The panther was limp and loose, although now and then his muscles would give a big twitch. Roelke walked along beside us. She said, "Watch those claws. *Never* get between a cat's front legs." We lowered the panther onto a blanket, then backed off a few yards. His breathing was slow and regular. Strands of saliva hung from his jaws. His eyes were open and blinking, although Roelke told us he couldn't see yet. After about fifteen minutes, he flopped his head up and down. Grunting sounds came from deep within his chest. He began pushing himself along on his side with his hind legs, his thick tail pinwheeling. "External walk-flop," Roelke said. "Now he's in the 'Oh shit, what's wrong with my body?' phase. When he gets past that, he'll just be exhausted and want to sleep."

I stayed with the panther for a while longer; he had to be watched, to make sure he didn't lurch off into a puddle and drown. People began packing up equipment, talking quietly as they drifted back to the trucks. Maehr had his receiver and antenna out, checking on the panther's collar signal. He told me that this was the first uncollared adult captured in almost five years. I wondered about that, about how many other panthers might be hidden away in forests and swamps and on the big cattle ranches to the north. I wondered about the wisdom of darting panthers to attach collars to them, let alone to take samples of their blood and tissues and semen. When the first cats were collared back in the 1980s, critics speculated that the collars would get hung up on vines or disrupt the animals' keen sense of balance. They did not like the idea of natural, noble beasts going around with electronic boxes on their necks. If the panthers were going extinct, they reasoned, let them do so with dignity.

I took a last look at the panther, still lying on his side on the ground. His coat blended perfectly with the dirt and leaves, his new collar shining in pale contrast. Overhead, the fog had burned off; the sky was blue, stippled with tiny pink clouds. Vultures soared and dipped in the thermals. A flickering, shifting light filled the hammock and the pop-ash slough. The generator was still thrumming. Palmetto fronds waved in the breeze. In the live oaks, the gray-green beards of the Spanish moss lifted and fell. I picked a wild orange from a low spindly tree and quartered it with my knife. The flesh, lemon-sour, puckered my mouth.

7

PIGEONHOLING THE PANTHER

Laurie Wilkins is Collection Manager of Mammalogy at the Florida Museum of Natural History, on the campus of the University of Florida in Gainesville. She is a small, vivacious woman with dark gray-streaked hair, lively brown eyes, and a direct manner of speaking. It is her responsibility to prepare the remains of Florida panthers for the specimen files of the museum.

"Let's say a panther gets creamed by a Buick on Alligator Alley," she said. We were sitting among a semiorganized rubble of computers, typewriters, books, mailing tubes, slide sleeves, and rolled-up maps. Wilkins's office is partitioned off in a section of the museum's basement—gray concrete walls, the tang of mothballs, droning ventilation fans, buzzing fluorescent lights. "The carcass is rushed to Gainesville," Wilkins said, "either by vehicle or on a chartered flight. It goes to the vet school, where it's X-rayed and necropsied. The veterinarians take tissue samples for biomedical studies and to determine the cause of death. I like to be on hand for the necropsy. I've been there on Thanksgiving; I've been there at midnight. The vets want to open the skull and take out the brain, to check for rabies. I need the skull left as intact as possible, to preserve certain structural features.

"Everything stays in isolation until it's cleared of disease. Then I pick up the remains—skin, skeleton, and skull. The bones go to the beetles—that's dermestid beetles; we put the skeletal parts in an aquarium with hundreds of beetles, and they strip off the flesh. Later we give the bones a final cleaning, catalogue them, and file them." Wilkins nodded at the ranks of tall steel cabinets receding

into the expansive room. Any sort of defunct creature is liable to
end up at the Florida Museum: Bats. Bobcats. Armadillos. Mice.
Raccoons. Monkeys. Shrews. Hippopotami that have expired in
zoos. Dusty big-game mounts with glass eyes and heroic horns,
gemsbok and sable antelope and kudu, with which some sportsman no longer wishes to exchange glances, there on his trophy
room wall. "We are the official repository for mammals in the
state of Florida," Wilkins said. "We have over twenty-eight thousand specimens, most of them from the Southeast, Florida, and
the Caribbean. We have an excellent collection of manatees. We
have another whole building just for whales. One week I had a
thirty-three-foot humpback whale beach on Monday, a Florida
panther die on Tuesday, and a minke whale wash up on
Thursday."

She handed me a black box. Inside it was a plastic bag containing a dozen squarish yellowed bones: tail vertebrae. The box
also held a lower jaw (wishbone-shaped, robust) and a skull with
UF19096♂ inked on the crown. The skull was grayish-cream in
color, oblong, a bit over seven inches in length, with a door at
the back where the brain had come out. I was struck by how
rounded the skull was, how abbreviated the jaw. (There is a Biloxi
Indian legend, from Louisiana, explaining how the Ancient of
Frogs got into a wrestling match with the Ancient of Panthers
and whipped him against a tree, beating him sorely and shattering
his jaw—which is why, to this day, all panthers have a short jaw.)
The panther skull looked slightly different from two other puma
skulls that Wilkins showed me, one from Meldrum Creek, British
Columbia, and another from Bocas del Toro province, Panama:
The Florida skull was blunter than either of the others, larger than
the Panamanian skull and smaller than the Canadian one. I picked
up the panther's skull and jawbones and, after handling them for
a while, was able to articulate them. The large upper carnassial
teeth, in the back, fit outboard of the lower carnassials. The edges
of the teeth were as keen as newly cleft flint. In the front, the
upper canines meshed neatly to the outside of the lowers; the
canines were stout at the base, tapering to dull points, each about
an inch long. The skull felt compact and sturdy. I tried to imagine
the force brought to bear by the clamping shut of those jaws.

Wilkins led me to another part of the museum, where a fresh

pelt lay skin side up on top of a three-foot cabinet. Salt grains and flecks of newspaper stuck to the remaining flesh. The hide gave off a mild reek, like the beef sticks sold in filling stations. A tag attached by a copper wire read FL PANTHER *#43 10–31–91*. Wilkins said, "The skins hang around here for a while, until we find the money to get them tanned." She got out a panther hide just back from the New Method Fur Dressing Company, Beacon Street, San Francisco. The pelage, although smooth and soft, was markedly less luxuriant than that of another hide, of a puma from the Canadian Rockies; the Florida pelt was also noticeably darker. Clearly visible on the back of the skin was the telltale cowlick, a whorl of fur six inches long by an inch wide, the hairs standing up roughly against the surrounding fur.

Zoologists have put forward several schemes for classifying the cats. One scheme divides the various species into Big Cats and Small Cats. The lion, tiger, leopard, and jaguar are Big: large in size, having eyes with round pupils, and able to roar. The Small Cats—some thirty species worldwide—cannot roar, but they can purr, something the Big Cats are supposed to be unable to do. (A few experts insist that the Big Cats *can* purr and we have simply failed to observe them doing it.)

The Small Cats have vertical oval pupils, in which special muscles cinch the opening to a tiny slit, smaller even than the pinprick contraction of a round pupil. Highly nocturnal, their eyes huge and sensitive for gathering light, the Small Cats need this sort of protection against the glare of day. Among the Small Cats are the familiar house cat; the margay, a lovely spotted creature of Central and South America; the Iriomote cat, found on Iriomote Island east of Taiwan, a feline so retiring that it went undiscovered until 1967; the sand cat of North Africa and the Middle East, which gets all the moisture it requires from the bodies of its prey; and the bobcat, widespread and common in North America.

Where does the puma fit into this dichotomy? It has round pupils, like the Big Cats. Its skull—short and broad, and relatively small in proportion to the rest of its body—links it to the Small Cats. Like the Small Cats, it purrs and cannot roar. However, the puma is a tad larger than the Afro-Asian leopard and nearly as large as the jaguar, both of which are considered Big.

A second scheme organizes the felines into the Great Cats, the Not-So-Great Cats, and the Lesser Cats. The puma ranks with the whimsically named Not-So-Great Cats, whose size is intermediate and who lack the ability to roar. Some zoologists suggest that, among the living cats, the puma is most closely related to the cheetah, and indeed the puma resembles the cheetah with its lanky limbs and smallish head. But the puma is ever hard to classify. No one has been able to isolate specific morphological features that are clearly shared by the puma and only one or a few other species—which suggests that *Felis concolor* has its own lineage, has been its own separate self, at least since the other modern cats diverged some fifty million years ago.

In the 1940s, the zoologist Ernst Mayr, now professor emeritus at Harvard University, proposed what he termed a "Biological Species Concept" that today enjoys wide acceptance. Mayr defined a species as "a group of actually or potentially interbreeding populations that are reproductively isolated from other such groups." In plain words, a species is made up of many small populations of animals whose members can breed with one another or with members of other small adjoining populations, but not with animals of other species. (Of course, things are not nearly so simple in nature. For instance, a lion, *Panthera leo*, can breed with a tiger, *Panthera tigris*—the resulting kittens are called "tigons" and "ligers." It seems that such cross-species mating occurs only in zoos; wild animals of different species avoid one another because their habitats and breeding behaviors differ.)

The Florida panther is not a full species. It is a subspecies, a race. A subspecies represents a partitioning within a species: as Mayr put it, "a geographically defined aggregate of local populations which differ taxonomically from other subdivisions of the species." That is, one subspecies may not look exactly like another subspecies (it may have slightly paler fur, smaller paws, a broader skull), but members of the two races can and will interbreed when they come in contact. Nor is there a sharp line of demarcation between neighboring races: where subspecies come together, they "intergrade," with individual animals showing traits of both races.

Mayr once observed that the splitting off of subspecies, as conducted by taxonomists, is "not necessarily a very accurate rendering of the situation as it exists in nature." He attributed this fetish for differentiating organisms to "the need of the museum worker to identify every individual and to place it in a definite pigeonhole."

The chief pigeonholer of the puma is Edward A. Goldman. In a 1947 issue of the *Journal of Mammalogy*, I found his obituary, written by Stanley P. Young, with whom Goldman had collaborated on *The Puma, Mysterious American Cat*, published the previous year.

Edward Alphonso Goldman was born in 1873. When he was a boy, his parents left their farm in Illinois and drove three hundred head of cattle overland to the vicinity of Falls City, Nebraska; there, shortly after they settled, a plague of grasshoppers reduced the prairie to stubble, causing the Goldmans' cattle to starve. The family pulled up stakes again and, in 1888, arrived in Tulare County, California. Goldman's interest in natural history was nurtured by his father, himself an avid naturalist. The elder Goldman gave his son a decrepit muzzle-loading shotgun to bag specimens of the local fauna on both the California and Nebraska ranches, for identification and study.

In 1891 a team of naturalists directed by C. Hart Merriam had just completed a biological survey of Death Valley, California. Merriam headed the Office of Economic Ornithology and Mammalogy, a division within the U.S. Department of Agriculture that eventually would become part of the U.S. Fish and Wildlife Service. After the Death Valley Expedition was disbanded, one of Merriam's lieutenants, Edward Nelson, was passing south through the San Joaquin Valley when the singletree on his buckboard broke. He sought help at a nearby ranch—the Goldmans'. Mr. Goldman arranged for Nelson to meet his son, by then eighteen years of age and working at a fruit-packing plant in Fresno. As it happened, Nelson was looking for an assistant. Impressed with the young Goldman, Nelson hired him at a salary of thirty dollars a month, plus board—half as much as Goldman had been making at the fruit plant. Presently the buckboard, its singletree mended, two 42-pound grizzly bear traps clanking on either side, proceeded south to Tejon Pass, the two naturalists sharing the wagon's seat.

Soon Nelson and Goldman embarked on a four-year collecting trip to Mexico. This was during the regime of Porfirio Díaz, and the country was troubled by banditry and incipient revolution. The two gringos kept six-shooters strapped to their hips by day and tucked under their pillows at night. On one occasion, twenty Mexican Indians, believing Goldman to be a government official with designs on their land, chased after him with pistols and machetes. (He managed to hide in a farmhouse.) Near Toluca, late one evening as Goldman was returning from his fieldwork, three men with serapes wrapped tightly about them approached him along a narrow path. The men exchanged greetings with Goldman, then one of them slugged him in the temple with a rock, knocking him out. The thieves made off with Goldman's bag of traps, an altimeter, and the shotgun he used for collecting specimens. Altogether, Goldman spent fourteen years trapping and studying the creatures of Mexico. He and Nelson accumulated 22,756 Mexican mammals, most of them now in boxes and drawers at the U.S. National Museum of Natural History in Washington. During construction of the Panama Canal, Goldman made collecting forays into the adjacent jungle. In Arizona, sitting under the eaves of an adobe, skinning out a desert pocket mouse, Goldman was approached by a cowboy on horseback. The cowboy dismounted, looked at the tiny pelt on Goldman's knee, whistled softly, and said, "Well, I'll be goddamned!" In the Charleston Mountains of Nevada, hunting for a mountain sheep specimen, Goldman recrossed his own trail and discovered puma tracks superimposed on his bootprints, following him. Later, Goldman wrote: "The lion was doubtless prompted merely by curiosity, and I had been in no danger of attack."

As his career progressed, Goldman devoted more of his energies to taxonomy. He became known as the Noah of the Division of Biological Survey, on account of the more than fifty animals and plants to which he and others had attached his name. These included genera, species, and subspecies of coyote, pocket gopher, shrew, jaguar, flying squirrel, weasel, wood rat, white-footed mouse, shrike, motmot, rattlesnake, turtle, frog, and univalve mollusk. There is a photograph of Goldman, a dark-haired, ascetic-looking man wearing a suit and tie, sitting at a desk and inclining his head toward a formation of tiny white skulls. The caption states: "Goldman in his favorite field, revising a group of mammals, pocket gophers of the genus *Thomomys*." The last specimen that Goldman collected was a pocket gopher taken in 1946 in Florida. During his career, Goldman described over three hundred mammalian forms, most of them subspecies. Wrote Young in his obituary: "Goldman was a strong believer in evolution. His philosophy, as exemplified in the great number of mammals he described, is that any amount of constant variation in a geographic population, no matter how small, is incipient evolution and as such should be recognized."

For his landmark taxonomic revision of *Felis concolor*—his contribution to *The Puma, Mysterious American Cat*—Goldman examined 764 puma specimens, mostly skins and skulls. Many of the U.S. specimens had been shipped to the National Museum by hunters laboring in the government's anti-predator campaigns (an especially prolific contributor was one B. V. Lilly). Goldman measured the relative lengths of skulls, tooth rows, and canine grooves. Using vernier calipers he obtained the dimensions of palates, nasal openings, maxilla, zygomatic arches, cranial cavities, postorbital processes, and interorbital constrictions. From Canada to Patagonia, over the great sweep of the puma's range, Goldman identified a whopping thirty subspecies, basing his designations mainly on minute differences in cranial structure. (Today, most taxonomists recognize twenty-seven puma subspecies.) Goldman used what is called the Seventy Percent Rule: If 70 percent of the individuals in one geographic area are discriminable from a neighboring population, they can be considered a separate subspecies. Goldman acknowledged in *The Puma* that "the boundaries between subspecies are more or less arbitrarily drawn," especially for places like South America, where "very extensive regions remain unrepresented by specimens"—a situation that holds true in South America to this day.

Goldman did not measure all those skulls just to make life complicated for humans at the end of the century, or in some kind of a contest to attach his name to more creatures than anybody else. (By all accounts, he was a shy and self-effacing soul.) Goldman and others of his own particular subspecies of *Homo sapiens* were trying to impose order on the vast number of animals still being discovered in various corners of the world. One of the things that Goldman and his colleagues did, for better or worse, was to provide standards upon which we now base critical environmental policies—in the case of the Florida panther, the extremely powerful federal statute, the Endangered Species Act.

Goldman had access to only seventeen Florida panther specimens. From them, he characterized the race as "a medium-sized, dark subspecies, with pelage short and rather stiff; skull with broad, flat frontal region; nasals remarkably broad and high-arched or expanded upward." (These cranial attributes give the panther a distinctive Roman-nosed appearance. One research scientist I talked to in Florida judged the aspect "noble" in the males and "homely" in the females.) Goldman considered the Florida panther "closely allied to *couguar* of Pennsylvania," an extinct subspecies. Compared with the neighboring *stanleyana* of Texas (Goldman named this subspecies for his chum and co-author, Stanley Young), the panther's skull differed "in the greater general width and upward expansion of the nasals." Goldman made no mention of a kink in the tail (most of the specimens he examined consisted of skins and skulls, not skeletons). Nor did he note the "cowlick," the distinctive swirl of fur above the shoulders assumed to have been brought on by inbreeding. However, it was there on some of the panther skins he studied.

Laurie Wilkins had just started working at the Florida Museum in the early 1980s when people began rediscovering panthers in the southern tip of the state. As Chris Belden collared more and more of the elusive cats, he reported characteristics that no one had remarked in other pumas: the kink in the tail, the furry cowlick. On a trip to Chicago, Wilkins stopped in at the Field Museum of Natural History. The Field Museum houses the skins and skulls of the first Florida panthers bagged by Charles Cory in the 1890s. Edward Goldman had studied the very same specimens. When the curator got them out for Wilkins to look at, all four skins had the telltale whorls of fur on the back. How had Goldman missed them? Maybe the light had been poor; maybe he had been more attentive toward skulls than pelts; maybe he had seen the ruffled fur and discounted it as damage caused by storage or handling.

Intrigued, Wilkins went and counted cowlicks at other museums. Altogether, she (and various curators and colleagues, at her request) inspected skins from 648 pumas of fifteen North American and fourteen South American subspecies. Wilkins checked seventy-four Florida panthers (museum specimens and living animals) and found fifty-nine cowlicks. Only twenty-nine other pumas, from six North American and four South American races, had cowlicks. Almost all the South American cowlicks came from Chile and Argentina, toward the southern end of the continent, where it becomes peninsular. It seemed probable to Wilkins that puma populations living on long, narrow land masses are hindered from exchanging genes with neighboring populations. Ten thousand years ago, at the end of the last Ice Age, a rising sea level turned what had been a broad Florida peninsula into a much narrower projection of land. Had the panthers there been inbreeding ever since?

Wilkins also looked at skulls. "Basically, I attached numbers to other people's observations," she told me. She set the skull of *UF19096♂* on the table. "I measured the contour relative to a straight line drawn from the tip of the nasal bone"—she touched her finger to the skull just above the nose opening—"to the top of the transverse thickening of the sagittal crest"—she touched the crown of the head. "I took a carpenter's contour gauge and made an impression of the skull, transferred the image to a piece of paper, and digitized the contour." The Florida panther's highly arched nasals—its distinctive Roman nose—had thus been quantified.

Wilkins scrutinized specimens of panthers from Everglades National Park and found the Everglades cats to be "morphologically different" from classic Florida panthers in the Big Cypress, a hop, step, and a jump away across Shark River Slough. The Everglades cats were smaller, their coats were redder, and none of them had the cowlick.

As an authority on the taxonomy of the panther, Wilkins found herself in U.S. District Court in 1987 as an expert witness in the trial of James Billie. Billie, a forty-year-old Seminole Indian, had been charged by the federal government with two felony violations of the Endangered Species Act: killing a Florida panther and possessing its skin. Billie was then, and still is, chairman of the Seminole tribe of Florida. The Seminoles arrived in Florida, driven down from the north by white settlement and tribal strife, two centuries after the Spaniards had occupied the peninsula. Today, Florida's Seminoles number some seventeen hundred people living on five reservations. (Several of the reservations are large, like the one in Hendry County where Billie killed the panther, 52,000 acres; some are tiny, like the square mile in Fort Lauderdale where the tribal headquarters are located. The tribe gets most of its income from selling tax-free cigarettes and running bingo games.) James Billie is said to be half Seminole, half white. He is a folksinger and a veteran of the Vietnam War. A promoter of Seminole culture, he often wears the brightly colored, patterned blouse that is traditional among the Seminoles, in combination with blue jeans, cowboy boots, and a Rolex wristwatch. One night in December 1983, Billie and a friend were driving in a pickup truck on the Big Cypress reservation, playing a spotlight through the brush alongside the road. The light illuminated a large animal with green eyes and a long tail. Billie aimed a high-powered pistol, and pulled the trigger. He killed kuwachobee, or "big cat." Billie skinned the panther, ate some of its meat, and draped its hide over a cypress pole. While Billie was digesting his meal the next day, two wardens for the Florida Game Commission showed up at his house. In addition to the federal charges, Billie faced state charges for killing a panther, one of thirty-seven animals on Florida's endangered species list.

In newspaper interviews Billie professed to be an apprentice medicine man and said he was engaging in a sacred Seminole rite when he killed the cat. His lawyer maintained that state and federal wildlife regulations did not apply on the reservation, where Indians may kill game at any time of the year. The lawyer said, "The irony is that there would not be any endangered panther if the white man hadn't developed South Florida. The Indians, left to their own devices, never would have needed an Endangered Species Act." When the case went to court, Billie's lawyer based his defense on the premise that Billie did not knowingly kill a puma of the subspecies *Felis concolor coryi*. Laurie Wilkins testified for the prosecution. The presence of a cowlick and a kinked tail, plus the highly arched nasal openings, she said, demonstrated that the animal was indeed a Florida panther. The defense lawyer pointed out that panthers recently captured in Everglades National Park lacked the cowlick and the kinked tail. He told the jury that even the experts were confounded: the verdict was not in on what constituted a Florida panther, and therefore his client could not be convicted of killing one. The federal case ended in a hung jury. Then Billie was acquitted in state court. When asked by a newspaper reporter if he would ever kill another panther, Billie replied that he would, "but probably up in Colorado"—Florida's panthers being a "sickly" breed, he said, weak and disease-ridden, the males with only one testicle. When I tried to telephone Billie at Seminole tribal headquarters, the woman who answered said she would take a message but that the Chief probably would not get back to me. "He doesn't like to talk to newspaper and book people," she said, "because what he says always gets, like, construed. He'll say the panther is beautiful, and it'll turn up in the papers that he's out butchering panthers in the Everglades."

After Billie killed the panther, the Florida Game Commission changed the state law to make it a crime to kill *any* puma in Florida—as Laurie Wilkins told me, "even if it's purple with pink polka dots." At that time, the Game Commission resisted advice from the U.S. Fish and Wildlife Service to work toward changing the panther's status from that of an endangered subspecies to an endangered population—a course that would have made it easier to address the myriad biological problems afflicting a sickly, inbred cat.

8

WALKING IN

O n a hot day in August, one careful step at a time, Dave Maehr
worked his way into a drought-parched pop-ash slough. He
did not slap at the mosquitoes that bit him. He refrained from
waving away the gnats that circled his head. He kept his eyes
roving, checking the ground in front: behind a fallen tree, in the
tall grass, at the edge of a palmetto clump. He was "walking in"
on a panther, a female, Number 19; from the way she kept returning to this site, Maehr believed she had given birth to kittens.

"Walking in" is a tactic that wildlife biologists often use. After
locating an animal's collar signal, they walk toward the signal's
source. They hope to spot the creature (with a wary animal like
a panther, they rarely do), or discover its lair, or find out what it
was eating and fit one more piece into the puzzle of how the
animal lives in the wild.

From fifty feet away, Maehr spotted Number 19 lying at the
base of a tree. She was asleep; mosquitoes hovered about her face.
Her radio collar looked gray and weathered. Her whiskers, caught
by a shaft of sunlight, were a dazzling white. Maehr counted the
small spotted kittens sprawled out around her. Four! He had never
known of a litter that large.

Stealing closer, he crouched behind a fallen limb. A kitten sat
up and looked at him. The kitten yawned, showing tiny, needle-
sharp teeth; it lay down again alongside its mother. Number 19
woke. She raised her head to shake off an insect pest, the white
fur at her throat glinting brightly. Seventy paces away, a twig
snapped. Number 19 sat up quickly. The noise came from another

biologist, Maehr's partner, walking in on a slightly different heading. Nineteen, Maehr noted, looked lean, almost gaunt. She peered intently toward the sound. Then she turned her head back, her gaze shifting slowly until she was staring at Maehr's face.

A low growl issued from her throat. The kittens scampered into a nearby palmetto thicket. Number 19 rose to her feet. Her eyes riveted on Maehr's, she crept toward him.

It had never happened like this before. Always the cat had stolen away before the humans got close. Nineteen took another step, her body tense and low to the ground. Maehr realized that to drop his stare, or to turn and run, would trigger an attack. As the panther took another step forward, Maehr took a step back. Again: the cat stepped forward, Maehr stepped back. Moving as carefully as he could, feeling behind him with his feet, he kept his eyes on the panther's. Five steps. Ten. Finally Maehr realized that he was the only one moving. Nineteen had stopped advancing and was no longer in a taut crouch. Maehr turned and walked away. Trying not to hurry, he retreated to the edge of the slough.

In 1944 a biologist named Lucille Stickel, studying box turtles in Patuxent, Maryland, wanted to chart where, in their diurnal trundlings, they ventured. She cut a coffee can in half lengthwise. She taped half the can to a turtle's back. She suspended a spool of thread inside the can, anchored one end of the thread, and let the turtle go.

A half century later, scientists can glue radio transmitters (the smallest, to date, is approximately the size of a pencil eraser) to turtles' shells, to the upper mandibles of ducks, to the carapaces of beetles—and follow their subjects' meanderings. They can chart animals' food preferences, find their dens, divine their breeding habits, learn of their illnesses. A friend of mine, a wildlife biologist who is restocking the rivers of Pennsylvania with otters, enlists a veterinary surgeon to implant radio transmitters inside the body cavities of the otters, where the wax-coated devices free-float among the intestines, liver, paunch. Elsewhere, researchers are putting bar codes on the backs of honeybees (the better to document their comings and goings at the hive), dusting mice with fluorescent powder (an ultraviolet light source reveals where the rodents venture in the dark), and equipping tree frogs with belts containing mildly radioactive powder (the frogs can be located through the use of a Geiger counter).

The standard method of following a wild animal is to fit it with a collar containing a radio transmitter and trail it about using an antenna. To achieve line-of-sight readings on a transmitter, a scientist may send the antenna aloft: in a balloon, attached to a kite, in an airplane, or (for widely peregrinating species such as caribou and whales) aboard a satellite in earth orbit. Biologists first began using radio telemetry to study wildlife in the early 1960s. They worked with wolves, porcupines, and rabbits. In Yellowstone National Park they put radio collars on grizzly bears and observed them mating, feeding, and hibernating. Since then, transmitters have been attached to moose in Minnesota, civets in Thailand, guanacos in Chile, clouded leopards in Nepal, Adélie penguins in Antarctica, snowshoe hares in Alberta, polar bears in Alaska, wombats in Australia, woodcock in Maine, starlings in New Jersey, brown noddies in Hawaii, feral dogs in Alabama, raccoons in Washington, D.C., bobcats in Oklahoma, lions in Africa, lynx in Switzerland, and jaguars in Brazil (the researcher following along over the jungle treetops in a Quicksilver-MX ultralight aircraft).

The puma has probably been studied more extensively than any other wild feline in the world. Maurice Hornocker began the first modern analysis of a puma population, in Idaho, in 1965. Since then, biologists have pried into the habits of *Felis concolor* in places as various as Texas, Manitoba, the Los Angeles Basin, and Patagonia. They have made careful observations of pumas while following jaguars in Belize and Brazil and Peru.

Hornocker (who had previously worked on grizzly bears in Yellowstone) studied the pumas in a two-hundred-square-mile area along Big Creek, a tributary of the Middle Fork of the Salmon River, in what has since been designated the River of No Return Wilderness. He chose that roadless, remote place because few people ventured into it to hunt pumas: Hornocker wanted to examine a stable population unaffected by the rapid turnover caused when humans kill cats. He enlisted a local puma hunter named Wilbur

Wiles. Using Wiles's hounds, Hornocker caught forty-six pumas
(a Westerner, he called them "mountain lions"), put ear tags on
them, and kept tabs on them for five winters.

Working from the ground, and walking an estimated six thousand miles during the study, Hornocker and Wiles puzzled out
the cats' ranges and interactions, their reproduction, what they
killed and ate. They found that the population revolved around a
nucleus of mature males and females well established on home
territories. Although a female might share some of her territory
with a neighboring female, the males adhered to rigid boundaries
between their ranges, carefully delineated with scrapes. Male
pumas roamed over much larger areas than did females; usually
the home territory of a male included those of two or three females.
Male pumas did not help in raising kittens. Hornocker theorized
that by ranging widely and keeping tabs on several females, the
males upped their chances of reproducing. The females increased
their chances of successfully rearing young by having smaller home
ranges and learning them intimately, locating safe den sites and
places where prey abounded.

Hornocker wondered whether pumas suppress the number of
big game animals, an assumption that had led to their persecution
for decades. From tracks in the snow he learned that, in fact, lions
are adept hunters: of forty-five stalks he documented, thirty-seven
ended in kills. The lions killed deer and elk routinely. Sometimes
they preyed on very young or very old animals, sometimes on
creatures in their prime. Hornocker estimated that a mature lion
would take five to seven elk, or fourteen to twenty deer, in a year.
During the five years' research, deer and elk actually increased in
the study area, while the number of pumas stayed the same. "Only
so many cats can live in a given area," Hornocker concluded.
"Food supply, hunting [by humans], and weather determine deer
and elk numbers."

As Hornocker's findings became known, wildlife departments
began refashioning their attitudes toward pumas. Today, most
Western states classify them as game animals. Hunters buy licenses
to shoot pumas. Biologists try to manage puma populations for
a sustained yield, or "harvest," just as they manage other species
from moose to mourning doves. In eleven Western states, the
combined puma population is estimated at sixteen thousand—an

increase of 20 to 40 percent over the last half century. Only in Texas does the puma remain a "varmint" that can be killed year round and with no limit on the number taken. At the other end of the spectrum is California, where in 1990 the state's voters banned the hunting of pumas for sport. In California, the game department estimates the puma population at five thousand and rising.

Hornocker's graduate student John Seidensticker, now at the National Zoo, continued the Idaho study in the 1970s. The first researcher to put radio collars on pumas, Seidensticker postulated a "land tenure system" among the cats. In most cases, only resident lions—those holding established home areas—actually got to breed. In addition to the residents, transient pumas came from outside the area and drifted through it. When a resident died, a transient might happen onto the vacant area, tighten his or her movements around it, and finally settle in and join the breeding population. "The most frequent 'social' behavior pattern in the mountain lion," Seidensticker wrote, "is that of avoiding other lions." Pumas would get together for mating, but otherwise would shun one another. When kittens reached adolescence, they left home—crossed rivers and mountains and did not return. Even if a local home area was open, the young still struck out on their own.

Wherever they have studied pumas, biologists have found the same general dynamics to prevail: resident adults, with each male's home area overlapping those of several females; young that disperse when they near adulthood; and transients in search of homes and a chance to pass on their genes.

In Florida, Dave Maehr determined that the home ranges of adult male panthers average two hundred square miles. Female panthers' homes are seventy-five square miles. Maehr learned that young panther females do not automatically leave the area in which they were born; in some cases they carve out territories from their mother's holdings. It is the young males who are the wild cards, the floaters, striking out for parts unknown or tiptoeing along the fringes of adult males' territories, waiting for vacancies to open up. Often they wait in vain: from 1985 to 1990, Maehr did not find a single dominant adult male who died or was driven from his territory. It is easy to imagine those tenured males mating with their own female offspring. As for the young males, in whichever direction they roam, sooner or later they run into housing developments, orange groves, cane fields, and croplands. They perish on the highway or, as Maehr puts it, get "crunched" by a dominant male. Some may sneak into densely overgrown river bottomlands and follow them northward. No scrapes do these sojourners find, no signs of other panthers to tantalize and hold them. So they keep on moving. Maybe they, and not people's imaginations or sentimental yearnings for a wild Florida that is swiftly diminishing, are the source of the hundreds of panther sightings reported across the state each year.

One evening I drove down a mile-long lane to the Fakahatchee Strand Hunting Club, along Route 29 just north of the Florida Panther National Wildlife Refuge. There I met with Roy McBride. McBride bunks at the club when he works on panthers in South Florida, staying by himself, except for his dogs, who barked at me before settling at his command. The swamp came right up behind the dwelling, a white trailer. Herons were croaking in the dusk as we sat on musty stuffed chairs on a screened-in porch. McBride was still wearing his Stetson hat, indoors. He had consented to be interviewed, but only if I agreed to let him inspect anything I wrote about him before it was published. He owns a business called Livestock Protection Company. His two sons, Rowdy and Rocky, also hunt lions, Rowdy hiring himself out to sheep ranchers, Rocky guiding hunters—"The hunters are more lucrative," McBride said, "but then you're kind of a high-priced babysitter."

In his work, McBride uses Walker hounds—lean, fast dogs from fox-hunting strains that cold-trail silently and give tongue only when they flush the quarry and get its body scent. He likes smaller dogs, weighing forty to fifty pounds, because they do not tire as quickly as big ones do. Like Ben Lilly, he methodically culls his pack, keeping only the fleet, the good noses, the dogs with the fire in them to trail a predator until the end. When in Florida, McBride gets up at four in the morning and someone ferries him into the woods or the swamp. With the dawn, his hounds work into the breeze a quarter mile in front of him. He hunts in the cool and quits when it gets hot. He carries a walkie-talkie to confer with the biologists. He may walk fifteen miles in a morning. Once the dogs drive it from cover, a panther will run downwind, double back, or weave through a thicket, trying to lose the pack. However, it will not run far. "If you hear the chase start," McBride told me, "you'll probably hear them bark treed."

McBride was open-faced, brown-eyed, loose-limbed. His voice had a West Texas twang: "can't" was "cain't," "drink" was "drank," as in "Here, have a drank." He handed me a can of Budweiser in an insulating foam sleeve. He told me, "I'm just a cat hunter" and "Talk to the biologists, guy, I'm not a big wheel here." He claimed to be a simple fellow, then would let slip a term like "large ungulates." During our conversation he addressed me as "guy" several times, and "man," as if trying to keep me at arm's length with the anonymous, familiar address. McBride has killed predators through the use of traps, dogs, cyanide guns, firearms, and snares. He has slain coyotes in Texas, gray wolves in Mexico, Andean foxes in Argentina, hyenas in Namibia, and snow leopards in Mongolia. He most enjoys hunting what he calls "the big stuff": jaguars, pumas, leopards. He has invented a collar that holds poison in a small bladder. A rancher losing sheep to any predator which kills with a throat hold (including wolves, coyotes, and pumas) can strap the collar onto sacrificial lambs and place them, unguarded, in a pasture, for when the predator returns. The collar kills selectively. Poison need not be spread indiscriminately or helicopters hired at great expense. McBride's collar is widely used in South Africa and Argentina; the U.S. Environmental Protection Agency, perhaps fearing secondary poisoning that might be caused by the toxin (or more likely, McBride contends, fearing political heat from environmentalists), has not certified it for general use, although it is employed by federal agents to eliminate particularly wary, untrappable animals.

McBride captured the red wolves that the U.S. Fish and Wildlife Service bred in captivity, the ones whose offspring were reintroduced into North Carolina in 1987. He tracked down a few of the remaining Mexican gray wolves for a breeding program at the Sonora Desert Museum in Tucson, Arizona. He believes that in the early 1960s, when predator control was at its strictest in Texas, fewer than twenty-five pumas remained in the state. In

Incident at Eagle Ranch, a book about the persecution of eagles in Texas (like pumas and coyotes, eagles kill sheep), the author Donald G. Schueler asserted that Roy McBride "had more to do with bringing the mountain lion to the verge of extinction in Texas than any other single person." Today, however, with sheep raising on the wane and predator control less of a necessity, fewer lions are being killed in Texas, and the puma population—boosted by cats wandering in from Mexico—has come back strongly. No one knows for certain, but some people think there may be a thousand pumas in Texas. "They're so common," McBride told me, "that they're considered a nuisance animal."

McBride pioneered the shooting of coyotes from helicopters, a technique still used throughout the West. He told me about the time a helicopter stalled out while he was riding in it. The machine nosed into the ground, flipped over, and slammed into the desert. Although the force of the impact bent the barrel of his shotgun into a U shape and sheared several shotgun cartridges in half, McBride remained uninjured. The front of one of the pilot's boots was torn off so that his toes showed; he was not moving, and blood trickled from the corners of his mouth. McBride smelled aviation fuel. He dragged the pilot out of the wreck and laid him on his back. After a while, the man's chest heaved in a breath. The pilot groaned. Slowly he turned over and pushed himself to his hands and knees. He gasped, "Roy, where are we?" McBride replied, "We're still in Texas. I just heard a coyote bark."

McBride was hard to keep on the subject of panthers, preferring to talk about his home state. I had read his master's degree thesis on mountain lions along the Texas–Mexico border, and it seemed to me that the work he had done—on cats that were not protected by law and, because of their abundance, were essentially expendable—had helped pave the way for work on the endangered Florida subspecies. In conducting the research for his degree, McBride had found that if pumas were chased and darted when the weather was hot, they usually died. He worked out practical drug dosages. He caught cats in the dry treeless mountains of West Texas, put radio collars on them, and released them in the jungle-like wooded lowlands of southeastern Texas, 450 miles away. There the cats had stayed.

. . .

Female panthers mature sexually at two and a half to three years of age. An exception to this generality is panther number 19, who, protecting her kittens, had menaced the biologist Maehr. Number 19 had her first kittens before she turned two, the earliest documented reproduction by a puma anywhere. Her first litter was four; the average Florida panther mother has two kittens, with one to four the norm across North America. (Larger litters have been reported. In the 1940s, in Utah, a female puma gave birth to six kittens while caught in a trap. In Arizona, around the turn of the century, a plainsman named Buffalo Jones is said to have killed a mother puma with nine unborn kittens, all of which he skinned and turned in for the bounty.)

In captivity, female pumas that are not bred go into estrus every seventeen to twenty-seven days. When a female goes into heat in the wild, she finds a male's scrape, leaves her own urine as a calling card, and hangs around in the vicinity. She advertises her receptivity by squawling and yowling. Old-time reporters have confused the puma's call with steam locomotive and steamboat whistles. Charles Cory, who collected the type specimen of the Florida panther, described the animals' vocalizations in this way: "The cry of the cub resembles the screech of a Parrot, but it often utters a soft whistle. The cry of the old Panther somewhat resembles the screech of a Parrot, but is much louder." Controversy reigns over whether the puma actually screams. Daniel Giraud Elliot, a zoologist, wrote of hearing the "shrill cry or shriek" of a panther one night in 1883 while camping along Florida's St. Johns River: "The animal seemed to be directly over my tent; and the unearthly yell made my flesh creep, and brought me out to the fire, that was burning brightly before the tent." Observers across the puma's range have compared the cry to "demoniac laughter," "the scream of a woman in extreme agony," and "the wail of a child in terrible pain." Perhaps the uniting description is supplied by Ross Allen, a Floridian who, in the 1940s, hid downwind of his wild animal compound and watched a panther calling:

[She] stood with her neck held straight out, and with her mouth pointed toward the ground. She then opened her mouth to about half its possible gape and voiced a series of loud, grating shrieks. The scream of this panther could be likened to a high, rasping human voice loudly shrieking "Ouch!", the sound being prolonged for about three or four seconds, and repeated from three to seven times in succession.

That perfectly summarizes the yowling I heard with Deborah Jansen at Big Cypress National Preserve.

Making his rounds, the male hears or scents the female. Pumas are most vehement in their courtship and copulation. The females are thought to be "induced ovulators": in order for them to release eggs, they must be stimulated by mating. The sexual act itself is often violent and may occur dozens of times in a single day. The rough play (which is almost universal among cats), the snarling and cuffing and biting, cause the female's uterus to undulate, conveying the semen to the ovaries.

Should two males converge on a female, the fur may fly. In Idaho, Hornocker found no evidence of fighting in the stable population he studied. But where vacancies keep occurring, where boundaries are in a state of flux, pumas do fight, sometimes to the death. In his Texas study McBride found several cats that had been injured in fights. In the 1920s, when California was trying to eradicate its pumas, a government hunter named Jay Bruce bagged a 145-pound male which, Bruce wrote, "showed evidence of having engaged in a desperate battle a few days previously. Two toes were missing from the cat's left forepaw, and his head, neck, and shoulders had been severely bitten and clawed." Bruce backtracked the puma, found the spoor of another, smaller puma, followed that trail, and discovered the smaller cat's carcass. The smaller puma, also a male, had deep wounds on his head, neck, and both front legs, and apparently had died from infection of the lacerations. Bruce concluded that "the larger lion had probably intruded after [a] lioness had accepted the attentions of the smaller one, and the latter, although mortally wounded, had apparently been the victor, as the larger lion had left the scene of combat and failed to return, while the lioness had faithfully lingered for two days near her mate's dead body, deserting it only when she heard the hounds approaching."

In Florida, Dave Maehr once followed a radio collar's mortality signal to a young male who had presumed to intrude on a courting pair. The young panther had been punctured and mauled from nose to tail. His skull had been crushed into an approximate cone shape between his antagonist's jaws. Soon after, the transmitter signal from panther number 12, a large resident male, lagged slower and slower and finally stopped. When treed by hounds a month later, 12 had sores all over his body, a ten-inch scar along his rib cage, and a front paw that had begun to heal from a severe dislocation or a fracture. His radio collar's transmitter had two holes in it, slightly less than two inches apart. In his office Maehr showed me the transmitter. He picked up a panther skull and held it against the device. The daggerlike upper canines fitted perfectly into the holes. Modern technology, Maehr believed, had saved Number 12's life.

In July 1990, Number 17, another resident male, died of unknown causes, perhaps simply of old age. For over five years he had dominated a huge chunk of territory around Alligator Alley, in a portion of Big Cypress National Preserve called the Stairsteps Unit. After his death, neighboring males, finding that 17's scrapes were not being renewed, began probing into his territory. At the same time, a newcomer, Number 28, stepped into the picture. Number 28 already was mildly famous. Two years earlier, in the wee hours of an October morning, he had stepped in front of a police car on a road at the Fort Myers airport. The collision fractured his shoulder blade and his skull just below one eye. The Florida Game Commission nursed him back to health and, with a flourish of publicity, released him at the Corkscrew Swamp Sanctuary, a large private tract owned by the National Audubon Society.

Number 28 drifted eastward. In October 1990 he broke all the rules. In the heart of 17's territory, he encountered two female panthers, numbers 41 and 18, and killed them. One biologist to whom I spoke labeled the killings "nonadaptive behavior" and speculated that his head injury had transformed Number 28 into a "crazy cat." I asked Dave Maehr why a male panther might have done such a thing. "Number 28 was a young, inexperienced male," Maehr said. "It's possible that he saw those particular females—neither of which was in estrus at the time—as rivals

rather than as potential mates." In any case, in three short weeks
an estimated 4 percent of the entire adult population of Florida
panthers was lost.

In the Northern Hemisphere most puma litters are born between
March and September—in Florida, from March through July,
although kittens have been born there all year round. Gestation is
three months. At birth, the kittens weigh about a pound and are
eight to twelve inches in length. Their tails are banded with black,
and their bodies are as dappled as a fawn's, except that the spots
are black. The pattern helps break up a kitten's body outline,
blending it into a variegated natural background. In different parts
of their range, pumas den in brush, beneath uprooted trees, under
rock ledges, and in caves. In Florida the favored site is that old
standby, a palmetto patch.

Most panther mothers locate their dens in quiet, out-of-the-
way places, although there are exceptions. Sonny Bass, the biologist at Everglades National Park, once drove me along the road
that leads to his office, about a quarter mile from the Park Service
campground where I was staying. We parked and walked off the
blacktop into bracken fern, briars, and saw palmetto growing
densely beneath straight slash pines. A stone's throw from the
berm, an antenna had been duct-taped ten feet up in a spindly tree;
a wire descended to a chart recorder, a setup Bass referred to as
a "biologist-in-a-box." From the box Bass removed a roll of chart
paper, inked with a pattern of spikes recording the comings and
goings of female panther number 14. Bass was sure she had given
birth to kittens in a clump of palmettos about fifty yards from the
box. Bass pointed; I peered, and could make nothing out. It gave
me an odd feeling, knowing that Number 14 (Bass called her Pearl;
he had captured her on Sunday, December 7, 1986) was lying in
her den, perhaps nursing her young, listening to our every word.

Bass is a short, solid man in his fifties, with a pleasant, forth-
right manner. When speaking, he has a habit of throwing up his
eyebrows as if suddenly astonished. In dress, he favors blue jeans,
a T-shirt, and Western boots. As a graduate student at the University of Texas, he studied herons. He is that rarity among Floridians over the age of forty, an actual native, born and raised in

Homestead, a few miles east of the Everglades, where he lives today. Bass used to do a lot of quail hunting. Now most of the land outside the park is covered with asphalt or crops: tomatoes, bunch beans, squash, okra, seed corn, flowers, onions, cucumbers, turf, mangoes, avocados, limes, strawberries, bananas. No room for quail. No room for panthers.

As we stood next to the biologist-in-a-box, I asked Bass about Pearl.

"She's nine or ten years old," he said softly, the faintest drawing out of his vowels suggesting his Southern origin. "Physically, she's in good shape. She's a very proficient deer killer. She has never been hit by a car, although she's seen fairly regularly along the road. This could be her last litter, since it will be a couple of years before she could have another one, and she might be too old to breed by then."

Unbeknownst to Bass, Number 14 was not in good shape, and this would in fact be her last litter. Two months later she was dead. An autopsy found high levels of mercury in her body. Bass never located her kittens and presumed that they too had died.

Young pumas depend on their mother for everything. She suckles them for the first two months of their life. She protects them from predators, including their father. When they are about two months old, and roughly the size of cocker spaniels, she starts taking them hunting. Because wild pumas are shy and reclusive, it is difficult to study the exact relationship between a mother and her kittens. Does she actually teach the young to hunt? Some observers believe that this would be impossible. The puma is a stalker, a layer of ambushes. How could a female get within killing range if she had a couple of playful kittens in tow? In Chihuahua, Mexico, the biologist Starker Leopold once watched a mother puma padding along softly, as her two young—almost as large as she—followed forty yards behind. When she stopped to scrutinize the cover for prey, they stopped as well.

Harley Shaw studied pumas in Arizona in the 1970s and 1980s. He described his experiences in a lively memoir entitled *Soul Among Lions*. Through radiotelemetry, Shaw found that a mother would lead her kittens—even small, newly weaned kittens seven or eight weeks old—to a kill, usually a deer or a cow, and there she would leave them, to go off in search of further prey. She might be gone for several days. Unprotected, the kittens themselves sometimes became prey, to coyotes, ravens, eagles, other pumas, and once, to Shaw's chagrin, to the biologist's own trail hounds. Kittens "have a glorious time at kills," Shaw wrote. "Grass and ground litter may be disturbed for fifty feet surrounding a carcass . . . The body is usually more fully consumed than one [fed on] by a mature lion alone. Leg bones, ribs, and even the skull are chewed into small pieces. Chunks of hair, hide, ears, and tail are torn and scattered, suggesting that such fragments are used as toys." When the female kills another animal, she escorts her young to the new carcass. "Kittens learn early to move around their range and not imprint upon a single home site," wrote Shaw. "Home is a large tract of land that they undoubtedly come to know as you and I know the floorplan of our house."

Pumas hunt when their prey is most active, at dawn and at dusk. They do not climb trees or rock ledges from which to jump on the backs of their victims, as is often depicted in illustrations; such an approach would be too dangerous. Tackling "large ungulates" is dangerous enough when tried from level ground. The hunting puma zigzags slowly through thick cover, whose lush greenery attracts grazers and masks the movements of stealth. When the puma sees, hears, or smells its quarry, it lets the animal approach or makes a slow, strategic stalk. When the prey is within ten or twenty yards, the puma launches itself. An onrushing puma is thought to be able to run at thirty-five miles per hour, which means it can cover twenty yards in a little over one second. The cat leaps onto the animal's back, biting through the neck vertebrae or into the back of the skull. Depending on the final angle of attack, and on the size and strength of the prey, the puma may clamp its jaws onto the animal's throat, crushing the windpipe and killing by suffocation.

A puma weighing one hundred pounds can kill a bull elk weighing eight hundred pounds. The technique, as interpreted from tracks in the snow, is exquisite. The puma crashes into the elk, the great deer bolts in terror, the cat wraps its forelegs around the elk's neck and wrenches it back—and the opposing forces cause the elk's spinal column to snap. If the puma botches the job, it may pay with its life. During his research study in Idaho, Hornocker found tracks in the snow showing where an adult female puma had tangled with an elk. The pair had skidded down a steep hill and slammed into a tree, after which the elk escaped. When Hornocker captured the puma three weeks later, he found that her jaw had been broken and her lower canines were torn out at the roots. Unable to feed, she had dwindled from one hundred pounds to seventy pounds. Dead pumas have been found with sharp sticks penetrating their rib cages and brain cavities. In Utah, biologists came upon a mule deer and a puma lying together, each dead of a broken neck.

Usually a cat will carry its prey to a place where it feels secure. Stories abound of pumas transporting fully grown horses, mules, and cows up steep hills, across water-filled ditches, and over fences. A cat may eat ten pounds of meat at a sitting. It may return for several meals. After feeding, it will usually cover its kill with sticks, grass, and leaves, apparently to hide it from scavengers. In Idaho, Hornocker located dead elk concealed under stacks of limbs that pumas had bitten off trees. In Arizona, Shaw came upon a mule deer buck killed in the middle of a boulder field. The cat, finding no other camouflage material available, had placed a single twig on the buck.

In various parts of its range, *Felis concolor* preys on horses, cattle, sheep, goats, and pigs. In *The Puma, Mysterious American Cat,* Stanley Young wrote of pumas: "These animals are so destructive to man's interests that they cannot be tolerated except in the wildest areas." Roy McBride makes a not-inconsiderable income "taking out," as he puts it, stock-killing pumas on ranches in his home state of Texas and in Central and South America. He told me, "Those cats kill sheep like Samson killed Philistines." It is nothing for a puma to knock off twenty sheep in a few minutes. The cat seemingly goes on automatic and keeps seizing and slaying, perhaps because the animals are weak and slow and have no way of escaping.

People have reported pumas killing moose, mountain goat, pronghorn antelope, bison (Daniel Boone is said to have shot a puma off the back of a bison it was attacking), bighorn sheep, peccary, porcupine, beaver, badger, armadillo, raccoon, opossum, bear, bobcat, coyote, pampas deer, huemul, guanaco, snowshoe hare, rabbit, pika, marmot, skunk, ground squirrel, pine squirrel, flying squirrel, rock squirrel, pocket gopher, wood rat, cotton rat, white-footed mouse, meadow vole, fox, coatamundi, agouti, brocket, rhea, turkey, ruffed grouse, fish, and insects. In Utah, a biologist once observed a puma with a porcupine: "The cougar watched the porcupine at close range for several minutes before seeing an opportunity to slip its paw beneath the porcupine. As it did so, it flipped the hapless animal into the air, disemboweling it in the process. The cougar licked its paw and then commenced devouring its prey on the spot," leaving a prickly hide that "gave the appearance of having been skinned out."

Deer are by far the favorite prey of the puma; it seems almost certain that the cat evolved specifically to kill them. In North America, deer have increased astronomically in the last half century, and, at least in the West, puma numbers have begun to follow. Pumas do not prey only on the weak. When I stayed with Deborah Jansen, the biologist at Big Cypress National Preserve, she had in her yard a number of wire cages containing the moldering remains of panther-killed deer. (She planned to use the bones in a feeding study.) Many of the skulls had wide, branching antlers that would have made human hunters envious. Panthers ambush many bucks during the autumnal mating season, when the deer grow amorous and incautious.

Some panthers eat more pork than venison. Florida is overrun with feral hogs, fast-breeding swine that descend from domesticated stock turned loose by early settlers. Some observers believe that the panther survived in Florida, while dying out across the rest of the South, because of the abundance of hogs in the Sunshine State. Hiking in the Fakahatchee Strand one time, in an area regularly used by panthers, I came upon a sow with a litter of half-grown piglets. All were snorting, squealing, rooting up the vegetation, shouldering one another aside. They were colored pinkish-white, black, and black banded with white. They appeared to be nice and chubby, and if I had been a panther, in front of me was a meal free for the taking.

Probably panthers kill at least some livestock in Florida (certainly they did so in the past), although you don't hear much about it. I spoke to a cowboy on a ranch near Immokalee, a man who had seen several panthers in his lifetime in Big Cypress Swamp.

He told me he had never heard of a ranch losing cattle to a panther. "Unless you had an old cat who was starved slap to death," he said, "I don't think it would go for a cow." With good reason: the cattle of South Florida, developed from Brahma stock originating in India (the locals call them "Braymers"), arc tough, contentious beasts.

A young puma loses its spots when it is six to ten months old. It stays with its mother for a year and a half or two years. One biologist estimated that a female with three year-old cubs must kill a deer every three days to feed herself and her young. In Idaho, Hornocker monitored a mother with three kittens. One female kitten weighed 98 pounds, a second female kitten was 102 pounds, and the third kitten, a male, was 135 pounds; the mother, who weighed 94 pounds, was feeding the whole crew.

No one knows how the family breaks up. Maybe the mother goes into estrus and a dominant male chases her young away. Maybe she gets fed up with her ravenous brood and sneaks off. Maybe the kittens drift away as they become more inclined to hunt and kill by themselves.

A hunting guide on the Kaibab Plateau in Arizona told Harley Shaw about a time, many years earlier, when he had guided the movie star Clark Gable on a hunt. They treed and killed a female puma who had a kitten with her, still bearing its spots; the guide judged the young cat to be four months of age and to weigh thirty pounds. Gable wanted the kitten for a pet, so the guide put a spare dog collar around its neck and chained it to a tree; when he returned the next day, the kitten had broken the chain and was gone. A year later the same animal, wearing the same and now extremely tight collar, was killed thirty miles west of where it had escaped.

As it matures, a puma refines its hunting technique. Some cats develop into proficient killers, while others weaken and die because they never become adept. Of two female panthers that Deborah Jansen studied in Big Cypress National Preserve, one of them, Number 38, killed mainly deer, taking one every seven to ten days. Number 23, Annie (the Everglades cat who was separated from her mother and spent much of her early life in captivity), concentrated on hogs and raccoons.

Killing prey is an instinctive act for a puma—for any cat. The difference between a house cat pouncing on a rabbit and a puma seizing a deer is simply a difference of scale. In central Florida, Robert Baudy runs a small zoo called Savage Kingdom. Baudy has several Florida panthers, descendants of cats already in captivity when the panther was declared an endangered species; he breeds these panthers and sells their offspring to zoos around the world. One night four panthers—littermates two years old—escaped from their pen. They went on a spree. Still inside the walls of Savage Kingdom, they killed one llama, seven goats, and numerous chickens, peacocks, rabbits, and ducks. They attacked two mules and cut them up severely, but were unable to deliver the coup de grâce. The cats dispatched their victims with neck bites and, using leaves, sand, and small limbs, covered their kills so expertly that Baudy had a hard time finding them—all this by cats who had received no training from their mother, had eaten a prepared diet from birth, and had spent their entire lives behind bars.

Proponents of captive breeding are fond of citing another episode suggesting that not-so-wild pumas can indeed make it on their own. A few years ago the ecologically minded television magnate Ted Turner, perhaps hoping to give the Florida panther a boost, turned loose two half-grown Western pumas, a male and a female, on his plantation near Capps, in northern Florida. (The Florida Game Commission laid charges against him for importing non-native wild animals. Turner, who did not bother showing up in court, was sentenced to pay a fine and to produce free public-service television advertisements for conservation organizations.) Six months later, the male puma ran afoul of a car on Interstate 10 not far from where he had been set free. At his demise he was in the pink of health and had an armadillo in his stomach. As far as anyone can tell, the female is still on the loose.

9

BIG GUY AND CITY KITTY

There is a zeal to Dennis Jordan that lets him spend his days in a windowless office in a brick building on the campus of the University of Florida, in Gainesville, two hundred miles north of the only confirmed population of Florida panthers. Jordan works for the U.S. Fish and Wildlife Service. Since 1986 he has been the Florida Panther Recovery Coordinator. That position does not authorize him as Panther Czar. He does not make decisions to buy land for panthers, or to manage land for deer so that panthers can eat them and increase, or to regulate human activities on land upon which panthers tread. Those decisions are ponderously, politically arrived at (or carefully shunted aside) by the four governmental entities more or less cooperating to keep the panther from going extinct: the U.S. Fish and Wildlife Service, the U.S. National Park Service, the Florida Game Commission, and the Florida Department of Natural Resources.

Dennis Jordan is the lightning rod. He fields telephone calls from journalists. From hunters. From animal-rights activists, conservationists, and business and agricultural lobbyists. He talks to people who believe they have seen panthers in Florida or Louisiana or Mississippi or Georgia. He drafts memos and organizes meetings. He assembles such weighty documents as the "Updated Implementation Schedule of the Florida Panther Recovery Plan," "Florida Panther Protection/Enhancement/Recovery: A Historical Review of Events to Date," and the Draft and Final Environmental Assessments of "A Proposal to Issue Endangered Species Permits to Capture Select Florida Panthers (*Felis concolor coryi*) for the Establishment of a Captive Population" (followed by the Draft and Final Supplemental Environmental Assessments of the same proposal, necessitated when an animal-rights group, the Fund for Animals, sued the Fish and Wildlife Service over the first environmental assessment).

Jordan is soft-spoken, thin, fiftyish, his brown hair going gray. He says, "There's been lots more gray show up since I've had to write all of those environmental assessments." He jogs three times a week and plays golf after church on Sundays. Answering the phone, he says, "Dinnis Jordan." He grew up in Ellisville, Mississippi, where his family lived on the edge of town, and beyond the town lay the swamp. "My daddy was a hunter and a fisherman," Jordan told me. "He used to carry me with him as a kid." Jordan, with a master's degree in wildlife management, has worked for the Fish and Wildlife Service for twenty-six years, primarily at wildlife refuges in the South (he speaks somewhat wistfully about uncomplicated tasks like counting waterfowl and flooding timber) and in the agency's endangered-species branch.

Jordan admits that he has rarely been out of his office lately, to see the orange groves, highways, and housing developments gnawing away at the pine woods and prairie in South Florida— or, for that matter, to understand the way the ecosystem of South Florida works, in the way that he understood the natural dynamics of such places as the Noxubee and Yazoo national wildlife refuges in Mississippi, and the Hatchee National Wildlife Refuge in Tennessee, where he once worked. Still, he remains optimistic about the panther's future. Patient and persevering, he keeps his ego tucked away, perhaps subverted to his religion (he carries a flat silver cross in his change purse) or to his steadfast commitment to saving endangered animals. Jordan once told me, "If a pregnant woolly mammoth suddenly emerged alive out of the polar ice cap, the Fish and Wildlife Service would do everything in its power to keep the species from going extinct."

One morning I rode with Jordan to White Oak Plantation, which housed the first wild-captured panther kittens, the nucleus of the captive breeding program that had taken so long to get started and that still faced opposition from animal-rights activists (they hated to see panthers in cages) and biologists (they didn't want to see even one kitten plucked from the meager wild population). A light frost lay on the fields as we drove out of Gaines-ville. It was late January; spring was proceeding northward through Florida, the maples showing their vivid red flowers, the sky a deep and unhumid blue, vultures tipping across it.

Jordan talked as he drove. "Last year we took two litters of two kittens each, and two partial litters, where we took one kitten and left the other one with its mother. Of the six kittens captured, five are at White Oak. The sixth is in Gainesville. It turned out to have a severe heart defect, a valve that doesn't close. In dogs, that sort of condition is fatal in one to two years. Obviously we wouldn't want to use that animal in a breeding program."

We passed roadside stands with signs for citrus, tomatoes, strawberries, collard and mustard greens, and hot boiled peanuts. "That's the way we like 'em down here," Jordan remarked, "boiled. Guess y'all don't eat peanuts that way up North."

I asked Jordan about the wisdom of devoting time and effort to the unproven stratagem of captive breeding—as opposed to buying up all the panther habitat that could be purchased. "If our society, our system, was more flexible," he said, "we could pour all of our money into buying land. But some funding comes from one source, and some of it comes from another—and all we can do with it is use it for captive breeding, for instance. Logically, we have to work on several fronts.

"Some people would like us to close down Alligator Alley." He smiled faintly, lifted one hand from the steering wheel and held it palm up for a moment. "We can't do it. But we can limit public access to lands that the Interstate goes across, and we can put in underpasses for wildlife, and we can fence the road."

We skirted Jacksonville and its rush-hour traffic and continued on toward the Georgia line. Turning off the blacktop, we followed a sand road into the pines. Where the road dipped to cross a creek, the pines gave way to tupelo, bald cypress, and swamp white oak, the trees hoary with Spanish moss and other air plants. After a mile we came to a gate house with a pike across the road; the attendant gave us a map and told us to continue on for another half mile.

White Oak Plantation belongs to the Gilman Paper Company, which sells its paper for newsprint and for heavy bags to hold dog food and concrete. The company is headquartered in the Time-

Life Building in New York City. Most of its holdings are in New England, but Gilman also owns 250,000 acres in Florida and Georgia, along with four sawmills and a paper mill. Almost every weekend, I was told, Howard Gilman jets down from New York to relax at his plantation, riding horses and hunting quail. White Oak consists of seven thousand acres along the St. Marys River, twenty miles inland from the Atlantic Ocean. It is located on the site of an earlier White Oak Plantation owned by Zephaniah Kingsley, a notable figure in Florida's history.

Kingsley was born into a wealthy family in Scotland in 1765. In 1782 he immigrated with his parents to Charleston, South Carolina; not long after, he moved to Florida. At that time Florida was lightly populated by Spanish and British colonists, escaped slaves, and Creek Indians who had come in from the north. Kingsley saw Florida as an excellent base for slave trading. Although a Quaker, he had no compunction about buying and selling human beings. From African chiefs he obtained prisoners taken in tribal warfare, his crews picking them up at a base camp on the Congo River, carrying them across the Atlantic on schooners, and selling them in Brazil or the West Indies or depositing them on one of Kingsley's Florida plantations. (During his lifetime, he owned eight plantations.) Kingsley trained the slaves as field hands and domestics, then sold them—illegally, the United States having outlawed the importation of slaves in 1808—across the St. Johns into Georgia.

Kingsley married several African women and had children by them. He is reputed to have said, "I always thought . . . that the coloured race were superior to us, physically and morally. They are more healthy, have more graceful forms, softer skins, and sweeter voices. They are more docile and affectionate, more faithful in their attachments, and less prone to mischief, than the white race." By all accounts, Kingsley was kind and charitable toward the slaves he himself kept. He believed that such a condition as "good slavery" was possible. "The idea of slavery," he wrote, "when associated with cruelty and injustice, is revolting to every philanthropic mind; but when that idea is associated with justice and benevolence, slavery . . . easily amalgamates with the ordinary conditions of life." When seventy years old, he was described by an acquaintance as "a small, spare man, who wore square-toed, silver-buckled shoes to the last, and was generally seen about the plantation sporting a Mexican poncho. His usual exclamation was 'Dear God Almighty!' "

Zephaniah Kingsley planted rice, cotton, sugar, corn, peas, and potatoes. He was one of the first agriculturists to grow citrus in Florida. Irrigation canals for his crop fields still etch the earth at White Oak Plantation, but today what is grown there are trees. Most of the trees are longleaf pine. A small fraction of the plantation, five hundred acres, yields a remarkably different crop: swamp wallabies, maned wolves, giant eland, dwarf forest buffalo, roan antelope, scimitar-horned oryx, Australian shelducks, Orinoco geese, paradise cranes, red-fronted macaws, and several dozen other rare and endangered animals. It is exhilarating to walk along one of the sand roads and suddenly come face to face with an enclosure full of tigers, their eyes following your every move, or a pasture studded with rhinoceroses, their skin gray and folded, their eyes squinty, grazing peacefully behind a fence. "It was altogether vain to argue with him about fixed principles of right and wrong," an interviewer wrote about Zephaniah Kingsley toward the end of the slaver's life. "One might as well fire small shot at the hide of a rhinoceros."

At White Oak Plantation, Dennis Jordan introduced me to John Lukas, who directs the wildlife conservation program. Lukas is tall, angular, and dark-haired, with the quick, clipped speech pattern of New England. His master's degree in zoology is from Northeastern University in Boston. He and a staff of twenty-four, including a full-time veterinarian, care for and breed endangered animals as a source for zoos, for release into the wild, and for exchanging with other breeders in a passing around of chromosomes designed to preserve species' genetic diversity. These efforts, in Lukas's words, "help keep the modern ark afloat." At White Oak, animals live in what is characterized as a "semi-wild state." The public may not visit. The animals mingle with others of their kind, their homes simulating a natural habitat: bontebok graze in pastures mimicking rangeland, reticulated giraffes browse in open woods, East African bongo antelope (twelve of them, perhaps fewer, survive in the Abadere Mountains of Kenya) keep to the shade of deep woods.

In 1985, White Oak Plantation approached the Florida Game

Commission and offered to house and care for a panther that had been crippled by a car. Since then, White Oak has become a safe haven where injured panthers can be rehabilitated for a return to the wild, and where, if captive breeding proves practicable, a new, separate population can begin.

We drove to a remote part of the conservation center in John Lukas's Jeep (a brand-new, sand-colored "Sahara Edition"). We stopped next to a pen, roofed at one end and lined with maroon-painted snow fence. At the far end of the enclosure, a panther lay stretched out on the ground. "Hey, Big Guy," Lukas said. The cat opened his eyes and raised his head. On November 11, 1984, a man driving a produce truck across the Tamiami Trail had spotted a panther, more dead than alive, lying alongside the road. The driver sped to a highway patrol station. A veterinarian was quickly helicoptered to the scene. The panther's two hind legs had been shattered; on one of the legs, jagged bone ends stuck out through the skin. The panther, a young male, was treated for shock and flown to an animal clinic in Naples, and thence by chartered plane to the University of Florida's College of Veterinary Medicine. Surgeons pieced his legs back together, reinforcing the bones with steel plates. At some point people began calling the panther "Big Guy." Newspapers picked up on the name. They followed the cat's progress closely. While recuperating, Big Guy attacked his cage and broke off his canine teeth; dental surgery provided replacements.

"Hey, Big Guy," Lukas said again, opening the door to the pen. He went inside and beckoned for Jordan and me to follow. Jordan went in, and so did I. Without bothering to rise, the panther bared his teeth. His prosthetic canines looked very respectable. He snarled, a soft, liquid muttering.

Lukas had strolled to within fifteen feet. "Don't let him bluff you," he said. "He's completely docile."

"You've got more confidence than I do," Jordan said, remaining at the far end of the cage.

Big Guy watched us with what seemed to be a mild and slightly disdainful curiosity. He might have been softened by his captivity, but he still projected an aura of power. His paws looked as big as boxing gloves. His forelegs appeared to be twice the circumference of my arm. "He weighs a hundred and ten pounds," Lukas said.

"He really *is* docile. I can scratch his head while he's eating. But as soon as we put him in a fifteen-acre enclosure, he just disappears."

"That's the most photographed Florida panther in history," Jordan remarked. "He's been in all kinds of magazines. He's on the cover of this month's *Audubon*."

Big Guy's injuries preclude him from ever returning to the wild. At first, hopes were pinned on him as a potential breeder. Perhaps he could be used to impregnate wild-captured pumas from Texas, whose kittens could later be released, both to replenish the population of Florida panthers and to give the beleaguered subspecies a much-needed injection of fresh genetic material. (That possibility was raised back in the early days of the panther recovery effort, when the powers of bureaucracy could entertain so simple and pragmatic a solution—and one toward which they are moving again today.) But Big Guy turned out to be a lousy stud. Presented with lusty females, all he did was beat them up. The Florida Game Commission would issue hopeful press releases, only to have Big Guy embarrass them by spurning his female consorts. After a while, some people began calling him "Big Gay." That perceived slur on the Florida panther's name may have been what prompted the Game Commission's unsuccessful effort to change Big Guy's name to the less overtly masculine "Jim." Press release: "Two female cougars from Texas were moved to White Oak Plantation, and 'Jim' and the older female have co-mingled—results unknown."

We left Big Guy and trod through the pine needles to the next pen, which housed Florida panther number 21. Sonny Bass had caught and collared 21 as a kitten in the Everglades in 1987. As she matured, she wandered out of the park and hung around on the outskirts of Florida City, a rather tacky municipality that borders the town of Homestead to the south; the biologists dubbed her "City Kitty." In 1988, on Palm Drive east of Florida City, a car hit her and broke her leg. She has been at White Oak Plantation ever since. Like Big Guy, City Kitty could never make it in the wild. Also, she has been diagnosed as carrying feline immunodeficiency virus, the feline version of the virus that causes AIDS.

Over the winter the foliage had died back in City Kitty's pen; I picked her out, frozen in a crouch behind a clump of palmettos.

Her yellow eyes were riveted on us. "They stay wild if nobody bothers them," Lukas said. We edged along one side of the pen for a better look. City Kitty maneuvered to keep herself behind the vegetation. Her back was parallel to the ground, her belly hovered about three inches above it. She did not run so much as flow, gliding silently, then stopping as suddenly as she had begun. "For nine months of the year, when the leaves are thick, we can hardly see her," Lukas said. "If we don't spot her every few days, we put up a video camera." The panther glided again, her ears pricked, the muscles quivering in her shoulders. "If we really need to check on her, we go in and get her up and moving. You can almost step on her tail before she'll move. Panthers are not aggressive toward people. All we carry with us is a little piece of PVC pipe."

Jordan reached a finger through the woven steel and touched the wooden snow fence. "What's this for?"

"So she can't see deer and armadillos going past at night. Otherwise, she'd rush at the prey and hurt herself on the wire." Lukas added, "We have loads of deer on the plantation. Also a panther. Did you know we have a wild one wandering around?"

Jordan lifted his eyebrows. "Is that so?"

"It's seen regularly in the area. We've gotten plaster casts of its tracks. Whether it's a pure Florida panther or not, I couldn't say—it could be a cat that somebody let loose. It's back and forth between Georgia and Florida all the time. Actually, it could be more than one cat."

Before we moved on, I took a last look at the tangible panther in the pen. I was struck by the unblinking eyes of City Kitty, by their total vigilance, a state that seemed compounded of fear and an utter wildness unquenched by her years of captivity. The fluidity of her movements made me feel like an oaf, snapping sticks, kicking over ferns, stumbling along precariously balancing on one leg, then the other.

Our last stop was at a pen shared by two male panthers, whom we observed from a distance. Both of the cats wore radio collars, so that they could be recaptured if they escaped. That they were young animals was evident from the faint dark banding on the upper front portions of their hind legs, juvenile markings that would fade away in another month or so. One of the panthers slept; the other paced around the compound, gangly, big-pawed, his slack belly swaying. These were two of the six kittens taken the previous winter to start up the captive breeding program. Because of the lawsuit filed by the Fund for Animals, the panthers had to be kept in a totally wild state, in case the captive breeding program was discontinued. Workers do not drive to the pen when bringing food, so that the panthers will not associate cars with meals. The meat is shoved in through different doors, at different times of the day.

On the way back to Lukas's office, he and Jordan talked about how captive breeding could help the panther. "You could capture eighteen- to twenty-four-month-old animals," Lukas said, "produce a litter or two in captivity, and once the individuals were represented well enough in the captive population, the adults could go back into the wild along with some of their kittens. You'd get 'em wild, keep 'em wild, and put 'em back wild."

"We could bring in non-reproducing adults," Jordan said. "With females that have some kind of reproductive obstruction, like an ovarian papilloma, we might be able to correct the problem with surgery." (Ovarian papillomas are tumors that have shown up in the ovaries and vaginas of several female panthers.) "Or at least we'd be able to take eggs and store them. We might be able to help males that aren't producing viable sperm by putting them on a better diet."

"Artificial insemination and in vitro fertilization would open up a lot more options," Lukas said.

"They're working on those techniques at the National Zoo right now," Jordan told me. "Five years from now, who knows what we'll be able to do?

"The ideal way," he continued, "would be to establish a wild population of Texas pumas—in northern Florida, or Georgia, or Louisiana, or elsewhere within the historic range. We could harvest eggs from captive Florida panthers and inseminate them with Florida panther sperm. Then we could pull back a Texas female temporarily, implant the panther embryos in her womb, and get her right back into the population's social structure. That way she would give birth in the wild, and teach her young to hunt, and someday we'd have a population of pure Florida panthers back where they belong."

. . .

While in Florida, I asked several scientists and a breeder of pumas what they thought about captive breeding.

"The biggest hurdle a captive-reared cat would have to get over is the ability to hunt if not trained by the mother," said Laurie Wilkins of the Florida Museum of Natural History. "And despite what they'll tell you, there really is a lot of handling in captivity, a lot of habituation to humans."

"The whole concept requires a leap of faith," said Sonny Bass, the biologist at Everglades National Park. "You have to believe you can take cats without harming the wild population, you have to believe you can breed them, and you have to believe you can put them back in the wild. If you can't put them back, what are you going to do with them? If an animal's not in the wild, it's functionally extinct.

"The problem for the panther," Bass continued, "and for all other wildlife in Florida, is the loss of habitat. Florida is caught up in uncontrolled growth. We haven't reached the crisis level yet, but we're getting close. It's time to say enough is enough, and stop the habitat loss. But agencies like to postpone tough decisions; they'd rather use quick-fix techniques instead of long-term planning. And captive breeding, while it looks like a long-term effort, is really just another quick fix."

The veterinarian for the Florida Game Commission, Melody Roelke, saw no alternative to captive breeding. "The wild population will never again be a pristine, unhandled, unmanaged population," she said. "Even if we get a hundred and fifty cats, three times as many as are out there now, we'll still need to use captive breeding to keep the genetic material flowing.

"The panther is going through a severe genetic bottleneck," Roelke continued. "We are in a crisis situation. If our goal is to save this subspecies—these particular animals, in this particular ecosystem—we need to go ahead and do the heroics. If all we want is a major carnivore sloshing around in the swamp, we should just bring in Western cougars."

Dave Maehr, the Game Commission biologist, disagreed. "Genetic concerns are just not that important," he said. "In the last five years, we have observed no trend up or down in the population. Reproduction is at a higher rate than mortality. This population could increase if it had somewhere to expand into. We need to acquire more land and manage it for deer to increase the prey base—that's a much better way to improve things for panthers than captive breeding."

Chris Belden, the biologist, said, "I really hate to see us turn to captive breeding. It's the beginning of the end—no, it's more like the end of the end. Like when you go into an old folks' home and realize that none of the people in there are ever really going to live again."

I also looked up a man named Frank Weed. Weed and his wife, Ellen, are in their seventies. They live in a mobile home set back into the woods a hundred yards from Florida Route 29, a few miles north of where it crosses Alligator Alley. In 1989 the Weeds found themselves and their five acres surrounded by the Florida Panther National Wildlife Refuge, created when the federal government bought 24,000 acres from a family named Collier. Although quite friendly, the Weeds are not the sort who like having neighbors. They used to live in Dade County near Miami, and then in Broward County farther north along the coast, but left when those places became too populated. Through the 1950s the Weeds took a wildlife show on the road: Frank wrestled alligators and did stunts with pheasants and bird dogs, and Ellen, dressed as a cowgirl, showed off a tame deer named Daisy Mae. "We were in New York City one time for the sportsmen's show in Madison Square Garden," Ellen told me. "We stayed in the Forrest Hotel because we figured Daisy Mae would feel more at home there. To exercise her, I walked her down Broadway on a leash. If a car horn blew, or if the people crowded in, I would assure her that everything was all right. One lady stopped me and asked what kind of a dog that was. I told her it was a deerhound."

A stone's throw from the Weeds' trailer live twelve pumas in cages. Also a tiger, black and spotted leopards, and an ocelot. Another fifteen of their pumas reside at a menagerie in Fort Myers. Frank Weed trains and breeds the cats. His animals, rented by the hour, are photographed for advertisements and magazine illustrations. Weed has collected his breeding stock from North and South America and claims to have all thirty of the puma subspecies represented in his kennels. Over the past ten years the Weeds have sold more than three hundred pumas as pets; the current price is $800 for a kitten, $1,500 for a breeding animal. Kittens are taken from their mothers when three days old and raised by hand; I watched Ellen bottle-feed a small spotted puma, its newly opened eyes as blue as huckleberries, its tiny white whiskers twitching. "If you wait until they're ten days old," Frank told me, "they may starve to death before they'll take to the bottle. If you're *real* lazy and leave them with their mother, then you can't do anything with them, and someday they'll bite your head off." Weed once told me, "There is no such thing as a Florida panther." With a smile on his face—he is green-eyed, square-jawed, and hand-some—Weed denied having freed any pumas in the wild, but implied that many people to whom he had sold pumas had done just that. Stanley Young, in *The Puma, Mysterious American Cat*, wrote: "When fully matured many pumas, though tamed and affectionate, may at times become so untrustworthy, fractious, and sullen as to cause their masters either to kill them or give them to some zoo." Or drive out into the boondocks, open the back of the station wagon—Weed gestured at the larger world of Florida outside his darkened, crammed-with-furniture trailer. "You might as well call it *Felis concolor weedi*," he said. "It's just as true as *coryi*."

I thought Weed might have some commonsense ideas about how to boost the panther population. "The best way to do it would be to take a wild pregnant female into an area where you want to reestablish the panther, and cage her there," he said. "You'd let her have the kittens. You'd let the kittens move out from the cage, through an opening that's too small for the mother, into a larger enclosure. In time, you would let the female out into the larger enclosure, where she could kill deer put into the pen. Ultimately, you'd take down the fence and let her hunt for herself."

Weed told me that the Fish and Wildlife Service was urging him to sell them his five acres and "go retire somewhere." He was not interested in selling. He hoped that his daughter would take over the business. He insisted that the Florida Game Commission's estimate of fifty panthers in the wild was low: "There's at least two hundred of them out there." Yet he held little hope for the panther's future. "In time," he said, "South Florida will be nothing but people. There won't be any cougars or panthers or pumas or whatever you want to call them."

While Dennis Jordan and I were driving from White Oak Plantation back to Gainesville, I asked him if, in another five to ten years, there would still be room in the wild for panthers bred in captivity.

"There's a lot of rural areas in the South—not just in Florida, but in other states, too—where panthers could do very well," he said. "Look at Colorado and California, where pumas live right up to the edges of cities. Panthers don't need wilderness to survive. They can live in places that also support commercial timbering and farming, places that have a sparse human population and not a heck of a lot of roads." Jordan spoke quickly and evenly; it seemed clear that he had given much thought to the subject. "The key is whether the hunting public will let the animals be there. My father hunted. I still hunt on occasion myself. Hunting is a traditional land use that has gone on for generations in the South. Unfortunately, hunters don't understand how panthers operate. Panthers don't densely populate an area. They make a kill, they stay and feed, and they move on. They don't deplete an area of deer. They do not lower the biomass available to hunters. Bobcats have a much greater impact on the deer herd.

"We need to do a better job of educating hunters," Jordan said. "Because hunters and panthers *can* coexist. I really do believe that. Hunters using dogs, now that's another story, and that's the way a lot of people hunt. They run deer with hounds, and if the hounds happen onto a panther's trail, they'll run it, too. A resident cat might not be bothered—he'd probably tree, and after the hunters took the hounds away, the cat would climb back down and go about his business. But with an introduced cat, you'd have a problem. Until that cat settled into a home area, dogs could push him out."

10

A TISSUE PACKRAT

The headquarters for Big Cypress National Preserve is a brick motel taken over by the Park Service when the preserve came into being in the 1970s. The building, landscaped with palms and shrubs, lies along the Tamiami Trail. It houses administrative offices and apartments for seasonal workers. One evening I parked in the lot and walked through a roofed entryway dividing two of the building's three wings. Around back, half a dozen people were swimming and lounging in a screened-in pool. Climbing the steps to the upper level, I looked out over the sawgrass, three feet tall and bathed in orange light, rippling in a breeze that carried scents of saltwater and decaying plants. Above the marsh, egrets perched in snags, their white plumage tinted the color of candle flame by the setting sun. Herons sculled past, their legs tucked up, their necks folded back against their bodies. Ibises came flocking north from feeding grounds along the Gulf of Mexico, hurrying toward roosts in the preserve.

In the two connecting rooms of the veterinarians' suite, Melody Roelke and her colleagues were not looking out at the view. Shelves, beds, and floor were littered with plastic bags, gauze bandages, tongue depressors, and pipettes; on a countertop sat stainless-steel canisters, a microscope, and a small gray machine that continually tipped back and forth a wire rack holding vials of blood. The blood came from a panther, captured that morning. "We'll be up until two, processing and analyzing samples," Roelke told me. She wore blue jeans, a T-shirt decorated with the faded image of a cheetah, Birkenstock sandals, a digital watch, and a clasp knife in a sheath on her belt. Her hair, pulled behind her head, was freeing itself in brown, curly wisps. She ushered me over to a microscope. "Have you ever seen panther sperm?"

I turned the focusing knob. Sperm cells jittered across the field of view, their tails gray and whiplike, their heads blue-gold and dazzling. Other cells—more of them than the motile ones—sat clumped and motionless. A few went around in circles, like broken toys. One appeared to be traveling, for God's sake, *backwards.* "Ninety percent are defective," Roelke said over my shoulder. "They're like a textbook of what can go wrong with spermatozoa. Bends in the midpiece. Bends in the tail—that's why they swim in circles. There are immature forms. About 40 percent of them have abnormal acrosomes—the acrosome is the sheath on the head of the sperm that carries the enzymes to unlock the egg and penetrate its outer layers. When you look at sperm like that, you wonder how the females ever get pregnant." The Florida panther, Roelke explained, has a higher frequency of malformed sperm than any other puma subspecies ever examined. The total number of motile sperm per ejaculate is eighteen to thirty-eight times lower than in other pumas; thirty times lower than in the cheetah, an inbred species with its own reproductive problems; and up to 270 times lower than in some other cats.

Roelke turned aside to confer with a young man from the U.S. National Zoo who was doing a study of panther sperm. She instructed an assistant packaging tissue and blood samples in dry ice, for air shipment to distant laboratories. She seemed keyed up, harried; when she did find time to send a comment in my direction, she spoke too rapidly and disjointedly for me to take notes. We arranged to meet again the following afternoon. In the morning, while McBride and the Game Commission biologists were out hunting for panthers, Roelke and the vets would be here at Big Cypress headquarters, waiting by the radio; if no panther was caught by noon (at which time the capture team would knock off, since the heat would put too much stress on a chased and drugged animal), we could talk.

.   .   .

"I'm in terror every time we dart one of them," Roelke said. We were sitting at a picnic table next to the now-deserted swimming pool. The afternoon sun shone through thin clouds. Traffic hurried past on the Tamiami Trail, semis, local pickup trucks, big gleaming autos heading west toward the Gulf Coast resorts of Marco Island, Naples, and Fort Myers. "I suppose it's like being an actor," Roelke said. "When you quit having stage fright, you should go get another job."

I asked why she had become a veterinarian. "I grew up on a farm in western Oregon," she said. "Neither of my parents were farmers. They were professional artists. We moved there from Southern California when I was eleven. I mean, we didn't know *what* the hell we were doing. I took care of the orphans on the farm—lambs, mostly, who got to live in the house. When one of them would die—well, it was frustrating, not knowing how to care for them."

While in veterinary school, Roelke got a summer job in the Pribilof Islands off the coast of Alaska, helping a marine pathologist studying fur seals. "We would climb around on catwalks above this seal colony, using gaff hooks to collect the dead pups. Then we would necropsy them, to see if microbes had played a role. There we were, in the wind and the rain, with these six-hundred-pound herd bulls growling and bellowing down below. I found it all very exhilarating." About twice a month the cloud cover would break sufficiently that an amphibious plane could land. The pilot would dump the mail on a table and then take off again, making it impossible for the scientists to answer a letter right away. "I was married at the time," Roelke said. "My husband and I managed to tough it out through vet school, which is when a lot of marriages fall apart. After graduation I got a job at a veterinary clinic in Roseburg, Oregon." Down the road from the clinic was Wildlife Safari, a foundation famous for its success at breeding cheetahs in captivity. Roelke began treating the Wildlife Safari animals. A year later, she went to work for the foundation full time. "My very first day on the job, we pulled a cheetah cub, and it was my job to hand-rear it. I took it home, and it slept in our bed." Roelke sighed, mugging a grin. "Poor man," she said. "Maybe *that* was the beginning of the end of our marriage.

"At Wildlife Safari I learned how to shoot a tranquillizing gun and handle big animals—elephants, wildebeests, elands, rhinos, tigers. The emphasis was on helping those species through captive breeding. Wildlife Safari had had twenty-eight cheetah births when I started working there, more than anybody else. Those were *my* animals. I was there every day, and they were long days. I remember driving to work thinking, I'm the luckiest person in the world." She glanced away, her eyes set against the glare of the sky reflected from millions of sawgrass spears in the marsh. "I don't do that these days," she said.

At Wildlife Safari, Roelke met visiting scientists. One of them was Stephen O'Brien of the National Cancer Institute in Frederick, Maryland. O'Brien was studying genetic variability in the cheetah. At his request Roelke surgically grafted small patches of skin between unrelated pairs of cheetahs. Weeks passed, and none of the skin grafts were rejected; four weeks into the experiment, the skin patches had healed and were growing hair and developing normal cheetahlike spots. In contrast, within twelve days the cheetahs' immune systems rejected grafts of skin from domestic cats. The compatibility of skin between unrelated cheetahs showed a lack of genetic variability—it was like receiving an organ implant from a sibling: the cheetahs' immune systems were essentially uniform.

In 1982 a crisis began that would yield even more convincing data regarding the cheetahs' immune systems—and would ultimately propel Roelke out of Oregon and diagonally across the continent. "We had forty cheetahs at the park," Roelke remembered. "In May, we brought in two new animals from another zoo." The pair, a male and a female, were on loan for breeding purposes. "At the time we didn't have a decent quarantine facility or even the philosophy of quarantining new animals." The visiting cats fell ill with fever, diarrhea, and jaundice. The female died. Then the male. "We diagnosed the cause of death as feline infectious peritonitis—it's caused by a virus. Both of the animals had been kept in a pen next to the Wildlife Safari animals. The virus swept through the colony. Gum disease, diarrhea, weight loss— the symptoms went on all winter." Although feline infectious peritonitis may race through a colony of domestic cats, it will seldom kill more than one in ten. But at Wildlife Safari the epidemic killed nearly half the adult cheetahs and three-fourths of the cubs. "We knew what was causing the problem," said Roelke, "but there wasn't much we could do about it. FIP is an immune-mediated disease; the immune system keeps trying to get rid of the virus, but it's an aberrant response, with the body going berserk and actually killing itself. The organs turn into a putrid yellow soup."

Wildlife Safari regularly sold the cheetahs it produced to other breeding operations and to zoos. At the time of the epidemic, a sale was pending. "I couldn't keep my mouth shut," Roelke said. "I told a zoo director about the FIP problem, and the next thing I knew I was looking for a job.

"I saw an advertisement in a veterinary journal for a residency in wildlife medicine at the University of Florida. I applied and got it. Four years out of vet school and I was making fourteen thousand dollars." She laughed. "Both of the jobs I've taken since the clinic have meant a cut in salary."

She began attending panther captures. It was her responsibility to set the drug dose. "The animal is sixty feet up in the air, and you're supposed to evaluate its kidney function by looking at its whiskers. Sometimes you almost have to be clairvoyant. I rely on Roy [McBride] to estimate the animal's body weight." Roelke, ultimately hired full-time by the Florida Game Commission, reckoned that she had been on hand for more than 120 captures. "I've called off captures because I was worried about the animal's condition," she said. "Since I started working on the project, there's been only one death—the actual cause was septicemia, blood poisoning—that was affected, if not directly caused, by a capture.

"Like I said, it can be terrifying. A male we caught last Friday—we gave him exactly the same dose of drug that we did a year ago, but this time around he decides he's not going to breathe very well. His breathing is shallow, he's showing gray mucous membranes, so we grab an endotrachial tube—it goes right down the windpipe—and breathe for him for a while, and get him hooked up to a bag and give him oxygen.

"You may have noticed that the tensions run high at a capture. I've heard it again and again: You were hired to take care of immobilized cats. Period. But it seems to me that we have a responsibility, both to the individual and to the subspecies. If we're going to run the risk of anesthetizing a cat, then we'd damned well better learn as much about it as we can. Blood, urine, feces, hair, skin biopsies, semen . . . I was never directed to take those samples. The whole thing just evolved." She flashed a smile. "I'm a tissue packrat. You should see all the biological samples I've collected. When I started analyzing them, I learned how compromised the panthers really were."

It was Roelke who first found that some panthers were loaded with toxic mercury. Most of the cats so afflicted came from the southern part of the subspecies' range—Fakahatchee Strand, Big Cypress Swamp, the Everglades. There, deer and hogs were scarcer than on lands farther to the north, because the soil was poorer, grew less forage, and supported fewer grazing animals. The biologists' field studies buttressed Roelke's findings: panthers living in those hardscrabble places often resorted to eating alligators and raccoons, lesser predators that accumulated mercury in their own bodies from eating fish. The toxin was passed on to the panthers. "Mercury has killed at least one cat directly," Roelke said, "and it may have contributed to the deaths of others. Certainly it has affected their breeding productivity. In domestic cats, mercury passes through the placenta and causes nerve damage in offspring—abortions, stillbirths, retardation, kittens that can't suck. With panthers, we have no way of quantifying those effects, but they're probably happening."

Since 1983—despite having immunized and given vitamins to every panther she handled—Roelke had seen a startling slide in the animals' overall health. The litany of ills terrified her more than the prospect of selecting how many milligrams of ketamine to load into a dart syringe. All of the afflictions, Roelke believed, could be traced, at least in part, to inbreeding and its inevitable outcome: genetic depletion and loss of individual vigor. Inbred animals were weaker, less able to survive. The kinked tails and the furry cowlicks were outward signs of inbreeding. More insidious was the terrible sperm, its low motility and 90 percent malformation. (I was told by another scientist that the Florida panther has "the worst sperm of any endangered species. When human reproductive specialists see the figures on panther sperm, they just laugh and say, 'Throw it away.' If it was a human donor, they'd tell him he was sterile.")

In 1992 and 1993, nine panther kittens were taken from their mothers to begin the controversial captive breeding program. One had a hole in its heart. One, a male, proved to be sterile when his testicles failed to descend: tucked up inside the abdomen, they remained in an environment too warm to produce sperm. Before 1975, no one had reported undescended testicles in Florida panthers; the condition, called cryptorchidism, had never been observed in any wild cats. Cryptorchidism is an inherited condition more apt to befall the offspring of incestuous matings. Between 1975 and 1979, six males were found with an undescended testicle. By 1989, 90 percent of the males had only one testicle. And then the double cryptorchid kitten showed up. "If all the males in a population have undescended testicles," said Roelke, "obviously the population will go extinct in one generation. The panther hasn't gotten to that point yet, but it's moving in that direction."

In 1990 two collared panthers, ages two and five years, died mysteriously. In each cat a necropsy revealed an "atrial septal defect"—a hole between the heart's right and left atrial chambers. Roelke diagnosed a third case of atrial septal defect in a young male with an extreme heart murmur. The animal, born of a father-daughter mating, died after an operation to patch up the hole. In other pumas heart murmurs are seemingly rare—a reported 4 percent, compared to 80 percent in Florida panthers.

In panther blood Roelke found antibodies for a host of diseases. The most ominous was feline distemper, a viral malady especially deadly to young animals. Many kinds of wildlife can contract feline distemper, including bobcats and raccoons, both extremely common in Florida. An infected animal sheds the virus in its urine and feces. The virus is hardy and can stay viable for up to a year. A panther could easily pick it up when sniffing another animal's droppings.

Roelke also found antibodies against feline calicivirus, which causes pneumonia in domestic cats and is especially virulent in kittens. And pseudo-rabies virus, capable of killing domestic cats in two days or less. (Feral hogs in South Florida carry pseudo-rabies virus, and where hogs are especially abundant, panthers, paradoxically, are scarce. In a medical report Roelke suggested that pseudo-rabies virus "has the potential to delineate the range of Florida panthers much as the tsetse fly prevented the movement of domestic cattle into tropical Africa.") In a fourth of the panthers she checked, Roelke detected feline immunodeficiency virus. Like the AIDS virus in humans, feline immunodeficiency virus may not cause death directly, but it saps the body's immune system, leaving it vulnerable to other pathogens or toxins.

As her medical study progressed, Roelke realized that Florida's panthers were far more fragile than anyone had thought. Perhaps it was not enough to protect them from poachers and to preserve their habitat. Now a nightmare scenario arose in which a disease would kill most, if not all, of the cats. Losing half of them would probably doom the subspecies: there would be no choice but to bring the survivors into captivity. If pathogens can kill cheetahs living the good life in a breeding menagerie, they can kill panthers scratching out a living in the wild.

It was 1990. Roelke was puzzled. It looked as if there were two kinds of panthers in South Florida. The main population cluster —thirty to forty adults—inhabited the northern reaches of Big Cypress Swamp and extended northward into the large private cattle ranches of south-central Florida. A smaller contingent, never more than ten animals, lived in Everglades National Park. Shark River Slough, the marshy outflow from Lake Okeechobee, seemingly separated the two groups. The Everglades cats were smaller than the Big Cypress ones. Their coats had a pronounced reddish cast. No kinks in their tails or cowlicks on their backs. The males had two testicles, and their sperm had a higher motility than that of their Big Cypress counterparts. Some scientists speculated that the slough had kept the two clusters apart long enough that they had evolved separately. It was strange. The smaller band of panthers ought to have been more severely inbred. Yet their genetic health appeared to be better than that of their neighbors in Big Cypress Swamp.

Roelke called on Stephen O'Brien, who had gone to Oregon to examine the genetics of the cheetahs at Wildlife Safari. A molecular geneticist, O'Brien heads the National Cancer Institute's Laboratory of Viral Carcinogenesis. Another geneticist once described him to me as a blustering, aggressive man with a fondness for chewing on cigars. In addition to the cheetah, O'Brien has studied the chromosomal intricacies of the Asian lion, the humpback whale, and the California Channel Island fox. He was once

asked to determine the sire of a panda cub that had died shortly
after birth at the U.S. National Zoo. Not only did O'Brien identify the cub's father, he also resolved a long-standing taxonomic
debate by proving that the giant panda is indeed a bear and not
an evolved form of raccoon, as many geneticists had come to
believe. O'Brien peers into an animal's genetic background by
analyzing the sequences of amino acids in the DNA of its cell
nuclei and mitochondria. The techniques he employs have names
like hypervariable minisatellite DNA probe, allozyme phoresis,
and restriction fragment length polymorphism analysis. Most of
the tests depend on a procedure called electrophoresis, in which
proteins of differing molecular forms, subjected to a mild electrical
current, migrate at differing rates through a stationary fluid.

Roelke went to O'Brien's laboratory in Maryland and learned
his arcane practices. She applied them to blood samples she had
been hoarding from Florida panthers. She compared the panthers'
genetic material to that of eight other North American puma subspecies and three South American subspecies. (These were all the
races from which biologists and veterinarians had secured tissue
or blood samples.) The indicator on which she focused was a
distinctive form of an enzyme called adenosine phosphoribosyl
transferase, or APRT. Roelke and O'Brien concluded that seven
panthers in Everglades National Park had descended, at least in
part, from pumas that came from Central or South America. Also,
the South American genes had crossed Shark River Slough (one
wandering cat could have done it) and infiltrated the main cluster
of panthers in the Big Cypress ecosystem.

Roelke studied the archives of Everglades National Park and
learned that a small private menagerie, Everglades Wonder Gardens of Bonita Springs, Florida, had turned loose at least seven
captive pumas between 1957 and 1965. Apparently park admin-
istrators had wanted to boost the panther population even then,
and no doubt they were under the impression that the imports
were pure Florida panthers. Thirty years later, Everglades Wonder
Gardens was still in business. Roelke went and checked on their
cats. She zeroed in on an ancient female named Fatima. With the
permission of Lester Piper, the menagerie's owner, Roelke
trimmed Fatima's toenails. Also, she snuck a syringe of her blood:
South American APRT.

"No one wants to admit it," Roelke said, "but apparently a tame female from the east coast of Florida was brought into the menagerie in the fifties." Maybe she came from Central America. Or from French Guiana, where the native puma has such a reddish cast to its coat that it is called *tigre rouge*. In any event, a cross-bred panther had made it into the wild. Five, six, seven generations later, the chromosomal contributions of at least one foreign cat could still be detected.

Which meant that Florida's panthers were cross-bred. They were still overwhelmingly *Felis concolor coryi*, but they were not purely so. In several scientific papers, Roelke and O'Brien referred to the cross-bred cats as "heretical," which was a polite way of calling them hybrids. It seemed that the outside genes had given a boost to the panthers' overall health. It was as if, say, several Haitian immigrants had somehow been accepted into an isolated Amish community in which, due to inbreeding, half the children were being born as dwarfs. After a few generations, there would be darker-skinned Amish plowing the fields, fewer of whom would be three feet tall.

Yet if the panther had been helped biologically by this influx of genes, it had been compromised politically. The Endangered Species Act bestows federal protection on the Florida panther. It provides funding to aid in its restoration. It disallows the wholesale plundering of its habitat. It scares hell out of corporations poised to turn thousand-acre tracts of panther-friendly pine forest into orderly, profitable rows of orange and grapefruit trees.

The Endangered Species Act does not apply to hybrids.

11

ORACLES

Everglades Wonder Gardens sits next to the Tamiami Trail, where the road curves inland several miles from the tonier beachfront properties. The menagerie could have been called Big Cypress Wonder Gardens, because it is geographically much closer to Big Cypress Swamp—but "Everglades" is the more attractive name, projecting an aura of mystery, of siren naturalness, that sucks in a tourist every time. Everglades Wonder Gardens is in downtown Bonita Springs, the sort of community to which Northerners of modest means might retire. Across the street from the menagerie is the pink stucco Pittman Funeral Home and Crematorium, where the Bonita Springs Church of Christ holds its weekly services. In the immediate vicinity are the Bamboo Mobile Village, the Driftwood Motel, Pop Warner's Grapevine Bar ("Proper Attire Required: Gentlemen, No Hats, Bandannas, Headbands"), Art Pinnow's Auto Wholesale, a shoe store, an insurance office, a pizza parlor, Shucklat Realty (the bricks painted blue and the mortar white), an automobile radiator repair shop, a coin-op laundry, and a Pick Kwik convenience store.

Everglades Wonder Gardens announces its presence in this dense region of commerce with a soaring orange sign featuring a raised-relief snake in a coiled pose. Above the snake, emerging from the top of the sign, is a bust of a rugged-looking man with a beard and a Stetson hat. *Les* is lettered on his shirt, and the head of a panther peers over his shoulder. The sign sprouts like a giant mutant from a bed of purple flowers and is surmounted by an American flag that stirs in the Gulf breeze.

In the stuffy shop leading to the menagerie, parrots sat in cages with faded hand-inked signs: WE BITE. One of the parrots began giving out raucous, ear-splitting squawks; an attendant strode over, thrust his face up to the cage, and shouted, "Shut up, bird!" The parrot kept squawking; the attendant kept yelling. This colloquy continued for more than a minute, until the parrot quieted down. Nearby, a display case held skulls of monkey, dolphin, manatee, crocodile, and (with that classic Roman nose) panther. The stuffed head of a panther stared from the wall; its bulbous eyes, cupped ears, and undershot jaw suggested the comedic television actor Don Knotts. On a shelf were shark jaws, alligator skins, and stuffed birds—wood stork, caracara, flamingo. Inside formaldehyde-filled jars floated snakes, frogs, fish, baby crocs, and a dog's heart infested with pale threadlike worms. A magazine excerpt, framed and yellowing, depicted the Piper brothers, Les and Bill, capturing a bobcat. The text stated, "The Piper boys consider the Everglades more dangerous than the cats they capture. The Everglades, extending over most of southern Florida, have never been explored in their entirety. Experts consider them worse than anything in Africa or Asia." Another clipping had a picture of a man restraining a panther with a rope around its neck: "Panthers are Lester's favorite wild animals, and he often frolics with them."

I forked over four bucks for the tour. Out in back, feathery Australian pines blunted the sun, and the cages were clean and newly brightened with red and silver paint. In our group of a dozen tourists, at least three couples spoke German. Our guide was a short, skinny man in his late teens or early twenties. He needed a shave. He wore a pale-blue shirt with a white oval on its breast bearing the name *Ron* in red script. We shuffled along behind Ron from one cage to the next, listening to his spiel, delivered in a monotone and with a thick Southern accent.

"Them there are nocturnal, they're up and about at night, they hunt mainly small rodents, rabbits, mice, and such. Called a bobcat."

Ron showed us owls, wood storks, otters, parrots, bears. In a pit in the center of the menagerie lounged the obligatory gaggle of sun-stunned alligators, eyes shut, sides pulsing in and out, bellies plastered against the concrete. "Brain's on'y about the size of a goffball," intoned Ron. "Called an American alligator." On we strolled, past hogs and turkeys, peafowl and ducks, goats and vultures. "These here have a lot of features about themselves, you might say they're the Cadillac of vultures, most vultures are a whole lot uglier. Called the king vulture from South America."

The tour halted in front of a pair of cages. Ron tapped on the wire and paused significantly; he even dropped out of his monotone. "These are some of the rarest animals in the United States," he said. "They live right here in Florida. They eat mostly deer and hogs. They're a type of mountain lion. We've let a good many of 'em loose over the years. Called a Florida panther."

One of the panthers was lying on its side, sleeping. It looked grizzled and old. (Fatima?) Its eyes blinked rapidly beneath their lids. In an adjacent cage, a larger panther, a male, was awake. From cage into sleeping chamber and back into the cage again, he padded on his limited circuit. His neck slabbed up to his smallish head. His tail ended in a black tip that crooked off at the famous ninety-degree angle. His ears stood up smartly. White whiskers sprayed out on each side of his muzzle. On his grayish-tan face, dark and light areas accented his greenish-yellow eyes. His glance, directed out of the cage, seemed not to take in the tourists, most of whom had begun drifting on toward the Gardens' next wonder. Nor did the panther's eyes follow the movements of the lone remaining observer, as I settled to a crouch outside the wire. At first the cat's expression seemed blank; it reminded me of a well-known painting of an American World War II combat soldier, whose face, erased of all emotion by exhaustion and horror, is fixed in what was known as a "thousand-yard stare."

In the background a radio blared stale rock-and-roll. Trucks rumbled past on the Tamiami Trail. A monkey yammered. An otter chittered. Ron's voice droned: ". . . five-hunnert-dollar fine if you're caught messin' with 'em in the wild. Called a black vulture."

The panther stopped pacing. He sat back on his haunches, on the big round cushions of his hind feet. He raised his stocky forelegs, extruded his claws, and hooked them onto the wire. His face hovered only a foot or two from mine. Yet he was not looking at me. He was looking through me. His pupils were black, round, and tiny in their yellowish orbs. I realized then that the cat's expression was one of attentiveness—as if he were waiting for someone to arrive, some important event to occur. He opened his mouth. A cry escaped from his throat, a hoarse, crowing yowl. The panther raised his haunches off the concrete floor, switched his tail back and forth, and yowled again. From out of the slur of noises, from somewhere on the far side of the compound, came an identical answering yowl.

I found Les Piper sitting at a counter in a hot, fly-infested shed, cutting up bread. "Panthers won't eat this crap," he said dismissively, slicing the bread with a long, thin knife, then using a sun-baked forearm to sweep it off the table into a plastic drum. It was Hyde Park Enriched Bread, out of date or mashed. "We give it to the birds and the deer." On the walls of the shed hung hooks, saws, axes, chains, ropes, pots, tongs. Piper got up shakily, wincing and rubbing his back. It was apparent that his days of frolicking with panthers were over. He lurched across the room and opened the door to a walk-in cooler. A horse, skinned and quartered, hung from hooks on a track in the ceiling. "We feed a lot of meat," the old man said. "Horses and cows. Fish—channel cat, ladyfish, sheepshead, grunt, whatever they're catchin'." Piper was stooped and gaunt. His skin was dark brown, thick, crazed with painful-looking pink fissures. He had pale-blue eyes, a gray mustache and chin beard, and a full head of crisp gray hair. Over the crown of his head curved a brown plastic band, ending in hearing aids that pressed against the temporal bones behind both ears. "Busted my eardrums," he explained. "The scaffold give way while I was workin' on my sign. Fell down and landed on my goddamn head."

He sat back down at the table and resumed cutting bread. He related his history in Florida. He had been born in Lancaster, Ohio. "My dad came down here in 1910. Came to Florida to raise strawberries. We starved out and went back North, but Dad still wasn't satisfied there, so he sold a little farm, five acres I think it was, and we come back down here again, and starved out again.

"I'm eighty-nine years old—be ninety in September. I worked in a shipyard in Michigan when I was thirteen. That was in World War I. Then we come down to St. Pete, went back to Michigan, come back down and went to Miamuh.

"In '29 we moved over here to Bonita. Me and my brother Bill, that's Wilford, he died three-four years ago, we went in together and bought eight sections of land. [A section is 640 acres.] Paid seven dollars an acre. We raised cattle on it.

"In the thirties we bought this place"—Piper swept his knife through the air, close enough to my chest that I considered stepping back—"when there wasn't nothin' but a few houses around, maybe a hundred and fifty people in the whole durn town. We opened up in '36. Charged a quarter admission. What's here"—again the grand arc of the knife—"took fifty years to collect.

"We got our first baby panthers in the late thirties. Got 'em from Edmund Brown, from over in Immokalee. Little-bitty kittens about this long." He held his hands a foot apart. "He found 'em under a goddamn stump somewheres. Then we got three from a litter up in Hendry County. We put panthers in the wild twicet. I never kept no records. I put two pair in there, one pair in the National Park down around Florida City—that must have been back in the fifties. The next time was in the sixties."

"I was told," I said, "that one of your cats may have come from South America."

Piper squinted. He pointed his knife so that its tip was three inches from my chest. "That's a whole lot of bullshit," he said. "My cats all come from Collier County and Hendry County, Florida. Put that in your book.

"I got four of 'em left. Lost one last year." He drew the knife back, sliced it through some bread. "Somebody left the pen unlatched, and it hit the door and went out. We hunted it for two days. It hadn't gone any farther than three-four blocks. It was very tame. It wouldn't have bothered anybody. Probably come right up to you and lick your hand. But a guy down there went and shot it. We never did find out who done it."

Lester Piper did not want to talk about panthers any longer. He told me he still owned 267 acres "over near the dog track" and another section and a half "out at Mule Pens."

"That land's worth millions," he said. "But what's the use of selling it? Money don't mean a thing. I'd rather somebody'd raise cows on it than put up houses. This whole coast"—he lifted his knife and swung it—"it'll all be built over someday. And then they'll have one hell of a mess when a hurricane comes along.

Everything, everybody, destroyed and drownded." He slit the wrapper on another loaf of bread, took out a handful of slices, and drew his knife through them. "I'll tell you," he said. "Florida'll never be Florida like it was."

Tom Gaskins is the proprietor of the Cypress Knee Museum, at Palmdale, west of Lake Okeechobee and south of Fisheating Creek. The region is classic panther country, lightly grazed upland, pine woods, and prairies interspersed with bay heads and cypress swamps. Gaskins was born in Tampa in 1909, making him an original Florida Cracker. He sells a booklet that he wrote himself, *Florida Facts and Fallacies*, which discusses the provenance of "Florida Cracker," a term that should be used with respect. It may come from Florida Civil War soldiers who were crack shots, or from cow hunters who herded cattle by cracking whips at them, or from settlers cracking corn by hitting the kernels with a wooden club. According to his booklet, Gaskins graduated from De Soto County High School in 1927, went to work as a salesman for Gator Roach Killer, married the former Virginia Bible in 1934, and thereupon quit Gator and started up "the cypress knee industry." His house is covered with 30,000 cypress shingles, every one of which he split by hand. He describes himself as a woodsman, a hunter, a trapper, a fisherman, a physical culturist who jogged eleven miles on his sixty-ninth birthday, and a member of the John Birch Society.

I stopped at the Cypress Knee Museum on a beautiful spring day. It doesn't get many tourists, lying so far off the beaten track. The museum proper is a low building filled with glass cases displaying cypress knees of various shapes and sizes. In nature, cypress knees stick up around the tree, projecting a foot or so above the swamp. No one is sure what function they perform. Maybe they prop up the tree. Maybe they act as breathing tubes. Most have simple shapes, like the knee of a skinny person thrust into the air. Others are twisted, lumpy, fantastical. Tom Gaskins is in the habit of sawing off the more intriguing forms, hollowing them out, peeling their bark, and sanding the wood smooth. Some of the knees he sells to tourists; some he displays in his museum, where he has labeled the shapes that he sees: "Queen Mary,"

"Statue of Liberty," "Eleanor Roosevelt," "the devil," "penguin," "lady in an evening gown," "snake after a Chinaman," "ape," "Stalin," "Donald Duck," "egret," "camel," "wild stallion," "Venus de Milo," "Flipper," "parrot," "mushroom cloud from the blast of an atom bomb upside down."

The museum predates the broad highway, which one must negotiate (fast cars, sparse traffic) to get to the cypress swamp and see some knees *in situ*. The tour group consisted of me and a chubby middle-aged couple, the woman in royal-blue stretch pants, the man in full camouflage, including an Aussie-style hat with the brim snapped up on one side. Gaskins was another blue-eyed, sun-baked codger, short and stooped, in bare feet, shorts, and a stocking cap. Coming up to us, he said, "Everthang suitin' everbody?"

He led us onto a catwalk consisting of two weathered-pine planks, each about eight inches wide, resting on pipes which extended from posts to supports scabbed onto the sides of cypress trees. We were about ten feet above the swamp. Below us were the knees, covered with flaking brownish-gray bark, orange at their growing tips. The catwalk had a handrail on one side only, and in places the railing was absent. The woman in the blue stretch pants hung back. "Y'all go ahead," she called to her husband, as he and I followed Gaskins.

Gaskins turned and walked backwards on the catwalk. "You will see, hither, thither, and yon, knees that I have *tampered* with for *over fifty years*." He pointed down. "There. I put that mule shoe in that knee in 1954." The knee had grown around and over the shoe. "That one, I tortured it, made some cuts so's it would grow up shaped like the human hand." He pointed again. "See where I stuck that Coke bottle in there?" The knee had grown up in three prongs, to surround and smother the bottle. The man in camouflage said to me, out of the corner of his mouth, "Is that *weird*, or what?"

The catwalk angled from tree to tree. It was April, the end of Florida's dry season, and except for a few waterholes, the swamp was dry. Ferns grew thick around the knees and the trunks. I asked why the water was so low. "It's all the ten hundred thousand ditches that's been dug," Gaskins explained. "We don't have *near* the water we used to have when I was comin' up. Used to be water in here up to your knees, even in the wintertime. They've drained the state of Florida dry, and that's a fact."

When Gaskins found out I was from Pennsylvania, he said, "You know, you *definite* have cypress trees growing in Pennsylvania. Oh, you bet, you bet. I've cut knees, and cooked 'em, and peeled 'em, north of New York City. Ohhh, yessir, yessir. If you figure the cypress is just a Southern tree, you are sadly mistaken. There's cypress trees in Ohio and Illinois and Indiana."

After the tour Gaskins invited us into his shop. He showed me a turkey caller that he makes out of cedar wood and sells for $12.50. "This will call in turkey—also bear, wildcat, and panther. The panther hears the turkey calling, he figures there's an easy meal. You'll have to watch out for that. Also for hunters. I've had *six friends shot* using this caller, fortunately none of 'em dead." When he learned that I was a writer, Gaskins got out a card, wrote my name on it, slowly and in an ornate script, then signed his own name. "This card states that Charles Fergus is an honorary vice president of the Tom Gaskins Cypress Knee Museum," he said. "The next time you come back, you will get in free. Whenever that may be! Till the cows come home! *Damn right!* You carry that card, if anybody gives you any trouble, you tell 'em, 'Kiss my ass!' "

Gaskins did not have many knees left for sale. As the years had settled on him, he was not getting out in the swamps to cut them. He finally found one for me, stuck up between the rafters. He refused to let me pay for it. I took it home. It looks like . . . a rhinoceros's head. A man came into my house to clean the rugs one time and spotted the cypress knee. "Did you get that from Florida?" he asked excitedly. I told him about Tom Gaskins. He said, "I know, I know, I saw that guy on TV! The Johnny Carson show, years and years ago. He came on wearing one of those cypress things on his head like a hat."

I asked Gaskins if he had ever sighted a panther while collecting cypress knees in Florida. "I don't believe I have," he said. "No sir. I've had a cat or two get *in* and *out* of one of my traps. I've gone hunting all through the Big Cypress and the Telegraph Cypress, down below Arcadia and inland from Punta Gorda. Never have I seen a panther. Seen plenty of rattlesnakes—I call the rattlesnake a bell boy. His rattles are his bells, and that's a tune that'll make the hair stand straight up on your head. I remember when they put the Tamiami Trail in, across that whole Big Cypress country. You could go down there and park your car and walk off the road and jump into some *waaalled* country, let me tell you. But panthers?" He rubbed his scalp and shook his head. "No sir. Panthers are shy and they are scarce."

I met a different sort of oracle on Florida's Atlantic Coast, in the posh town of Coconut Grove, once a discrete community but now engulfed by Miami. Marjory Stoneman Douglas was 101 years old when I spoke to her. In the year she was born, 1890, the U.S. Cavalry massacred Sioux women and children at the Battle of Wounded Knee. In Florida in 1890 Henry Flagler was extending his railroad south along the Atlantic Seaboard, attaching the state to the rest of the nation and preparing it for development. Flagler had gotten as far as Daytona, a third of the way down the peninsula; for every mile of track his company laid, it received, from a grateful state government, land in the tens of thousands of acres.

Marjory Stoneman grew up in Massachusetts. Her great-great-uncle Levi Coffin, a Quaker, had headed the famous Underground Railroad that had spirited slaves out of the South before the Civil War. In 1912 Marjory was graduated from Wellesley College, where she majored in English composition; in her autobiography, *Voice of the River*, she described herself at that time as "unattractive, overweight, and [with] a kind of nervous giggle which ensured that no boy would take me anywhere." Soon afterward, she readily married a man thirty years her senior, who, although he turned out to be an alcoholic and a swindler, was a kind and instructive partner in bed. She wrote: "Without the experience of marriage, brief though it turned out to be, I wouldn't have been able to meet the rest of my life with the balance which I seem to have been able to attain. In other words, I got sex out of the way."

After her marriage failed, she moved to Florida to get a divorce and to become reacquainted with her father, from whom her mother had separated when Marjory was a child. Frank Stoneman had recently started up a newspaper, *The News Record*, which would one day become the *Miami Herald*. Marjory began writing for the paper. Later, she became a free-lance writer of essays, articles, and short stories, many of which she set in the Everglades, that vast, watery, mysterious, and lightly populated region west of Miami. She crusaded for women's rights, for poor people, for nature. In 1927 she helped form a committee that sought to place the Everglades under National Park Service protection. In 1947, Rinehart and Company published her book *The Everglades: River of Grass*. Before the book came out, most people had considered the Everglades nothing more than a snake-infested swamp too remote to have yet received the full attention of the dredgers. Mrs. Douglas described it as a complex living system, a body of fresh water moving, in waltz time, toward the ocean. The Everglades was a river, she explained, that replenished the aquifers from which people, plants, and animals drank; a river that humidified the air, which in turn cycled the moisture back to the ground as rain; a river inextricably tied to all of life in South Florida.

Her book begins with this passage: "There are no other Everglades in the world. They are, they have always been, one of the unique regions of the Earth, remote, never wholly known. Nothing anywhere else is like them: their vast glittering openness, wider than the enormous visible round of the horizon, the racing free saltness and sweetness of their massive winds, under the dazzling blue heights of space." She described the "brown deer" and the "pale-colored lithe beautiful panthers that feed on them." She wrote about panthers eating turtle eggs on ocean beaches. John Gomez, a reformed pirate, lived on an island in lower Florida where he started a goat ranch, but a panther ate all the goats, and the place thereafter was called Panther Key. A mailman, Long John Holman, in the 1860s carried the mail on foot from St. Augustine to Fort Dallas; he walked along the beach, because there were too many panthers in the palmettos. Hattie Carpenter taught the few high-school students in the single grammar school in Miami in 1905; on one occasion, bicycling home to Brickell Hammock with a beefsteak in her basket, the schoolmarm was chased by a panther, which did not catch her.

In 1947, the same year that *The Everglades: River of Grass* came out, Everglades National Park was established. Since that time, Mrs. Douglas has been its most visible champion. She is frequently characterized as Florida's most powerful environmentalist. (She was an environmentalist long before the word was coined.) In the 1960s she helped stop a jetport for the city of Miami that would have carved the heart out of Big Cypress Swamp. She worked to get Big Cypress declared a National Preserve. To this day, bureaucrats and politicians court her. The founder and leader of an influential environmental group, Friends of the Everglades, Mrs. Douglas is such an institution in Florida that the state Department of Natural Resources named its headquarters building in Tallahassee after her—a tribute that did nothing to allay her periodic chivvying of that governmental agency.

I met Mrs. Douglas at her home in Coconut Grove. The house, built in 1926, has no driveway or garage. (Mrs. Douglas was said to frown on automobiles; she had never owned one or bothered learning how to drive.) In the neighborhood were well-groomed ranchettes and Italianate manors; Mrs. Douglas's small dwelling was hidden behind bristling shrubbery, askew to the street, as if it had been there before the road went in. Its asphalt-shingled roof wrapped strangely around the gables, like thatching. The door, of dark wood, was arched.

A well-dressed middle-aged woman answered my knock; she said she was a friend of Mrs. Douglas. Inside, the house was musty and dim, the ceilings fourteen feet high (to let the heat rise: unlike most Florida houses, Mrs. Douglas's is not air-conditioned). Moisture had stained the plaster walls. Books occupied all visible shelf space. Mrs. Douglas sat on a couch. Small and frail, she reposed at a slight angle to the perpendicular. Her sparse white hair had been done in limp curls. She wore a piece of red yarn for a hair ribbon, a string of white beads around her neck, and a floral print dress. Her hands, twisted and mottled, lay in her lap. Her mouth was at a slant, not level in her head. (In her autobiography she described her face as "crooked.") Photographs taken of her outdoors show a wizened woman in dark glasses and a huge floppy hat that has been described as making her look "like Scarlett O'Hara as played by Igor Stravinsky." She sometimes jokes, "They call me a nice old woman, but I'm not."

Mrs. Douglas had on thick glasses and kept her eyes closed behind them. I had to speak loudly for her to hear me. Yet if her body had aged, her mind remained supple. When she learned I was interested in panthers, Mrs. Douglas immediately volunteered that twice she had seen a panther in the wild. "Once was over on the west coast, on Marco Island." Her voice was strong, her tone brusque. "I was staying at the Barfields' hotel, which was probably the dirtiest hotel in the state. I was out for a stroll one morning and a panther came out of the mangroves and walked across the road not twenty feet away. He looked at me, and I looked at him. I saw the markings on his face. He was a large, mature cat. That was some years ago. Since then, I've also seen a panther's tail disappearing into the brush."

Mrs. Douglas, I soon understood, was opposed to putting radio collars on panthers. She has a house cat named Willie Terwilliger. "He hates a collar," she told me. "A cat is a cat. Any cat would hate to have something around his neck. It makes him feel unbalanced. A collar can get stuck on a branch, and the cat can choke to death. It's a dangerous nuisance. I suppose the collars are helping them learn about panthers, but the simple fact is that panthers are in trouble because we are destroying the places where they live." I mentioned that the collars had helped biologists identify precisely the lands used by panthers, lands that perhaps could be protected. Somewhat grudgingly Mrs. Douglas acknowledged this utility of scientific surveillance. I brought up the difficulty inherent in saving land for panthers—trying to persuade people and corporations of the need to leave prime land undeveloped, and getting federal or state agencies or private conservancies to actually buy the huge acreages that panthers need. "Well," she said dismissively, "we not only *can* do it but we *must*. It's exactly the same thing as saving the Everglades. There is nothing esoteric about protecting land or wildlife habitat. We can't possibly stop population growth, but we can and we must guard Florida's natural resources against damage."

Mrs. Douglas's Friends of the Everglades has pressed for a moratorium on hunting deer and hogs in Big Cypress National Preserve to benefit the panthers there. "The government could stop it in an instant if they wanted to," she told me. "But the government is dominated by the hunters."

Our conversation shifted to the Everglades themselves. Casually I remarked on how foreign they seemed to me, how inhospitable—"Well, they *are* inhospitable," she snapped. "People are not supposed to live there. It's too buggy and too wet. I hardly ever go into the Everglades. I've ridden across them in a car from time to time. I know they're out there, and I know they're essential to life in Florida, and that's enough for me."

Later, as I myself drove back across the Everglades, I saw the land stretching gray and drab in all directions. Flat, utterly flat. The sun was headed down. Tangerine-tinted clouds hung high in the north, probably smoke from burning cane fields. No birds did I see, except for a few glossy grackles perched in pines above a trashy-looking restaurant, and here and there a heron as immobile as a yard ornament on the bank of the dredge-cut which paralleled the Tamiami Trail. It was the end of the dry season, in late April, when the Everglades and the Big Cypress country look their worst. One wonders if they will ever become green again—and year after year they do, beneath the soaking thunderstorms of May and June, the rains that "trample across the land," as Mrs. Douglas wrote in her everlasting book, which continues to sell ten thousand copies a year.

People have been working to save the Everglades for decades. Lawsuits have been filed, politicians have waxed eloquent about the need to preserve the environment. (Today it would be political suicide to suggest draining the Everglades, just as it would have been political suicide to have suggested saving them a hundred years ago.) Influential though Marjory Douglas may be, and strong indeed the sentiment for saving the natural lands, the Everglades—and all of South Florida—are in deep, some would say terminal, trouble. There is simply too much money in cane and citrus, too much power concentrated in the land and the water for its present tenants to give it up for panthers.

That evening I got together with some wildlife biologists in Everglades City, across the tip of the peninsula. (It is only about a two-hour drive from the Atlantic Coast to the Gulf. People commute from Miami and Fort Lauderdale to jobs in Naples.) We bought pizzas at a restaurant and carried them to a picnic pavilion at the Park Service's Gulf Coast Ranger Station. The place was closed. Lights from the town winked on the black water. We slapped mosquitoes, ate pizza, and drank beer. Herons croaked. An outboard motor buzzed somewhere off in the darkness. I told about meeting Marjory Stoneman Douglas. There was a pause in the conversation. One of the biologists said, "Does Marjory know that her Everglades are dead?"

12

THE POLITICAL PANTHER

After I lucked onto the capture of panther number 46, back home in Pennsylvania I got a phone call. On the line was an administrator for the Florida Game Commission. He said that Melody Roelke had recommended me as a neutral person who might be willing to comment on the capture: specifically, on how the field biologists and the veterinarians had worked together, and whether the biologists had conducted themselves in a cooperative, professional manner.

I had noticed the friction between the two groups. During interviews I had heard plenty of complaints: The veterinarians were trying to take over the research project; the repeated anesthetizing to collect tissue and semen samples was needlessly endangering the cats. The biologists were obstructing new initiatives that might help the panther; they were fighting to control the research, no matter the cost. Plainly, several of the participants did not like each other, and the personal animus seemed to be getting in the way of the science. (I had even heard that her antagonists tried to annoy Roelke by urinating on the tires of her automobile, and that someone, presumably a biologist, had stuffed a dead water moccasin down the gullet of a white-tailed deer that Roelke had been given to autopsy.) From what I had read about efforts to save other endangered species, infighting among scientists was common: some felt that every effort should go toward saving habitat, while others wanted to give technology a try. I realized I could not involve myself in any feud and still have access to all the people working with the panther. I told the Game Commission administrator that I would not comment. Such squabbles bored me; I was more interested in the animal itself, its physical capabilities, how and where it lived, its history, and what the future might hold for it. But the phone call made me realize that to understand the panther, to appreciate its plight, I would have to know the policies and power struggles affecting it.

Already I had begun to see the panther as existing beneath layers of invisible polygons. The smallest polygons defined the home ranges of the cats themselves, worked out from radiolocations made by Dave Maehr and his colleagues, who flew around in airplanes checking on the animals' whereabouts. Superimposed on the panthers' ranges were the larger territories of the biologists and the veterinarians. Stretching even wider than the biologists' and the vets' domains were the realms—including the boundaries of preserves and parks—staked out by the various government agencies charged with keeping the panther from becoming extinct. And larger even than the bureaucrats' territories (more nebulous, perhaps, but ultimately more powerful) were influences like the citrus industry, Big Sugar, the users of water, the creators of resorts and housing developments and shopping centers and office complexes, the moneyed forces changing Florida from a natural, undeveloped place to a fragmented, urbanized one.

On my next trip South, I sought out another man who was writing a book on the panther, focusing on the bureaucracies and their behind-the-scenes maneuverings. Ken Alvarez is a biologist for the Florida Park Service. In the 1970s he had made plaster casts of what he thought were panther tracks on the dirt trails of Fakahatchee Strand State Preserve. Alvarez had served on the Florida Panther Recovery Team, a group of citizen experts and government biologists whom the U.S. Fish and Wildlife Service asked in 1976 to assess the status of *Felis concolor coryi*. (The Fish and Wildlife Service routinely sets up a recovery team as part of its effort to save any endangered species.) The Florida Panther Recovery Team drafted a plan for determining how many panthers were alive in Florida and where they lived, and suggested possible avenues of research and restoration; the team disbanded in 1982. Alvarez had also chaired the Florida Panther Technical Advisory Council. This was the group of five wildlife authorities appointed by the governor of Florida in 1983, during the furor that arose when Chris Belden accidentally killed a panther he was trying to anesthetize. The Technical Advisory Council was to give advice to the Florida Game Commission. Alvarez served on the council for four years until, frustrated by what he saw as the incompetence and intransigence of the agencies working with the panther, he quit and began writing his book.

Alvarez's office is in a low building shaded by orchid–clad live oaks at Oscar Scherer State Recreation Area, on the Gulf Coast south of Sarasota; turning off the commercialized Tamiami Trail into the recreation area suggests going from Atlantic City, New Jersey, into the Garden of Eden. Alvarez is tall, rawboned, with dark graying hair, a clipped mustache, and a sober mien. His roots in Florida go about as deep as they can. He descends from one Don José Alvarez, born in Spain in 1771 and appearing in the early 1800s on the tax rolls of Fernandina, a settlement in the Spanish colony of Florida, on the peninsula's northeast coast near present-day Jacksonville. "You could presume that Don José was an impoverished aristocrat," Alvarez told me. "Otherwise, why would he come to such a godforsaken place as Florida was back then?" Ken Alvarez grew up in the 1950s in Ocala, in central Florida, then a town of 14,000, where his father was chief of police. (Today, hemmed in by trailer parks and retirement villages, Ocala has swollen to 42,000.) On the day I met with him, Alvarez had a head cold and was recovering from kidney surgery; he drank glass after glass of water, and kept leaving every few minutes to use the bathroom. Probably I added to his discomfort, since he seemed to regard me as a competitor. To many of my questions he replied, "It'll all be there in my book." In fact, it is all there (and then some) in his book, a self-published volume that came out in the summer of 1993. *Twilight of the Panther* goes on for 450 pages, exhaustive, brave, insightful, tedious, bitter.

Alvarez's book describes the four agencies brought together by the panther, and I draw on it here in presenting them.

Of the four, the most directly involved is the Florida Game Commission (whose full, formal name is the Florida Game and Fresh Water Fish Commission). The commission was set up early in this century and assigned the task of stopping Floridians in their constant and consummate poaching of fish and wildlife. By 1915 deer were so scarce in Florida that the carcass of one would bring fifty dollars. (To help restock, the Game Commission imported deer from Wisconsin and Texas—deer, it should be noted, of two different subspecies than the whitetails living in Florida in the first place.) The human denizens of Florida filched birds' eggs, trapped ducks by the thousands, slew bear, bobcats, quail, wild turkeys, otters, opossums, raccoons, skunks, alligators, turtles, fish—anything that could be skinned, eaten, sold, or otherwise consumed. They shot nearly into annihilation the wading birds—egrets, herons, ibises, and spoonbills—whose feathers went to decorate ladies' hats. William Hornaday, the chief taxidermist for the U.S. National Museum of Natural History and, with Theodore Roosevelt, one of the nation's two leading advocates of wildlife protection at that time, wrote in 1913: "In the destruction of wild life I think the backwoods population of Florida is the most lawless and defiant in the United States . . . At present I can see no hope whatever for saving even a good remnant of the wild life of the state."

That same year, the Florida legislature established the Game Commission, whose wardens would finally check the slaughter. Today, five commissioners appointed by the governor direct what has become a large and influential agency with more than three hundred employees and a yearly budget of $30 million. While the Game Commission has managed to suppress poaching, hunting continues to be a major, traditional activity. The hunters, well organized into sportsmen's clubs, form a strong political force. The Game Commission listens to them carefully.

A second group involved (reluctantly, as will be seen) with restoring the panther is the Florida Department of Natural Resources. As part of its mission, this agency seeks to return the lands it administers—parks, recreation areas, and preserves—to a condition of originality, a naturalness that will recall for modern Floridians what the peninsula was like "prior to ecological disruptions caused by the arrival of European man in 1513" (this phrase comes from the policy manual of the Florida Park Service, Ken Alvarez's employer and a sub-unit within the Florida Department of Natural Resources). The most prominent state-owned tract inhabited by panthers is Fakahatchee Strand State Preserve, part of Big Cypress Swamp. The Department of Natural Resources administers Florida's program of land acquisition, which,

Alvarez writes, is "second only to the federal government's in the amount of land it annually purchases." Alvarez describes this land-buying effort as "the tool of final configuration for the remains of a native landscape now being rapidly reduced and sundered by the onrush of asphalt and agriculture."

The Endangered Species Act of 1973 rather blithely instructs the U.S. Fish and Wildlife Service to protect and restore threatened and endangered species—everything from Oregon silverspot butterflies to Tennessee snail darters to Florida panthers. The Fish and Wildlife Service originated in the 1880s as an obscure branch within the U.S. Department of Agriculture concerned with "economic ornithology": how birds affect farming. (Bad birds got blasted, good ones received protection.) Along the way, part of the unit split off to control predators injurious to livestock, including pumas, bears, coyotes, and wolves. In the early 1900s, the agency evolved into the Bureau of Biological Survey, its mission expanded to include studying the distribution of animals and plants in North and Central America. The Bureau of Biological Survey was transferred to the Department of the Interior in 1939, and in 1940 it merged with the Bureau of Fisheries. Called by the name it has kept to this day, the U.S. Fish and Wildlife Service continued its efforts at building a system of national wildlife refuges. The first refuges were for ducks and geese, places where these fowl could breed and rest during their annual north-south migrations. Other refuges followed, for elk, antelope, bison, bighorn sheep, whooping cranes—and, in 1989, for the Florida panther. The Florida Panther National Wildlife Refuge, in the northern reaches of Fakahatchee Strand, contains thirty thousand acres, an excellent habitat (it serves as a home territory or a travel route for as many as nine cats), but only a small fraction of what is needed to save the panther.

The fourth agency holding sway over the panther is the National Park Service, which controls more potential panther habitat in South Florida than any other entity. The Park Service administers Big Cypress National Preserve and Everglades National Park—together a great sprawl of land, some two million acres, or 3,125 square miles. (By comparison, the state of Delaware contains 2,057 square miles; Florida itself is 58,560 square miles.) The Park Service cooperates with the Florida Game Commission by allowing state biologists to snoop around in the northern part of Big Cypress, called the Bear Island Unit, while monitoring collared cats; and they let the Game Commission set hunting seasons and bag limits for all species of game throughout the preserve.

The Park Service manages parks, preserves, monuments, and seashores nationwide—jewels like Grand Canyon, Yellowstone, Yosemite, Bryce, and Everglades, as well as hundreds of lesser-known places. In the early 1960s, the Park Service asked a committee of scientists, chaired by Starker Leopold, son of the pioneering ecologist Aldo Leopold and himself a prominent wildlife authority, how the service should be managing the creatures in its parks. Leopold wrote: "We would recommend that the biotic associations within each park be maintained, or where necessary re-created, as nearly as possible in the condition that prevailed when the area was first visited by the white man. A national park should represent a vignette of primitive America." Guided by this dictum (blinded by it, Ken Alvarez says), the Park Service has refused to play favorites among creatures, including endangered ones.

"The Florida panther has survived five centuries of post-Columbian travail," Alvarez told me in his office. "We have the technological tools to save the panther. We have the money—I figure that between thirty and forty million dollars have already been spent, for captive breeding, field research, highway underpasses. The Florida Panther National Wildlife Refuge alone cost over twenty million dollars. So the resources are there. What we don't have are agencies that can or will use those resources effectively."

According to Alvarez, the group that might have unified and directed the disparate efforts on behalf of the panther was the Florida Panther Technical Advisory Council. The following people originally made up the council: Alvarez, who as a regional biologist was responsible for managing Fakahatchee Strand State Preserve, where the mishandled panther had perished. Robert Baudy, formerly of France and now of central Florida, a man vastly knowledgeable about cats, a trainer and a breeder of tigers, leopards, jaguars, and pumas. (At Baudy's compound, Savage

Kingdom, you drive up to the gate, lean on the horn, and a worker comes and lets you in. The place is bigger and more successful-looking than Frank Weed's setup. Baudy's cats live in sturdy wire pens shaded by live oaks. He has induced even the clouded leopard to breed, a shy, arboreal feline of Southeast Asia that, in the wild, appropriates eagles' nests as places to rear its young. Baudy sells kittens to zoos, menageries, and circuses. People take pictures of his cats for whiskey and automobile advertisements. He was once seized by a caged Florida panther, which let go when a worker bashed it over the head with a shovel.) A third member of the council was Sonny Bass, the biologist at Everglades National Park, where panthers were rumored and where Bass would, within three years, capture several panthers and begin his own research. John Eisenberg was an ecologist from the University of Florida who had studied wildlife all over the world, including leopards and deer in Sri Lanka. (I met him at his office in the Florida State Museum in Gainesville; a large man, graying and bearded, supporting himself with a cane, Eisenberg is astute, philosophical, capable of recognizing concepts and placing local issues within a larger context.) The fifth and final member was Mel Sunquist, a professor of wildlife biology at the University of Florida who had investigated the social lives of tigers, leopards, and ocelots, and who had once had his Nepalese colleague plucked out of a tree by a tigress protecting her cubs.

These five independent members of the Florida Panther Technical Advisory Council—respected scientists and academicians and one lay member, Robert Baudy—met, discussed, and gave to the Florida Game Commission their recommendations.

In 1984 they recommended that the Game Commission immediately start a captive breeding program, or fund someone else to start one. Robert Baudy insisted that the panther was dangerously inbred, based on the crook in its tail and the cowlick of fur on its back. (Baudy had actually raised the specter of inbreeding as early as 1976, when he served with Alvarez on the initial Florida Panther Recovery Team appointed by the U.S. Fish and Wildlife Service.) Baudy and other members of the Technical Advisory Council felt that a captive population would ensure against the subspecies' dying out because of disease or inbreeding; also, it would provide a reservoir from which to restock panthers in other parts of Florida. Their recommendation came years before the veterinarian Melody Roelke arrived, to find biological evidence of a sick, inbred bunch of cats. It came years before so much attention was focused on the panther that captive breeding would necessitate filing thick federal documents and weathering a lawsuit brought by an animal-rights group. It came before many panthers had died—of old age, of mercury poisoning, under the wheels of cars and trucks—draining away their own unique genes from the sub-species' dwindling pool. To the recommendation that a few Florida panthers be removed from the wild and bred in captivity, the Game Commission did not deign to reply. (Monsieur Baudy, already fed up with the glacial pace of bureaucracy, started his own breeding program, using panthers borrowed from Les and Bill Piper's Everglades Wonder Gardens, the menagerie that had released the quasi-panthers into the Everglades in the 1970s.)

The Advisory Council recommended that key panther habitat be identified, protected, and managed as a unit—a step that had greatly benefited tigers in India, Bangladesh, and Nepal. The Game Commission did not reply to this recommendation, either. Alvarez believes the commission did not want to alarm influential ranchers and corporations who owned lands where panthers lived, lands that were also used by hunters. Perhaps the agency did not want to risk closure of those lands.

The Technical Advisory Council warned the Florida Game Commission and the U.S. Fish and Wildlife Service against de-fining the panther as having a cowlick and a crooked tail, char-acteristics that had long been trumpeted as evidence of the cat's uniqueness. The subspecies *Felis concolor coryi*, John Eisenberg ex-plained, had been split off because of certain key skull dimen-sions. If the agencies kept affirming a uniqueness based on traits having no taxonomic value—traits that also conferred no survival advantages, and which actually pointed to the unhealthiness of inbreeding—then they might box the recovery strategy into a position that precluded outbreeding, the bringing in of new ani-mals to boost the panther's genetic diversity. The council pointed out that, under the Endangered Species Act, the Fish and Wildlife Service could relist Florida's panthers as an endangered population of pumas in Florida—a step that would greatly simplify managing and protecting them. (The same thing had been done with bald eagles and grizzly bears in the lower forty-eight states—two species that remain fairly plentiful in Alaska and Canada.) The Fish and Wildlife Service said they would discuss this option with their lawyers in the Department of the Interior. The lawyers, for reasons that remain unknown to this day, demurred at changing the panther's status. The Game Commission likewise preferred not to alter the current understanding of "Florida panther."

The Technical Advisory Council then addressed that thorniest of issues: hunting. Big Cypress Preserve, 570,000 acres, had few deer and fewer panthers (and apparently old and malnourished ones at that). Was the preserve barren because humans hunted it so heavily, cropping off the hogs and deer, suppressing the prey base for the cats? Hunting camps dotted the woods and prairies. Hunters used hounds to pursue their quarry. More and more people were hunting in Big Cypress every year. Six thousand off-road vehicles had been registered there, including an expanding number of the all-terrain vehicles that had begun flooding the market in the 1970s—shiny, inexpensive four-wheeled conveyances that could be hauled in the back of a pickup truck and could penetrate almost anywhere.

The Technical Advisory Council recommended that the Florida Game Commission consult with the National Park Service and cut back on hunting in the preserve: Reduce the number of hunters and off-road vehicles. Shorten the deer season (at the time, it was two months). Forbid the use of dogs. Close certain areas so that local prey populations could bounce back. To the suggestion that hunting be limited, the Florida Game Commission replied as it always had: "The panther has coexisted with hunting for years."

At that point Alvarez blew the whistle to an environmental activist group. An article criticizing the Florida Game Commission's protectiveness toward hunting appeared in a state conservation magazine. Under pressure from the governor, the Game Commission accepted two of the Advisory Council's suggestions: They would ban dogs for hunting deer and hogs. They would bar the new all-terrain vehicles—but not the traditional swamp buggy, an automobile-like rig more expensive than the new machines and owned by far fewer hunters. The hunters screamed at even those limitations, and the Game Commission backed down. Renewed pressure from the governor brought about a compromise on the already-compromised recommendations. In the end, the Game Commission prohibited the use of dogs, except during the first nine days of the hunting season, which was when most of the deer and hogs were killed anyway. All-terrain vehicles were not banned, although it was prohibited to hunt from them or to use them for carrying guns.

If, in 1985, the Florida Game Commission appeared to be intransigent, the National Park Service would prove even more so, adhering to its policy of re-creating "a vignette of primitive America." Roy McBride, walking the trails of Everglades National Park, had found signs of five, maybe six panthers—about a quarter of the total then estimated for all of Florida. At the time, nothing was known of these cats, except that there were few of them and they seemed cut off from the main pocket of panthers in the Big Cypress and therefore seemed in danger of dying out. The Florida Panther Technical Advisory Council recommended that the Game Commission ask the Park Service for permission to do radio-telemetry research on both panthers and deer in the Everglades. The Game Commission requested, and the park superintendent refused. He agreed that the research ought to be done—but not on the "undisturbed" animals in his park. Ever the gadfly, Alvarez wrote to William Penn Mott, a former director of the California state parks system recently appointed by President Ronald Reagan to head the National Park Service. Alvarez pointed out that Mott himself had proclaimed a new commitment to preserving endangered species—and here one of his park superintendents was turning down a chance to help a highly visible, extremely endangered animal. Mott replied with what Alvarez calls "a soothing epistle backing the park superintendent." (Alvarez's superiors in the Florida Park Service almost took his head off for bypassing the chain of command: " 'What do you meeean,' said the voice in a rising inflection, 'using words like DILATORY?' . . . I hadn't thought 'dilatory' such a venomous adjective," wrote Alvarez. "I promised to try and do better in the future. In this I would fail.")

The Florida Panther Technical Advisory Council recommended that the Park Service plant forage for deer on lands newly added to Everglades National Park, thousands of acres of old farmland overgrown with non-native plants. (The most widespread of these exotics was Brazilian pepper, an aggressive shrub on which native wildlife, including deer, do not feed. Another pest—it has swept across much of South Florida—is melaleuca, an Australian tree that grows rapidly, seeds itself six times a year, and dries out the marshy ground that it invades.) More deer, the Advisory Council suggested, would make for more and healthier panthers. Again the Park Service refused. To manage for a single species flew in the face of their long-standing policy of re-creating primitive America. Never mind, Alvarez notes, that the Brazilian pepper and melaleuca were crowding out native plants; never mind that the Endangered Species Act superseded all other federal wild-life management policies.

In 1986 the National Park Service finally did let Sonny Bass study the waning population of panthers in the Everglades—a cell that would quickly fall apart. Today, perhaps five panthers hang on in most of the federal holdings, the two million acres of Everglades and southern Big Cypress: two females that the Park Service biologist Deborah Jansen monitors, Number 23 (aka Orphan Annie) and her daughter; and the two males, numbers 16 and 42, father and son, who wandered west out of the Everglades to join the females. The National Park Service, contends Alvarez, refuses to this day to do anything substantive for panthers. He labels the service "the most inflexible of all American land management agencies . . . blind to the contributions it could make to preserving biological diversity and oblivious to the harm it can do."

Alvarez must have been a pain in the neck to his own agency, the Florida Department of Natural Resources. He wrote embarrassing letters, he called out for promptness, he clamored for the public to be told how endangered the panthers really were, how far they had been sucked into the vortex of extinction. The governor had placed Alvarez on the Florida Panther Technical Advisory Council, where he was essentially untouchable. At one point an anonymous directive from the upper echelons of the Florida Park Service, delivered over the telephone by one of Alvarez's superiors, ordered him to resign as chairman of the Advisory Council. Alvarez asked that the directive be put in writing and signed by whoever it was that wanted him to step down. That was the last he heard of the matter.

Alvarez found his own agency reluctant to manage its lands to help the panther. The Florida Park Service, like its federal counterpart, has, according to Alvarez, "vested the original landscape with a near-mystical aura." A Park Service official once told Alvarez that it was not logical for the agency to take major steps toward saving the panther, because "it would be counter to the agency's own interest to risk having the program fail." In one of the more bizarre scenarios, the agency seemed willing to increase the panthers' food supply in Fakahatchee Strand—not by planting grasses to boost the deer herd, as Alvarez had suggested (such planting being deemed "unnatural"), but by putting out feeders that would scatter corn for deer, and by tethering goats for panthers to snack on. (Ultimately, even this proposal was shelved.)

Twilight of the Panther explains that the U.S. Fish and Wildlife Service is considered the "lead agency" in the effort to save the panther. However, the service holds little power over the three bureaucracies it is supposed to be leading. In regard to such critical issues as captive breeding, hunting, habitat preservation, and educating the public, the Fish and Wildlife Service must coax, suggest, never demand. "The endangered species branch of the Fish and Wildlife Service," Alvarez writes, "is purely an administrative organ [that] has no zealous band of constituents and thus no political base." Elsewhere in his book Alvarez is more succinct, describing the service as a "great federal wimp" and "a political weakling that can be elbowed aside at any time."

A ploy that the other three agencies used to keep the Fish and Wildlife Service elbowed aside—and one that also made the Florida Panther Technical Advisory Council (the governor's group of meddling academics and upstart biologists) appear superfluous—was to create yet another committee, this one giving the appearance of an official, professional consensus on how to tackle the panthers' problems. The Florida Panther Interagency Committee sprang into being in 1986, composed of leaders from the four cooperating agencies—the Florida Game Commission, the Florida Department of Natural Resources, the U.S. National Park Service, and the ever-compliant U.S. Fish and Wildlife Service. The Interagency Committee quickly designated its own technical subcommittee, stocking it with scientists from within the agencies themselves, to evaluate any future proposals, efforts, or research. Naturally, these hand-picked critics cause their parent agencies little discomfort. The Interagency Committee feeds information to the press. According to Alvarez, it downplays the gravity of the panther's endangerment. It seeks in all ways to avoid raising controversy and agitating hunters, landowners, and park visitors.

The greatest sin committed by the Florida Panther Interagency Committee, says Alvarez, is its refusal to educate and involve the general public. The committee assumes that the citizens of Florida and the United States are not capable of grasping the principles of endangered-species biology: the perplexities of genetics, the precariousness of small populations, the arbitrariness of the sub-species designation, and the need for special—and, to some people, troubling and excessively expensive—measures such as captive breeding, shuffling animals around to prevent inbreeding, and protecting large areas of essential habitat. Indeed, writes Alvarez, the Interagency Committee itself may not fully understand those principles.

When Ken Alvarez quit the Florida Panther Technical Advisory Council in 1987 and began writing his book, the group's influence had already begun to wane. Over the years, several of the Technical Advisory Council's recommendations have been put into practice, but, Alvarez contends, too few of them to help a creature whose habitat and genetic health are fading so swiftly. In his office at the state park, Alvarez told me, "In most cases, about seven years seem to pass between when a crucial step is advocated and when it finally gets implemented." Even then, he said, the step is usually taken only because of outside pressure, such as a lawsuit by an animal-rights group that forced the U.S. Fish and Wildlife Service to write a habitat preservation plan for the panther.

More recently, over the telephone, I asked Alvarez how *Twilight of the Panther* had been received. He had heard through the grapevine, he said, that "the Florida Game Commission pronounced it a compilation of half-truths. Officially, nothing has been said to me at all," he continued. "It's a little like the silence you'll get after somebody farts out loud in church.

"The book is selling well. I hear it's being used in a university course on endangered-species management." Alvarez, a career service employee, did not believe he was in danger of being fired over the book. "Actually, a lot of my old opponents have retired," he said. What's next for him? "I may try to get a deer management

project started in Fakahatchee Strand next year. And I may sue
the National Park Service to make them manage for more deer."
Alvarez sniffed into the receiver a little, in lieu of laughter—he
still sounded a most sober and serious fellow. "Well, it's the wildest kind of an idea," he said, "but I must admit it's attractive."

I asked what he thought the future would hold for the panther.
"If the trends continue, the inbreeding and the loss of habitat, I
don't see how it can possibly survive," he said. "To save the
panther, we'll have to preserve huge tracts of interconnected wild
land—which would be a good thing, because it would keep us
from being overrun by people. All of the problems in Florida—
the endangered animals and plants, the saltwater intrusion into the
freshwater aquifers, the air pollution, even the crime—stem from
too many people, too much growth. What we're seeing right now
is the Los Angelesization of Florida. The tremendous asset of
panther restoration is that it will put limits on growth—and that's
an asset to Florida's human population as well."

13

SAVING THE PANTHERS

D. J. Schubert was thirty thousand feet above Georgia when he decided to help save the panthers. It was early in 1990. Schubert, the newly hired Director of Investigations for the Fund for Animals, was in a jetliner on his way back to Silver Spring, Maryland, after having infiltrated a rattlesnake roundup in southern Georgia. He was reading a Florida newspaper (his flight had originated in Tallahassee) when he came upon an article describing the proposal to capture wild panthers and breed them in captivity.

"I was sickened by what I read," Schubert told me. We were in the office of Fund for Animals, on the third floor of an eight-story building in Silver Spring. Outside, sirens wailed down Georgia Avenue; traffic droned. Schubert is in his thirties, fair-skinned and chubby, with a thatch of brown hair and a boyish, ingenuous face that lets him pass for a college student, a guise he often uses when penetrating groups that he believes are abusing animals. "I take a harder position on zoological parks than the fund does in general," Schubert continued. "The fund isn't opposed to captive breeding *per se*, but in the case of the panther, it looked to me like the agencies were putting all their eggs in one basket by using this gee-whiz technological approach. There didn't seem to be a lot of discussion taking place about protecting habitat for panthers, or how—or even *if*—the cats could be put back in the wild if they succeeded in breeding any."

The Fund for Animals is a thorn in the side of the U.S. Fish and Wildlife Service—although Schubert insists that at least some people within the agency appreciate the outside pressure to protect the environment. In 1992, the Fund for Animals won a lawsuit compelling the Fish and Wildlife Service to speed up its listing of endangered plants and animals. (Because of the paperwork involved, and the great number of imperiled species, there is, in essence, a waiting list to get onto the endangered species list; at last count, some three thousand species were scheduled to be considered for inclusion.) "Before we sued, they were adding about fifty species a year," Schubert told me. "Some species were going extinct before they could even be listed. Under the settlement agreement, the Fish and Wildlife Service will more than double their previous pace." He added, "The Fund for Animals is responsible for getting more species onto the endangered species list —one hundred seventy-five so far—than any other conservation organization."

The Fund for Animals is not precisely a conservation organization. It is an animal-rights group founded in 1967 by Cleveland Amory, a former critic for *TV Guide* magazine and a writer about animals, chiefly house cats. Today, Amory is president of the group, which is bankrolled by donations from its 200,000 members and by monies awarded following successful lawsuits, such as the one hastening the listing of endangered species. The Fund for Animals has its headquarters in New York City, as well as ten regional offices spread across the country. At the one in Silver Spring, anti-hunting posters decorated the walls, and about a dozen young people sat behind scratched and dented desks on which computer terminals made their soft rushing noise and telephones buzzed. According to its promotional brochure, the Fund for Animals opposes "cruelty to animals—whether wild or domestic—wherever, however, and whenever it occurs." No doubt a whole book could be written about a group that maintains a sanctuary for injured rabbits ("Hope for the Hopless"); whose president has proclaimed on television talk shows that, ideally, predatory animals should be separated from their prey in the wild, to minimize suffering (Schubert rolled his eyes when he told me about that one); and whose members have smeared seal pups with "harmless red organic dye" to make their pelts useless to furriers, rammed icebreakers into whaling ships, and harassed hunters across the country. The Fund for Animals has an especial antipathy toward hunting. Through litigation, it has temporarily or permanently closed hunting seasons on creatures as various as bears, bison, and mourning doves. In California the group worked to pass a ballot initiative banning the hunting of pumas—"I went out and coordinated leafletting for the Bay area," Schubert said. "It was a close vote—51 percent to 48 percent, or something like that, but we got it shut down." The Fund for Animals would like to shut down puma hunting everywhere it occurs. From the fund's brochure: "Mountain lion hunters often use radio-collared dogs to track, chase and tree mountain lions. Sometimes vicious, bloody dog–lion fights occur before the lion flees to the tree. Then the hunter simply follows the radio signal from the dogs and shoots the trapped lion off the branch." In fact, using hounds to find a lion, trail it through broken, rocky terrain, and finally run it up a tree is far from the sure thing that the fund's brochure implies, at least according to the biologist Harley Shaw, who traced pumas for many years in Arizona, using his own and professional hunters' dogs.

I myself have never wished to shoot a puma. However, in visiting the Fund for Animals, I considered myself to be in hostile terrain. I hunt game birds and deer and have written books and articles dealing with hunting. I figured that, as Director of Investigations, Schubert would have checked me out; but if he had, he did not reproach me for my barbarism. I found him convivial and forthcoming—much more so than the bureaucrats with the Florida Game Commission. Schubert's enthusiasm bubbled over as he described the projects he was working on: Preventing hunters in Montana from shooting bison that wander out of Yellowstone National Park. ("Basically, we put our bodies between the hunters and the bison.") Gaining protection for gulls at John F. Kennedy International Airport. ("The feds have been shooting the gulls as they enter JFK airspace, to reduce the number of bird strikes on aircraft. They haven't done any risk assessment, which they ought to do before just going out and blasting the birds.") Exposing rattlesnake roundups in Georgia. ("They pour gas into the dens to drive the snakes out. They keep the snakes in big metal drums, where they suffocate and starve.") Stopping bear hunting in Pennsylvania. ("We follow the hunters around and make noise to scare the bears away. We came pretty close to getting beaten up a couple of times.") In regard to the panther, it was clear to me that the

Fund for Animals had accomplished more for the subspecies than
had any of the mainstream conservation organizations, the extent
of whose involvement with *Felis concolor coryi* seemed to consist
of plastering Big Guy's picture on their fund-raising brochures.

Donald John Schubert grew up on the outskirts of San Jose,
California. His mother was a teacher, his father an engineer for
Lockheed Missiles and Space Company. From childhood onward,
Schubert possessed a keen interest in animals. "I had lots of pets
when I was young—mostly dogs and cats. I was active in the
4-H; I even raised some sheep that were sold for slaughter." He
sighed and shook his head. "I didn't know any better. I was eating
animals myself back then. I've been a vegetarian since 1987—
actually a vegan." He pronounced the word "VEE-gun"; I asked
him what it meant, and he replied, "A vegan doesn't even consume
any dairy products." Schubert was wearing a canvas belt to hold
up his chinos and oddly textured black shoes undoubtedly made
from a leather substitute.

"I was sort of into Save the Whales, Save the Seals," he told
me, "but I was pretty unfocused." A turning point occurred when
Schubert visited his uncle, a biologist working in Nevada for the
U.S. Bureau of Reclamation. "We went out in a boat and counted
fish eggs in Lake Mead, which is backed up by Hoover Dam. My
uncle was involved in making a refugium for the Devil's Hole
pupfish. At that time, there was only one place in the world where
the Devil's Hole pupfish was found, and that was in Devil's Hole,
a hole out in the desert. Down in the hole was this pool, and that's
where all the fish lived. My uncle helped choose a site for a second
colony. They built a big spring-fed concrete pool at the base of
Hoover Dam and moved some fish into it."

After high school, Schubert enrolled in the wildlife sciences
program at Arizona State University. "All of my classmates were
concerned with wildlife," he said, "but in a very different way.
They were hunters. I was the only anti-hunter. I quickly learned
that wildlife management meant providing enough animals for
hunters to shoot." After graduation, finding jobs in wildlife management scarce and not wanting to work for a state game and fish
agency, Schubert applied to the Peace Corps. Sent to Burkina Faso
(the former Upper Volta), he worked on an experimental game
ranch whose purpose was to increase the number of wild grazing

animals so that some could be killed and eaten by the local people or sold to markets in the capital city, Ouagadougou. "Two of the best years of my life so far," Schubert said emphatically. "The killing was not actually going on at the time, and I felt that the benefits of the project outweighed the negative things. Basically, we created waterholes. The place was a wildlife haven! It was a warthog paradise! Roan antelope, hartebeest, buffalo, duikers, oribi . . . Some mornings I'd wake up to the sound of elephants feeding right outside my house.

"One day, out in the bush, I witnessed an elephant funeral. I was walking along, when all of a sudden I realized there were, like, a hundred and fifty elephants right in front of me. Off to one side stood a group of eight. In the middle of this group, a very small baby was lying on its side. Every so often it would try to stand up, but then it would fall over and let out a piercing scream, and one of the adults, probably its mother, would also scream." The elephants detected Schubert's presence, and an adult female, her ears flared, drove him off. When he crept back later, only the group of eight were still present; the baby elephant was lying motionless, now covered with dirt, grass, and stones. "The mother was standing over her baby, rocking back and forth. This went on for half an hour, until it was dark. Other elephants would come up and stroke the mother's back and intertwine their trunks with hers. Seeing this was an incredibly powerful experience."

After his stint in the Peace Corps, Schubert returned home and was hired as a biologist by the U.S. Fish and Wildlife Service. He was stationed in East Lansing, Michigan, where his job was to review development projects for their impacts on wetlands. Schubert could nix projects that would have damaged wetlands, but he could do nothing to save the uplands. "I was really bummed out by the amount of habitat destruction I was seeing," he said. After eight months he quit and joined an organization he had long admired: People for the Ethical Treatment of Animals, or PETA, based in Rockville, Maryland. "They fight against biomedical research that uses animals, against the fur industry, and against factory farming," he said. As a PETA investigator, Schubert would get a job in a laboratory conducting testing on animals and document any cruelties or violations of the federal Animal Welfare

Act. On one occasion, he worked in a lab where beagles were fed pesticide in their kibble, killed after six months, dissected, and their organs checked for the presence of toxins. "Did torturing those dogs tell us how a pesticide was going to work in the real world?" Schubert said to me. "There are so many variables that the experiment failed to take into account." When infiltrating a lab, Schubert often employed the alias Kyle Owens: he had a cousin Kyle, and he had worked with a biologist in East Lansing named Owens. "After twenty-three months I was pretty burned out," Schubert said. "PETA is a very powerful organization, on the cutting edge of the animal-rights movement, but it's a really stressful environment to work in. When I quit, I took three months off. I slept a lot."

Emerging from hibernation, Schubert went to work for the Fund for Animals. One of his tasks as Director of Investigations is to review federal plans that deal with wildlife. He writes detailed comments on the plans and, if a lawsuit is filed, works closely with the fund's lawyers. To spice up his routine, Schubert heads for the field. In Montana, one of Schubert's companions was arrested for jabbing a bison hunter with a ski pole. Later in the same fray, hunters stole the keys to Schubert's snowmobile and left him stranded. In Colorado, Schubert procured video footage of bear hunters; to gain their trust, Kyle Owens said he was making a film for use in discrediting the anti-hunting movement. "Unfortunately, or fortunately, depending on how you look at it," Schubert said, "they didn't get any bears."

In his office, poring over documents, writing comments, Schubert works an eighteen-hour day. He opened a filing cabinet and showed me dishware and utensils. A box of groceries sat in the space beneath his desk. Clothes hung from rods between bookshelves. "I was renting a room in a house, but I was staying there only one or two nights a month," Schubert said. He cooks in the office microwave or eats at local vegetarian restaurants. He takes sponge baths in a utility sink across the hall—"I learned how to do that in Africa." At night he gets a blanket and a pillow and stretches out on the carpet, in front of the television in the windowless library, with its boxed magazines ranging from *Vegetarian Times* and *Wild Earth* to *Sports Afield* and *World Bowhunters*, its collection of incriminating hunting videos, its taped talk-show appearances by Fund for Animals members; the indefatigable Schubert is in the process of reorganizing the video files.

Schubert and I were joined by a lawyer for the Fund for Animals, a young man named Sidney Maddock. We sat in chairs in the office of Wayne Pacelle, the group's chief spokesman. Unfortunately, Pacelle was on vacation that day; I had wanted to meet this handsome, polished activist, about whom I had read a recent article in *Sports Afield*. In his late twenties, full of carefully selected statistics, Pacelle appears frequently on national radio and television shows, condemning hunters and espousing the Fund for Animals' position. According to *Sports Afield*, Pacelle accosts people on the street and berates them for wearing fur. He once remarked about the Inuit natives of Greenland, whose trapping and subsistence hunting of seals and narwhals bothered him: "Why do they stay there? . . . It seems like a barren place to live."

Maddock sat in Pacelle's chair. He wore a starched shirt and a tie; his light-brown hair was in a longish coif. He clasped his hands behind his head and leaned back in the chair, revealing perspiration blots under his arms. Maddock grew up in Palm Beach County and practiced law in Florida before joining the Fund for Animals. He addressed me in a sort of legalese, with frequent pauses so that I could take down his comments. "In Florida there exists a significant political agenda that is in opposition to . . . no, that is *hostile* to . . . any regulations protecting the environment." He cleared his throat. "Florida is faced with a huge biological crisis. The state has seven of the ten fastest-growing metropolitan areas in the nation, and four of them are south of Highway 60." (Highway 60 crosses the state from east to west at roughly its midsection.) "The persistent efforts of Florida's powerful agricultural bloc are resulting in the biological collapse of the Everglades." He paused again, fixing his eyes on me; they were slanted and protuberant. "In the case of the sugar industry, litigation has been ongoing for three to four years, while the environment . . . has steadily deteriorated. Now the same thing is starting to happen on Florida's west coast." Maddock leaned forward in the chair and placed his hands palms down on the desk. "One thing that I hope you make clear in your book is that protecting the panther's habitat will benefit *people* . . . If development is allowed to continue at the current rate, recharge areas for groundwater will be destroyed, and poor-quality water from agricultural runoff will enter the aquifer. If we fail to protect the panther, the quality of life in Florida will go steadily downhill."

Maddock had to leave and attend to other business. Schubert spoke about the lawsuit that the Fund for Animals had lodged against the U.S. Fish and Wildlife Service over captive breeding of Florida panthers. The case was settled when the service agreed to capture only kittens and to keep them as wild as possible so that they could be put back in nature if the captive breeding effort fizzled. Further, the agency had to compose a habitat preservation plan: a thick document with color maps showing where panthers live today and where they might live in the future.

"They really blew it," Schubert said, referring to the habitat plan. "The service should have talked to the individual landowners that the plan would affect. There are only about a dozen and a half people they would have needed to contact."

Instead, the Fish and Wildlife Service released a draft of its plan to the news media and the public. It was received with approximately as much welcome as a twenty-five-degree night in an orange grove, or a bomb threat at Disney World. Landowners screamed that the government meant to buy up all of South Florida for the panther. (Actually, the Fish and Wildlife Service proposed buying only the most critical lands, and then only if the owners were willing to sell. They hoped to sign leases with other landowners, who would receive money in return for not converting their sloughs, forests, and cattle ranges into citrus and housing developments.) County commissions went on record as opposing the habitat preservation plan: The panther would become the spotted owl of the Southeast, all profitable development would cease, thousands of acres would be withdrawn from the local tax base, and South Florida's economy would topple. Ominously, the theory was trotted out that the panther is not really a panther at all, it is nothing but a mongrel cat, and hence deserves no special protection.

Schubert noted that the Florida Game Commission had not been pleased with the Fish and Wildlife Service's plan, which called for the federal rather than the state agency to lead the way in acquiring acres and signing easements with landowners. "Since the plan first came out," Schubert said, "it has gone through seven or eight drafts. It's been watered down until there's nothing concrete left in it. The rumor is that the Game Commission has been working behind the scenes to rile up local landowners. The Fund for Animals is watching very closely. When the final version comes out"—Schubert shrugged—"if we have to sue . . .

"At some point, we've got to draw a line in the sand," Schubert continued. "Let's say there's this big cattle ranch in South Florida with panthers living on it. We have to say to that rancher, what you are doing now—low-impact cattle grazing—is okay. But you can't go and put in a four-hundred-acre citrus grove." Schubert claimed he had fostered relationships with field biologists and clerks in regulatory agencies who would clue him in on proposed projects—citrus, housing, roads—that might harm the panther. He implied that the Fund for Animals might move to stop those projects. "The Endangered Species Act protects not only panthers but the places where they live," Schubert said. "If you destroy panther habitat, you destroy the panthers that live there.

"We have to take a hard look at firearms hunting in panther habitat. Does it alter the panthers' behavior or affect their breeding? I don't think that *all* forms of hunting affect the panther. Bow hunting for deer, for instance, even though it's brutal and cruel, probably doesn't hurt the panthers—if the hunters walk to where they are going instead of driving there on off-road vehicles. But if hunters are disturbing panthers, then they're violating the Endangered Species Act.

"According to the biologists, the habitat in South Florida is at its carrying capacity. That may be so, as the habitat is currently being managed. But that doesn't mean you can't change your management strategy. Plant forage for deer. Get rid of the ORVs. Reduce or eliminate firearms hunting. Increase the number of prey animals—basically turn the clock back about forty years. All of those things could boost the number of panthers. The state perceives us as an anti-hunting organization, which we are, but we got involved with the panther because we want it to survive. We also believe that the current level of hunting may not be conducive to panther recovery."

Considering the virulence with which the Fund for Animals

opposes hunting, I asked Schubert, "If you could use the panther to do away with hunting in Florida, would you do it?"

Schubert looked at me. He looked at the floor. A long pause ensued. "Uhh," he said. "I'd have to say that . . . uhh . . ." He squeezed the bridge of his nose between his thumb and forefinger. He looked up. "Yeah, we would." He nodded. He spoke slowly and carefully, as his colleague Mr. Maddock had done. "I guess you could say that we would use the panther to the extent possible to limit hunting. We would hope that the hunting community would be interested in maintaining the presence of the panther . . . We would hope that the hunters would want to preserve what's left of the ecosystem, with a top predator in place."

14

PATH OF THE PANTHER

One morning before dawn I drove to Corkscrew Swamp Sanctuary, ten thousand acres owned by the National Audubon Society on the northwestern edge of Big Cypress Swamp. The visitors' center was not open yet, so I stepped over a low wooden fence and walked along on one of the bark paths. The trail led off through pine flatwoods. The trees' arrow-straight trunks were topped by complicated crowns of twisted branches black against a faintly brightening sky. Dew lay on the ground. The air smelled sweet and pure. I sat at the base of a tree and listened: night herons croaking from the swamp, a crested flycatcher giving its strident *wheep-wheep-wheep*, a bobwhite quail whistling. A few yards away a sizable animal went rustling past. Probably it was a raccoon or a bobcat. Unlikely, but it could even have been a panther: the big cats live in and about Corkscrew Swamp and use it as a travel corridor.

As the dawn strengthened, the breeze came easing through the limber pine needles, scraping through the clustered palmetto fans. It brought from the west the faint intermittent static of highway traffic. The sky brightened to a deep rich blue, in which the last stars twinkled; another beautiful morning, the type of January day that draws so many of my friends' aging parents to Florida each winter.

I stood and continued along the path through the quiet woods until I came to a boardwalk. The walkway crossed a broad stretch of wet prairie and a band of pond cypress, then entered the swamp. Among the tall cypress trees it was still night. A clean, slightly acidic smell filled the clammy air. Birdsong ricocheted. Soon there would arrive the nature-minded retirees from nearby Naples and Fort Myers, the lifetime Audubon Society members with their sun hats, field guides, binoculars, and tripod-mounted spotting scopes—but for now I had the walkway to myself. As the light worked its way into the forest, the trees began to emerge, gray and smooth-barked, like huge concrete columns.

Corkscrew Swamp Sanctuary protects the country's largest stand of virgin bald cypress trees, seven-hundred-year-old giants like those logged in Fakahatchee Strand in the 1940s. Wood storks—Florida's largest remaining colony—build their sloppy stick nests in the tops of the trees. Around and on the cypresses grow creepers, ferns, shrubs, and air plants, the vegetation layered and dense, in every shade of green: yellow-green, blackish-green, verdigris, kelly, sea-green. Shafts of light angled in, reflecting from varnished leaves and from black water moving so slowly that it appeared to be stagnant; the sunbeams spotlighted the tips of fern fronds, loops of hanging vine, filigrees of Spanish moss, air plants plastered to trunks. From where I stood, hundreds of air plants were visible: prickly, angular ones; small, unobtrusive, lacy things; big bristling masses. An air plant is an epiphyte, requiring from its host nothing more than a reliable perch above the swamp's fluctuating water level. An air plant subsists on sunlight, rainwater, and the slow swirl of detritus in the air: bark flakes, pollen grains, leaf crumbs.

Birds flitted from bough to bough. The swamp resounded with their croaks, rasps, buzzes, chirps, trills. Pig frogs grunted. From somewhere came the heavy splash of an alligator. A red-shouldered hawk flapped into the crown of a maple a few feet from where I stood. Immediately the smaller birds in the vicinity fell silent. The hawk had a white-banded tail and rufous patches at the tops of its wings. It shuffled and settled on its perch, immobile now except for its head, which shifted up, down, left, right, in tiny increments. After a minute, it hopped off the branch and, on set wings, glided away between the trunks.

·　·　·

In the car, heading south from Corkscrew Swamp, I entered an area known as Golden Gate Estates.

Under a dazzling sun, Everglades Boulevard lay dead straight and north-south. At every quarter mile, a sand or a gravel road right-angled to the east and the west. No utility lines. No houses in sight, although street signs (24th Avenue, 33rd Avenue, 46th Avenue) announced the crossing roads. A thick diamondback rattlesnake lay tire-hammered and fly-attended in the northbound lane; vultures knobbed a nearby snag. A pickup truck passed me, going north, the driver wearing sunglasses and a cowboy hat, lifting a finger from the steering wheel in greeting. The country was flat. The plants were dry-land types, pines and grasses and legions of cabbage palms, stocky, rough-trunked trees whose fronds, enlivened by the breeze, caught the clear Florida sunshine and reflected it in dazzling spears and winks.

I began seeing a fair number of realtors' signs pointing off down the side roads. I turned onto one of the roads and bumped slowly along it. A few tenths of a mile brought me to another sign indicating that somewhere in the vicinity—amid the cabbage palms, wire grass, slash pines, and saw palmetto—lay a lot for sale. Golden Gate Estates is the world's largest housing subdivision. You can buy a lot in the northern half of Golden Gate Estates and build a house there. If the property lies too far from other development, and the cost of running a power line to it is prohibitive, you can install a diesel-powered electric generator; you can get a radio-telephone. You can build your own little fortress on top of the mostly drained swamp. Indeed, something of a fortress mentality is said to prevail among residents of the remoter parts of the subdivision, and there is nothing quite so embattled-looking as a split-level with vinyl siding, an attached garage, a trailered boat parked alongside, a lawn with manicured tropical shrubs—all by its lonesome in the scrubby Florida boondocks. Such an outpost may well include an alarm system and guard dogs. Or guard cats. Because, as they say, parts of Golden Gate Estates are "wide open." Drug planes use the road grid as a landing zone. Their clients on the ground find an isolated spot, switch on a couple of pairs of truck headlights, the plane touches down between them, the trucks load up, the aircraft zooms off into the night. A few years ago, a couple living in Golden Gate Estates were arrested for importing numerous tons of marijuana. Warren and Linda Stewart had surrounded their home with an eight-foot electric fence, behind which six pumas were allowed to roam. When officers of the federal Drug Enforcement Agency made the bust, they took along several Florida game wardens to deal with the pumas, most of which, fortunately, were in their cages that morning. Two of the pumas, however, were sleeping with the Stewarts, and when the officers entered the couple's bedroom, one of the pumas pounced on a warden and knocked him to the floor. The officer, unharmed, credited his bulletproof vest with warding off the puma's claws.

To the west, Golden Gate Estates resembles an actual development, with houses standing shoulder to shoulder, schools, and convenience stores; a lot on the western fringe, convenient to the burgeoning city of Naples, may sell for $100,000. Overall, Golden Gate Estates is twenty-five miles from its northern to its southern end. It varies in width from five to fifteen miles. Its grid is easily discernible in satellite photographs of Florida, like metal fencing pressed into a lawn.

Golden Gate Estates was the brainchild of two Baltimoreans, Leonard and Jack Rosen, who got their start in the world of commerce by selling refrigerators on time to poor people. They progressed to peddling hair tonic on television and, in 1957, found their true calling: selling lots in Florida. The Rosens created and sold the town of Cape Coral out of what had been mangrove swamp and miasmic coastal lowland, just across the Caloosa hatchee River from Fort Myers, about ten miles west of Golden Gate Estates. My parents, like many other Northerners, bought a quarter-acre lot in Cape Coral for $2,000 plus interest, on the installment plan. (I remember thinking, every time my parents mentioned the lot, that we must be richer than I thought to have afforded land in Florida. I also felt edgy, because I didn't want to move there.) The lot was always referred to as an investment, and I do not believe my parents ever really intended to build on it. After my father died, my mother considered selling the property and asked me to check on it some time when I was in Florida. With the aid of a real-estate map, I finally found the lot, on the edge of Cape Coral, a desolate, narrow rectangle of sun-scalded weeds and sand, nowhere near a cape, a bed of coral, or a view of the ocean. A few modest tract houses were scattered about, surrounded by imported turf and planted palms braced up by two-by-fours. When one of the residents saw me, she hurried over and asked, in a hopeful voice, if we were planning on building any time soon. She was from New Jersey. She and her husband had retired to Florida not long before. A school was coming, she exhorted, a grocery store was going in down the road, and rumor had it—a bright light suffused her eyes—that a Wal-Mart was on the way.

Gulf American, the Rosens' company, projected Golden Gate Estates as a community of 400,000. The Rosens' strategy, as it had been for Cape Coral, was to buy land ($150 per acre was the going rate in the 1960s), carve it into lots, sell them, and use the payments that came flooding in to secure options on more land. Salesmen sold parcels—two and a half and five acres—over the telephone and at banquet events in Northern communities, often held during the depths of winter. Potential clients were flown for free to the developed portion of Cape Coral (at one time Gulf American owned twenty-five airliners), where deals for Golden Gate properties were struck. Few customers actually looked at their land, a practice that the sales force discouraged. The salesmen implied the presence of roads, utilities, and plenty of Florida sunshine. Usually they could deliver on the sunshine.

North Golden Gate Estates was surveyed and sold. Then South Golden Gate Estates. Speculators and retirees bought the plots. By the time the Rosens got out of the land business, their company had made them a fortune. It had built, within the bounds of Golden Gate Estates, 800 miles of road and 180 miles of drainage canals. Depending on where their lots were located, the new landowners had either made a satisfactory investment or been royally ripped off. (As with most Florida real-estate ventures, for Golden Gate Estates the dividing line between a legitimate deal and a swindle was somewhat blurry.)

Despite all the ditching, every year from May to November many of the lots lie under varying depths of water, especially the twenty thousand tracts (totaling forty thousand acres) in southern Golden Gate Estates, lower and wetter than the northern development. South Golden Gate Estates is known locally as the Blocks. The Blocks are truly wide open. To reach them, I drove south over Interstate 75, the former Alligator Alley. I stopped at a bank of eighteen mailboxes (most of them riddled with bullet holes) next to a utility pole on which was nailed a large metal sign with the message:

"ACCESS"

SATURDAY 10:00 A.M.

EVERGLADES BLV. OVERPASS

"MEETING" EVERY WEEK!

Grouped together were mailboxes for residents at 4601 64th Avenue, 5760 104th Avenue, 1655 56th Avenue, 1501 58th Avenue. The implication was of settlement widely scattered. The "Access" referred to in the sign connoted entry to Interstate 75, which, humming along below a tall overpass, no longer exchanges with Everglades Boulevard. Now residents of the southernmost Blocks must drive a circuitous forty miles to get their groceries in Naples, as opposed to eighteen miles when Everglades Boulevard met with Alligator Alley. In the Blocks, people inhabit fancy houses (generators purring), mobile homes, wood-and-tarpaper shacks, and the rusting nether portions of tractor trailers hauled off into the brush. Many of the residents are said to be squatters, with no idea who owns the land on which they live. They bathe in the canals. They trap rainwater for drinking. Some of them grow illicit crops and surround their plots with trip wires and set guns. An ornithologist I know was out looking for nests of the swallow-tailed kite (a graceful insect-eating tropical hawk, whose range extends north into Florida) in an isolated part of the Blocks, whose gridded layout is ideal for plotting out coordinates in the flat, featureless terrain. The ornithologist stepped out of the brush onto a street and saw people at work around a large U-Haul truck. He focused his binoculars. Men carrying tall, bushy, potted plants were trooping single file up a ramp into the cargo section of the truck. He noticed another man standing near the truck, exchanging stares with him through binoculars. Across the man's chest, on a sling, was a submachine gun.

Cuban-American paramilitary groups conduct training exercises in the Blocks, which sometimes resounds with the rattle of automatic weaponry. ("We hear 'em in there," a local law-

enforcement agent told me, "and we just back off.") People poach
game in the Blocks blatantly: deer, hogs, alligators, wild turkeys.
I know a botanist for the state of Florida who worked in Fakahatchee Strand State Preserve, which adjoins the Blocks to the
southeast. He once encountered a woman walking along W. J.
Janes Scenic Drive (named for a member of the Janes family, who
owned land in the vicinity), a road that links the Blocks with
Fakahatchee Strand. The botanist said that the woman was "very
hard to age, since she was so drastically weathered." She wore a
cut-off shirt and cut-off trousers, had a rifle slung over her shoulder. She accepted a ride back to her home in the Blocks (the
botanist asked her to unload her weapon before getting into his
truck). She said that recently she had chased off, at gunpoint,
"some drug people from Miami," because she did not want the
feds connecting her with the marijuana the Miamians were planting. The botanist drove the woman through the maze of roads
(left on this road, right on that one, left again) until suddenly she
asked him to stop. She disembarked, walked down the gravel
street, stepped into the brush, and vanished.

I met a family camped at a turnout next to a canal in the Blocks.
Children in swimsuits were fishing in the canal and scampering
about throwing rocks. A man of considerable girth sat in the sun
in a wheelchair, watching the children. He shook my hand and
gave me his name. He was from Alabama. He had fixed up an
old Ford panel truck as a camper. A generator and a small washing
machine and drier sat in a trailer behind the truck. His refrigerator
ran on batteries, which he kept charged by driving the truck or
by running the generator. His wife had long blond hair, her eyes
highlighted by a generous amount of purple eyeshadow. She had
once worn pop-bottle-thick eyeglasses, she told me, but the Lord
had healed her ("A miracle's real sudden," she explained, "but
healin' takes time"), and now she could see perfectly well without
her lenses. She gave me a bologna-and-tomato sandwich made
between flopped-open hot-dog buns and a cup of instant coffee.
Another man with a round face, stubs of teeth, and hair that stuck
out in all directions came over and offered me some vanilla creme–
filled cookies in a clear plastic tray. He was the heavyset man's
friend, and he was also from Alabama. He had been a truck driver
and had hauled up through Pennsylvania to Caribou, Maine,

where, he said, he had seen mountain goats peering down from the heights (I did not dispute his story, although there are no mountain goats east of the Rocky Mountains); and once, on a farm that he'd lived on in West Virginia, a cougar got into his chicken coop, and when he pegged a stone at the cat, it took a great bound, lit between his legs, and took off running.

The man in the wheelchair told me he had been a police officer. He had survived two severe automobile accidents, the second of which had paralyzed his legs. A white Cadillac had rammed into the side of his patrol car, leaving him beneath the wreckage, staring at the sole of one of his shoes an inch in front of his face. On the way to the hospital, he said, he died and woke up in a grave with red clay all around him, pinning his arms against his sides; worms began boring into his head through his nose, mouth, and eyes, and when he screamed, he saw a little white light that got bigger and bigger until it blinded him, and that was the Lord. Now that he had been granted an extension on his life, he regularly conducted direct conversations with Jesus and was engaged in spreading His word. He preached at revival meetings. He ran a house in Alabama where homeless people could eat and sleep, and he didn't turn anybody away, black or white. He had been in the Blocks, camped on this spot, for two months, and he liked it just fine. He said he sometimes heard panthers screaming at night. He had had no problems with anyone bothering him, although sometimes a ray, or some other kind of force, passed over his trailer, causing his battery-powered television to go blank for a while; he guessed it was the radar they used to watch for drug planes. He told me, "When you go, take this thought with you: 'Choose you this day whom you will serve. Whether the gods which your fathers served, that were on the other side of the flood, or the gods of the Amorites in whose lands you dwell. But as for me and my house, we will serve the Lord.' "

One of the keys to saving the panther lies in preserving places like the Blocks. Panthers occasionally pass through the Blocks, but none are believed to live there, perhaps because of the unrestricted and rowdy human activity. Conservationists would like to buy the Blocks and link it with other secure holdings, such as Corkscrew Swamp Sanctuary and Fakahatchee Strand State Preserve.

Big Cypress National Preserve, ten miles east of the Blocks, is the most important tract of protected habitat used by panthers today. In the southern part of the preserve are the females, numbers 23 and 55, and the two male refugees from the Everglades. In the northern sector of the preserve—perhaps cut off from the south by Alligator Alley, although its new underpasses may rectify that situation—live more than a dozen radio-collared cats, which range back and forth between the preserve and the adjacent private cattle ranches. To date, the National Park Service has not tried to make the preserve more attractive for panthers. This reluctance may stem from the fact that, even though the preserve was established twenty years ago, the government does not own all of Big Cypress: it is still buying one-, two-, and five-acre tracts that remain in private hands. Until the government buys out a landowner, it is probably illegal for the Park Service to, for instance, fill in a drainage canal, remove a road, or burn off vegetation to encourage a lush growth of grass.

In Naples I visited the Park Service's Southeast Region Land Acquisition Field Office, occupying two floors of a modern office building close to a neighborhood of expensive, manicured homes. There I met a cartographer who showed me how a modern land-acquisition system operates. In addition to buying up inholdings in Big Cypress, the cartographer told me, the Park Service is adding a tract of 146,000 acres to the preserve's northern boundary, and expanding Everglades National Park to the east. I was especially interested in the Blocks and wondered how an agency might go about purchasing land in such a place.

"South Golden Gate Estates is a state initiative, not a federal one," the cartographer informed me, while booting up a computer terminal. "That means we won't be the ones buying the land. The state of Florida—their Bureau of Land Acquisition—will decide when and how fast to do it. Actually, we'd love to go after the Blocks." Punching keys, he darted through electronic menus. "That's the kind of project you could really sink your teeth into." He whistled softly. "Ten years of acquisition work, easy." The computer hummed, made digestive noises. A map of South Florida constructed itself on the screen in blue, yellow, green, and red. "This is a vegetation map," the cartographer said. "It's a digital rendition of a satellite photograph, showing the kind of vegetation that panthers like to hang around in." Staring at the screen while guiding a mouse across a rubber pad, he boxed in a portion of the map, which suddenly leaped into enlargement, showing a grid of squares.

"Each square equals one square mile. South Golden Gate Estates has about seventy of those square-mile sections. See the number in each one? That's the total number of people who own land in that particular square mile." The numbers in the squares were 220, 260, 306. "We're talking about a whole bunch of people," the cartographer said. He changed maps, contour lines emerging like a huge green fingerprint. "These are elevations. At the top of the screen, eleven. That's eleven feet above sea level." The mouse scurried, stopped, clicked. "Here's a six right here. This is true swamp. In July this is under water." He pursed his lips and made an explosive blowing sound. "If we get a hurricane, I can't begin to describe how wet this place gets." The maps were linked to local tax rolls. The cartographer picked a tract at random and called up the owner's name: Helen O. Dwyer, of Rochester, New York.

"People from all over the world own land in Florida," the cartographer said. "Europeans, Asians, Central and South Americans—although mostly it's people like Helen here, from the Northeastern states. I'd bet that less than 10 percent of them have actually set foot on their land." According to the cartographer, real estate is still selling briskly in South Florida, including many acres (and acre-feet of water: land sold "by the quart," as the saying goes) already targeted for addition to the public domain. "In one of the more popular scams," he said, "people from Miami buy land in southwest Florida for $300 an acre, then turn around and resell it at $3,000 an acre, mostly to Hispanics, who feel that if they own land in the United States they can get citizenship more easily—and land in Dade County is way too expensive. We're hiring bilingual people to negotiate with the Hispanic owners."

Since I interviewed the cartographer, the state of Florida has bought over 15,000 acres in and around South Golden Gate Estates; it intends to buy another 27,000 acres. The tract will be called Picayune State Forest, named after Picayune Strand, a landform that perhaps still exists beneath the canals, ditches, and roads of the Blocks. I spoke with a state forester working there. One day while walking along a road, she looked off into the palmettos and saw a black object bobbing behind the vegetation. The object seemed to be moving along with her, parallel to her course. When the forester stopped and looked harder, she realized that the black object was the tip of a panther's tail. The cat was twenty-five feet away. It stood and stared at her for a moment, then faded into the brush.

In the last sixty years, Florida has lost a quarter of its forests and two-thirds of its wetlands. Since Europeans arrived, eleven species of wild animals have vanished, including the bison, red wolf, Carolina parakeet, passenger pigeon, ivory-billed woodpecker, and dusky seaside sparrow. Today, 117 species are thought to be at risk of extinction (classified as "threatened" or "endangered" by the Florida Game Commission), from the obscure, diminutive sand skink (a legless lizard that slithers through sandy soil) to the charismatic panther. Conservationists consider the panther a "landscape animal," because it roams widely across the landscape in its search for mates and food. They call it an "umbrella species," because saving the amount of natural land required by panthers will automatically save scores of smaller creatures, such as the skink, whose realms are less sweeping.

Florida, with the breakneck pace of its development, has become a proving ground for conservation schemes. One new approach is "mitigation banking": Suppose a corporation wishes to drain several hundred acres of wetlands to put up a theme park. (Since this is Florida, we might as well imagine that it is a theme park honoring the microwave oven or professional wrestling or the nation's preeminent bass fishermen.) (Fact: Wayne Huizenga, the owner of a business empire that includes Blockbuster Video and the nation's largest garbage-hauling company, proposed building his Blockbuster Park on 2,500 acres of canals, quarries, and wetlands on the eastern fringe of the Everglades. At one point, Huizenga was contemplating a billion-dollar complex to include a domed stadium for his baseball team, the Florida Marlins; a "virtual reality amusement center"; movie and television recording studios; and an indoor arena for his professional ice hockey team, the Florida Panthers. In 1994 the entertainment conglomerate Viacom acquired Blockbuster, and plans for the park are now on hold.) But before the bulldozers can roll, the corporation must first contribute, say, $10 million to a fund; the $10 million are combined with other millions paid by other corporations with similar plans, and from this lump sum come the millions needed to buy a big cattle ranch (up for sale because its dissipated heirs would rather snort cocaine in Bal Harbor than herd cattle somewhere west of Lake Okeechobee), a lonely stretch of pine, palmetto, and cypress that is home to panthers. Mitigation banking can save large tracts of land—one thousand, five thousand, ten thousand acres. There, natural processes can continue, creatures can exchange genes with individuals who are not their siblings, and offspring can disperse in the species' habitual manner rather than perishing while trying to make it from one tiny green island, across an inhospitable urbanized landscape, to the next tiny green island.

In Florida, the Nature Conservancy, a privately funded national organization, is actively buying land and giving it to the state and federal governments. A state program, Preservation 2000, enacted by the Florida legislature in 1990, provides for spending some $300 million per year during the last decade of the century to preserve wildlife habitat. As of 1991, 8 million acres of Florida had been set aside in public and private preserves; the land targeted for Preservation 2000 would add to this figure over 3 million acres. Another 6.3 million acres are coveted by conservationists, and if these could somehow be acquired, they would bring the total protected land area in Florida to 17.5 million acres: 47 percent of the state.

A man in Oregon has the clearest and most radical view of how to reshape Florida to accommodate the panther. Reed Noss is an ecologist and conservation biologist living in Corvallis. Under the pen name "Diamondback," Noss has written numerous articles for *Wild Earth*, a publication of the environmental group Earth First!, whose members have been arrested for lying down in front of bulldozers, driving spikes into trees to thwart loggers, and, through the use of explosives, attempting to free rivers from the constraints of large dams. Noss, who received a Ph.D. in wildlife science from the University of Florida, has also achieved stature within the scientific community as editor of the journal *Conservation Biology* and as an architect of the Wildlands Project, a plan that the journal *Science* characterized as "the most ambitious proposal for land management since the Louisiana Purchase of 1803."

The Wildlands Project would transform America from a place where nature exists as a string of redoubts in a landscape dominated by humanity into something approaching the opposite. Such scientific notables as Edward O. Wilson of Harvard and Paul Ehrlich of Stanford have endorsed the concept. The Wildlands Project is seen by many conservation biologists as the last, best chance to preserve the biotic diversity of North America. In 1993, the Pew Charitable Trusts, a respected philanthropic organization, chose Noss as a Pew Scholar in Conservation and Environment, and granted him $150,000 to begin working out the details of what has heretofore been a largely theoretical exercise: where to allow human settlement to remain, and how to integrate it with lands dedicated to wildlife.

Noss presented a blueprint for Florida in an article published in 1991 in *Wild Earth*. What he has in mind for the Sunshine State exemplifies how the Wildlands Project might work nationwide. Noss's map shows a peninsula liberally blotched and banded with natural lands. At the heart of his proposal are ten core wilderness areas. A core wilderness would be a truly wild place. People would be barred from it, except for professionals working to restore the landscape or to help out endangered species. To protect against poaching and the effects of human activities, a buffer zone several miles wide would ring each core. (The buffer zone would simultaneously shield humans and their property from fire, predation, or pests originating within the core wilderness.) In the innermost ring of the buffer zone, people could hike, canoe, watch birds, or engage in other activities that would not interfere with nature. Progressively more human influence and activity would be allowed toward the outer part of the buffer: primitive hunting (with weapons such as bows and arrows) and long-rotation forestry; then firearms hunting and more intensive forestry and grazing use; and, at the perimeter, low-density housing, including scattered farms and small towns. Undeveloped corridors linking the wild reserves would, for the most part, follow rivers, streams, and swamps. These green pathways, writes Noss, would "facilitate the flow of nutrients, individuals, genes, habitat patches."

In Florida, the wilderness cores would center on public land, such as the complex formed by Everglades National Park, Big Cypress National Preserve, Florida Panther National Wildlife Refuge, Fakahatchee Strand State Preserve, and the new Picayune State Forest; the Ocala National Forest in central Florida; the Apalachicola National Forest farther north and west; Blackwater River State Forest and the huge Eglin Air Force Base in the Panhandle; and southern Georgia's Okefenokee National Wildlife Refuge, linked through Pinhook Swamp (recently bought by the Nature Conservancy) to Osceola National Forest in northern Florida. Buffer zones would include public and private holdings; the private land would be bought by government agencies or secured through conservation easements and management agreements. Where corridors cut across roads, the roads would be relocated, fitted with underpasses, or eliminated.

If I read Noss's map correctly, he would like to see something more than 47 percent of Florida return to its natural state. The concept of cores, buffer zones, and corridors is intuitive, commonsense, and increasingly accepted by conservationists as a means of keeping ecosystems intact and evolution functioning. The consensus vanishes, however, when people start drawing lines on the map.

For the panther—top predator, landscape animal, umbrella species—the scale would have to be grand. In the early 1990s the U.S. Fish and Wildlife Service set as an objective five hundred panthers by the year 2000, distributed in three populations in Florida, with at least two of those populations in the wild. (At the current rate of bureaucratic achievement, this goal appears impossible to reach.) Noss, in a report commissioned by the Fund for Animals, chided the Fish and Wildlife Service for setting a goal that, if apparently unreachable, nevertheless remained too modest. He wrote (with more than a little of "Diamondback" shining through): "It is doubtful that any single reintroduction area will ever provide for thousands of panthers, at least not until after the collapse of industrial civilization." To keep the subspecies genetically healthy, to let it recover from its endangerment and become self-sufficient in the wild, the Fish and Wildlife Service, declared

Noss, must reestablish ten "subregional metapopulations," each containing one hundred to two hundred adult panthers. The metapopulations would be scattered throughout the South. Each would require a huge wilderness core (or a system of cores), plus buffers and corridors. The panther, in essence, would become the tool with which to wrest the landscape from human influence and return it to nature.

Writes Noss: "A well-distributed, viable population of panthers throughout the southeastern states would be a sign that the land is reasonably healthy and that the human population has the tolerance and humility to share resources with another large and demanding creature."

The Fish and Wildlife Service, as part of their settlement agreement with the Fund for Animals, looked around for places to put panthers. They identified twenty-four candidate sites, eleven of which were judged to be better potential homes—larger in area, with fewer roads, fewer people, and less potential for human population growth—than South Florida. Among these wild places were Okefenokee Swamp in Florida and Georgia; the Smoky Mountains in Tennessee and North Carolina; southwestern Mississippi and adjacent Louisiana; the Ozark and Ouachita Mountains in Arkansas; along the lower Alabama River; and along the lower Pearl River in Louisiana and Mississippi.

North Americans are not alone in their wishes to preserve and reshape the landscape for animals. Even now, conservationists are promoting a green corridor to run the length of rapidly developing Central America: from Mexico south to Belize and Guatemala, Honduras, Nicaragua, Costa Rica, Panama, all the way across the isthmus (an overpass spanning the canal?) to Colombia. Such a passage would link biosphere reserves, national parks, coastal bays, islands, and lowland rainforests. It would protect the homes of native people living in traditional ways. It would foster a continued biotic exchange between North and South America. It is not a modest proposal, and for all the talk about it, it is still a dream. Just as the Wildlands Project for North America is a dream. Just as ten, three, and even one viable population of Florida panthers is a dream. In Central America, they call their vision Paseo Pantera, Path of the Panther.

15

A LINE IN THE SAND

The only way I could get an interview with Jeff McDaniel was on horseback. McDaniel had cows to move on the day I wanted to visit. We would meet on the highway, two-lane Florida Route 833, soon after dawn. Waiting for him, leaning against my car, I watched wood storks flying overhead, singly and in small groups, heading out from their roosts—perhaps on the McDaniel ranch—to forage. Wood storks, more properly called wood ibis, are four feet tall. They wade in ponds and sloughs and eat fish, reptiles, and amphibians. In *Birds of America*, published in 1917, the ornithologist T. Gilbert Pearson wrote of seeing "at least five thousand of these birds in a drove feeding on a grassy prairie of central Florida. When disturbed by the report of a gun they arose, a vast white and black mass, and the roar of their wings coming across the lake resembled nothing so much as the rumbling of distant thunder." Today, if you see a dozen wood storks feeding or flying together, you feel lucky.

McDaniel drove down the lane from his house, stopped, and shook my hand through the open window. I followed his pickup, which was towing a brand-new gooseneck horse trailer, down the highway, then onto a bumpy road that led into a pasture. McDaniel, a solid, freckle-faced, sandy-haired man in his thirties, had a manner at once leisurely and efficient. He greeted the four cowhands waiting in the pasture. He joshed with them while he unloaded horses, tack, and dogs from the trailer. He introduced me to the men, who were named Snuffy, Jabbo, Jesse, and Tom. They grinned liberally, perhaps at the thought of this greenhorn, this Northerner, perched on a horse. I had worn precisely the wrong clothing: light trousers, boots with lug soles, a flat-brimmed hat that would have been at home in a canoe or a duck blind, and no gloves. They had on blue jeans, plaid Western-style shirts with pointed collars and shiny snaps, cowboy hats, cowboy boots, leather gloves, and sunglasses. Jabbo, a stocky, musta-chioed, exuberantly profane man, wore chaps that ended in a fringe at his knees—"chinks," he called them, useful because they helped him grip his fucking horse, warded off the fucking briars, and did not get wet when he had to dismount in the fucking swamp that fingers into the fields and woods of the McDaniel ranch.

The ranch, McDaniel explained, had been in his family since 1936, when his grandfather bought it. It lies twenty miles north of Alligator Alley in Hendry County, east of Immokalee, south of Clewiston, and north of the Big Cypress Seminole Indian Res-ervation. Arpeika, also called Sam Jones, a Seminole shaman who led a bitter fight against the U.S. Army in the 1830s when the nation tried to evict the tribe from Florida, is buried on the ranch. "Sometimes the Indians come out and have a ceremony," McDaniel said. "They have this skull, supposed to be from Sam Jones, but for all I know, it could be from some ole bluegum." Deer and turkeys abound on the ranch. Panthers, including several collared ones, prowl through its pine woods and cypress sloughs, an excellent habitat with sufficient prey to produce healthy, fertile cats.

The McDaniels, like most ranchers, are less concerned with raising panthers than with raising livestock and crops. In recent years the family has been diversifying, branching out into the triumvirate that the local agricultural establishment terms "the three C's": cattle, cane, and citrus. Two sections of McDaniel land, or around twelve hundred acres, have been planted in citrus. Three sections—close to two thousand acres—are in cane. Other sections are leased to farmers, who grow vegetables, and to quail hunters, who do not tamper with the land. The majority of the ranch, around sixteen thousand acres, remains devoted to cattle. The cattle are Jeff McDaniel's responsibility, while his father and his three older brothers handle the cane and citrus. "Of the three C's," McDaniel told me, "cattle are the safest. They're dependable. You never have to worry about freezes or floods."

We mounted up. McDaniel had given me his wife's horse, a sleek buckskin gelding—"Bombproof," he had pronounced it. The dogs that had gotten out of the trailer, a half dozen or so of them, milled about at the horses' feet. They were lean, scarred canines, close-coated, in various houndish colors (tan, lemon, white): crosses, McDaniel said, between the Florida cur dog—"a type of cow dog, real rank, real feisty"—and the Catahoula leopard dog, a working breed from Louisiana.

We set off at a trot, heading for a distant field. Grackles rasped from the trees. A pair of swallow-tailed kites circled high in a thermal. "We worked cows on horseback till I was eleven or twelve years old," McDaniel told me in his booming voice. "Then we switched to trucks." To keep Bombproof in proximity to McDaniel's horse, I had to keep kicking him in the ribs. "But you have no management with a truck," McDaniel continued. "A cow gets into some thick cover, you can't get her out of there. So a couple of years ago we moved back to horses, and I brought in the dogs, and it's been the best way to handle cattle that we've ever found.

"We're what's called a cow-calf operation. We run twenty-five hundred, twenty-seven hundred head. We keep a cow about ten years. In the fall we sell our calves to feedlots, most of them in Mississippi, Texas, and Oklahoma. We use a video auction through the Okeechobee Livestock Association. The feedlot owners look at the video and bid on the herds."

The horses trotted along through a series of open gates. The sky was dappled with small rounded clouds, sidelit by the rising sun. To the west, nascent cumuli rose up like pink mushrooms. A distant pop-ash head looked like an island at sea. Around us, patches of thorn trees and palmetto interrupted the planted grasses, which had been closely cropped by cattle. We were crossing what a wildlife biologist would term "improved pasture," a land-use type that does not encourage panthers, since it offers limited brush for hiding and stalking. Elsewhere on the ranch, explained McDaniel, where the soil is thinner and the underlying limestone closer to the earth's surface, pine trees predominate. Cows graze on the native grasses beneath the pines, and the timber is periodically harvested—a cycle that keeps the land fit for wildlife. McDaniel spoke with pride about stands of virgin cypress tucked away in remote parts of the ranch. He told of how he liked to get away from the business of ranching by going into the woods and hunting deer.

The cowhands spread out. We rode in a semicircle toward a bunch of fifty or sixty cattle: Braymers. The cows were as close-coated as the cow dogs. They were pretty rank-looking themselves, lean and flop-eared, some of them with sweeping, sharp-tipped horns. They stood and stared as we approached.

McDaniel loosed the dogs. With a chorus of excited yelps they sprinted straight at the cattle. The herd closed ranks. The dogs swerved, some going to one side of the group and some to the other side. Running as fast as they could go, mouths agape, tails low, still barking, they looped around the cattle, angling in, tightening the huddle. When a cow tried to get away, a dog would cut her off, snarling and snapping. If the cow charged at the dog, the dog would dance back out of reach of her horns, then dart in and slash at the cow's face, or lunge at her calf and send it bawling back toward the herd. Dogs gripped cows by the ear and by the nose. Dust rose. Cows bellowed. By now, all the dogs were running in the same direction, in orbit around the bunched cattle. The cowboys were riding into thickets, pushing out stragglers, hooting at them, cracking whips to drive them into the herd.

When McDaniel called in the dogs, they retired, grudgingly and with an occasional foray against a cow that was edging out from the bunch, to trot at the heels of his horse. With a cowboy out in front, and the others arranged around the herd's perimeter cracking their whips, the cows started walking.

After penning the cattle on a new range, the cowhands dismounted to rest and palaver. High on the list of subjects was "cooter," which I inferred to be the female genitalia. As in "That old boy? You smash his head, and a cooter'd fall out, that's all he's got on his brain." There was some inveighing against blacks, whom the cowhands referred to as "bluegums"—"That's a nigger so black his gums are blue. The ones from Haiti who work in the groves." McDaniel, sitting quietly on the frame of his horse trailer, did not take part in the banter; he had told me he was a Christian and had advanced the theory that I was one also. "You're a Baptist, aren't you?" he said, pronouncing it "Babtist." I supposed it was because I didn't swear or talk about cooter. "You got this kind of aura about you," he said. Jabbo and Snuffy allowed that they liked to manufacture their own aura by smoking a little reefer after work. Jabbo asked if I didn't think that Rush Limbaugh had things figured out about right. He confided that he had made considerable money dealing drugs back in the 1970s; he was arrested, did some prison time, and, when released, moved inland from the east coast of Florida. In Hendry County he learned how to cowboy. He hired out to different ranchers. He was a skilled rider: while moving the cattle, twice he had cantered up to me, spun his horse around, and walked it neatly backward while telling me one thing or another.

I asked about panthers. Jabbo had never glimpsed one, although he hoped to someday. Tom, an older man who had lived in the Big Cypress all his life, guessed that he had seen twenty. "I haven't heard of anybody losing a calf or a cow to a panther on any of the ranches around here," he said.

"Well, they're not 4-H stock," McDaniel offered. "I suppose a panther might kill a calf now and then, especially a poor calf, but what the heck." He commented on the supposed scarcity of panthers: "If you see one deer, the old hunters will tell you that there are seven you didn't see. I think it's the same with panthers. I think the numbers are higher than what they say." McDaniel mentioned that his wife, while sitting in a tree to ambush a deer, had watched a panther stroll past beneath her stand. He said that his mother had seen a panther in the yard at her house, inexplicably playing with her house cats. He also reported the existence of "black panthers," which he said were bigger than a bobcat but smaller than a tan panther. (Such an animal is not known to exist, although sightings persist in Florida of dark, medium-sized cats that some people think are jaguarundi. The jaguarundi, native to Central and South America, has a black or rusty-brown coat. It weighs up to eighteen pounds and is sometimes called the "otter cat" because it loves the water.) McDaniel had spotted a pair of panthers recently. The cats had jumped out of a pop-ash head and loped away, one following the other, down a dirt road. Neither panther paid attention to the men on horseback watching them, and neither appeared to be wearing a radio collar. McDaniel guessed that the cats were a mating pair. I considered that, had the same encounter happened only twenty years ago, the humans might have pulled rifles out of saddle scabbards and started blazing away.

We arrived at the touchy subject of preserving land for panthers. I had expected McDaniel to strongly oppose any restrictions on his family's ranch and its operations, but he was less adamant than I had thought. "By law, this is our land," he said. "But God puts us here to be good stewards. We don't own the wild animals. We should be giving something back to the land. I want my children to enjoy nature, the same as I did when I was growing up.

"I don't think the government has the right to take your ranch away, or prevent you from doing what you want to with it. But there ought to be real incentives to keep it natural. Once you convert a piece of land to citrus—once you recontour it, change the drainage, turn the sloughs into runoff ponds—you've changed it so much you won't ever get it back to a natural state." McDaniel suggested regulating development through taxes. "You could put a high tax on land that's converted to cane or citrus," he said. "You could reward people with lower taxes for leaving their land as it is." If a rancher owns land where panthers are living, McDaniel said, he ought to be able to look upon the cats as a resource rather than a burden. McDaniel would have welcomed receiving a conservation easement to keep the land undeveloped —but then he was the brother who liked raising cattle, not the brother who tended cane or citrus. "I'll tell you," he said, "they'd better do something pretty quick. Because if they wait ten years"—he shrugged—"Hendry County will be all changed. There won't be much natural land left."

Before leaving the McDaniel spread, I stopped at the ranch office, where Jeff's wife, Vonnie, is secretary for the family business. A slender, striking, dark-haired woman, she showed me a wall map detailing land ownership in Hendry County. Alico, a corporation composed of several families, controls 197 sections, or over 125,000 acres. U.S. Sugar owns 46 sections, or 30,000 acres. Hilliard Brothers owns 32 sections, or 20,000 acres. The entire Florida Panther National Wildlife Refuge, in neighboring Collier County, eight miles south of the McDaniel ranch, is 30,000 acres. The average home range for a female panther is 48,000 acres; for a male, 128,000 acres. It was unclear how long the mosaic of citrus, cane, and grazing land would continue to accommodate panthers.

The more I traveled in South Florida, the more familiar I became with the countryside. I would be driving along a back road past flatwoods and prairie, remembering and looking for a certain patch of pines (I had seen deer browsing there at dusk on a previous trip). Or a stretch of grassland where a caracara had hopped down to the ground from a fencepost (a bizarre bird, looking like a cross between an eagle and a vulture, with long springy legs, a red face, and a black crested head—the locals call them "Mexican buzzards"). Or a stand of cypress that had been solidly white one day with ibis: and suddenly, instead of cypress or prairie or pines, there would be a brand-new orange grove. Waist-high trees in ashy-gray soil. White plastic sheaths around their spindly trunks, black tubes to give them water. The straight jade rows converged at the horizon. (It is said that the Japanese are developing a taste for orange juice and that Japan will become a huge new market for citrus.) Invariably, around the border of the raw new grove was a sturdy barbed-wire fence hung with signs warning against trespass.

Theoretically, the U.S. Fish and Wildlife Service could stop all development on lands where panthers live. They could stop it tomorrow. They could, under the Endangered Species Act, prosecute people for destroying panther habitat. I have a copy of the Act in my files. It is a booklet forty-five pages long, whose cover is decorated with the Fish and Wildlife Service logo: a duck taking flight, a leaping trout, a winding river, a mountain, the sun. The Endangered Species Act has been called a bill of rights for non-humans. It has been called the pit bull of environmental laws: short, and with a hell of a set of teeth. The teeth include prison terms and fines of up to $25,000 per infraction, per day. The Endangered Species Act considers "species" to mean an actual species, a subspecies, or a distinct population segment of a species. The Act says that no one is allowed to "take" any endangered animal, and goes on to define "take" as "to harass, harm, pursue, hunt, shoot, wound, kill, trap, capture, or collect." In the case of the panther's habitat, the operative word is "harm." If you develop your ranch—if you change it from rangeland to citrus—you make the land unfit for the panthers that live there. You cause them harm (in plain words, you kill them) by destroying their home.

Farther north, in the sandy uplands of central Florida, there is an ecosystem called the Florida scrub. The scrub is swiftly unraveling in the face of citrus, shopping centers, roads, and suburban sprawl, the whole dreary litany of development in Florida. In the Florida scrub lives a bird called the Florida scrub jay, a disjunct population of a species, otherwise unendangered, that lives in the desert Southwest. The Florida scrub jay is listed as "threatened" under the Endangered Species Act, which means that the authorities believe it to be slightly less imperiled than an "endangered" species such as the Florida panther. Like the panther, the scrub jay has a certain charisma: lively and cute, it arouses protective emotions in humans. In 1991, the Fish and Wildlife Service sent certified letters to 550 people owning one or more acres of scrubland in a two-county area in central Florida. Noting that the population of the Florida scrub jay had fallen from more than twenty thousand to about ten thousand in the past one hundred years, the letter warned that the service would prosecute anyone destroying scrub jay habitat. The letter drew the "line in the sand" that conservationists so often call for. It stopped a lot of bulldozers in mid-rumble. A federal refuge is planned, not only for the jay, but also for a suite of endangered scrub plants. However, plants and scrub jays are nothing like panthers. The scale is wholly different.

The Endangered Species Act was signed in 1973 by President Richard M. Nixon. No doubt he figured he was saving beloved, dramatic creatures like eagles and bears and whales. It is certain that he did not foresee the economic disruption the Act would cause. It delayed the completion of a $100 million dam in Tennessee, to benefit the snail darter, a two-inch fish. It changed the way boats harvest shrimp in the Gulf of Mexico, to protect sea turtles. It stopped the construction of golf courses and resorts in Oregon, to safeguard the habitat of the Oregon silverspot butterfly. It slowed logging in the Northwest, in consideration of the spotted owl. It stirred scientists to begin the restoration of gray wolves to Yellowstone National Park. The Endangered Species Act prompted another Republican President, George Bush, to characterize it as "a sword aimed at the jobs, families, and communities of entire regions." President Bush had appointed a Secretary of the Interior—whose job includes enforcing the Endangered Species Act—who labeled the Act a gross impediment to economic progress that needed to be changed or repealed. (The Secretary, Manuel Lujan, also said he did not believe in evolution.)

Despite its reputation as a "pit bull," the Endangered Species Act must also be considered something of a token gesture. It is supposed to recognize endangered species worldwide—creatures such as the giant panda, snow leopard, gorilla, Asiatic lion, Arabian oryx, and blue whale, as well as hundreds of less-well-known bats and cats and deer and lemurs and sloths and seals and wallabies, coots and doves and flycatchers and bullfinches and pheasants, caimans and geckos and monitor lizards and salamanders, catfish and chubs and dace and shiners, clams and snails, insects and arachnids, pitcher plants, snapdragons, mahoganies, mints— around fifteen hundred species at the latest count, with thousands more being considered for listing. Of that threatened and endangered fifteen hundred, a thousand are native to the United States and five hundred are foreign. (The foreign ones initially were added to control the traffic in items such as elephant ivory, rhinoceros horn, and leopard pelts.) According to science, these creatures and plants represent a small fraction of Earth's endangered life forms. Edward O. Wilson of Harvard, a renowned entomologist, suggests that the world may contain on the order of one hundred million different species—fungi, bacteria, and insects vastly outnumbering the more obvious birds, mammals, reptiles, amphibians, fish, crustaceans, and plants—of which only 1.4 million have been named. Worldwide, Wilson estimates that fifty thousand species wink out each year, almost all of them invisibly. Species that someday might become useful to humans (such as the endangered Lake Placid scrub mint, a Florida scrub plant from which a powerful insect repellent has been isolated); and species that deserve to exist simply for their own sake. Extinction is a natural process. Scientists estimate that all but 1 percent of the species that have ever lived are now extinct. But clearly, human-caused extinctions are on the rise.

It seems that as soon as scientists apply modern surveillance or censusing techniques to any marginal or seldom-seen species, they find it is imperiled—along with a troop of even more obscure organisms with which the subject interacts. People grow numb to the news of yet another endangered species. Scientists project that a quarter of the world's current species will have been extinguished by the year 2050. Although few species are unsavable today, it would seem impossible—with the human population surging, taking over the landscape—to rescue them all. Charles C. Mann and Mark L. Plummer, in an article about endangerment in *The Atlantic Monthly*, wrote: "In this deficit-ridden age Fish and Wildlife Service budgets will not climb to the altitude necessary to save the few hundred species on the [endangered species] list, let alone the thousands upon thousands of unlisted species that biologists regard as endangered. Like cost-conscious Noahs, Americans will pick which creatures to bring with them and which to leave behind."

Fortunately for the panther, Americans want to bring it with them. Increasingly, the thrust in saving wildlife is to focus on protecting ecosystems that support maximum biological diversity—and the panther, a large and roaming animal, encompasses ecosystems.

As this is being written in 1995, Congress is considering several proposals to weaken the Endangered Species Act. The Supreme Court is reviewing a decision by a lower court that would allow landowners to change or degrade the habitat of an endangered species in a way that might kill or injure the endangered animals, as long as the actual killing or injuring was not done intentionally. In part, this assault on the Endangered Species Act is an attempt by property owners and timber interests to disable any restrictions on what they can and cannot do to the land. And, in part, the assault probably grows out of a backlash against what many citizens perceive to be an overly restrictive—and sometimes abused—set of statutes.

Want to stop a landfill, a toxic-waste incinerator, a housing development, a sewage disposal project? Find a panther using the site. Or, if you can't find a real Florida panther, borrow a pet puma and lead it around on a leash, leaving tracks and scat— something that was reportedly done in Sarasota County on the Gulf Coast.

At the crux of the panther's status as an endangered animal is the way in which we define it. The genetic studies by Melody

Roelke and Stephen O'Brien showed that the panther has received outside genetic material and that the heretical genes have spread within the population. Almost certainly, those genes came from a subspecies of puma in Central or South America—a race, to this day unknown, with which the panther, for reasons of topography, could not have naturally interbred. The Florida panther has been hybridized. Since the Endangered Species Act was made law, three opinions from the Solicitor's Office of the Department of the Interior have ruled with the force of precedent that hybrids between endangered species, subspecies, or populations are not covered by the Act. These opinions concluded that protecting hybrids would not serve to help an endangered species recover and would probably jeopardize the species' continued existence. In the case of the panther, the infusion of outside genetic material seems to have had precisely the opposite effect. The panthers with Latin American genes are healthier than the panthers lacking them.

Without the Latin influence, *Felis concolor coryi* is easily classifiable as a subspecies. Even with it, the cats ought still to be considered a distinct population segment and therefore eligible for protection. But a judge might not see it that way. A judge might see only the hybridization. And so the Fish and Wildlife Service has been careful about telling landowners what they can and cannot do with panther habitat.

In 1993, faced with overwhelming evidence of inbreeding and an ongoing slide in the panthers' health—the cryptorchidism, the lousy sperm, the heart defects, the diseases—the Fish and Wildlife Service and the Florida Game Commission, on the advice of Ulysses Seal and his coterie of small-population biologists, proposed bringing in outside genetic material from a subspecies with which the panther once did interbreed naturally: *Felis concolor stanleyana*, the Texas puma. If humans had not eliminated the pumas in Mississippi and Louisiana, the Florida subspecies would have flowed seamlessly into the Texas one. This latest step, called "genetic restoration," will not affect the way the animal appears on the endangered species list: It will still be the Florida panther rather than *Felis concolor* in Florida or in the Southeastern United States. By all accounts—biological, logistical, legal—the step is a radical one. It took a year, and pressure from everyone from the governor of Florida to the Fund for Animals, for the director of the Fish and Wildlife Service, Mollie Beattie, to agree to the concept; she assented in July 1994.

In the spring of 1995, Roy McBride was in Texas, west of the Pecos, hunting down cats and capturing them. Passengers on certain commercial airline flights between Houston and Fort Myers, Florida, would have been surprised to learn that, in the cargo hold of the jetliners they were riding on, pumas crouched in plywood crates.

After a month's quarantine, the Florida Game Commission set the cats free in Fakahatchee Strand and Big Cypress Swamp. None of the cats were males, who might have fought with their Florida counterparts or, with their higher fertility, outbred them. Females, and not too many of them—a total of eight were scheduled in 1995—for fear of causing "outbreeding depression," an expunging of specific genes that may carry adaptations equipping the Florida panther to live in its damp, pathogen-ridden home. Over time, perhaps a dozen Texas pumas will be added to the Florida subspecies, as handmaidens to the dwindling race.

16

PANTHER REDUX

After Chris Belden accidentally killed panther number 3, after he carried her out of Fakahatchee Strand on his back, after he left South Florida burdened with the knowledge that panther habitat was shrinking there, after he read *The Power of Positive Thinking* and accepted Jesus Christ as his Lord and Saviour, after he got his marriage repaired and his life back in order, he went searching for places where panthers could live.

One goal in restoring the Florida panther is to put the animal back into various parts of its historic range. However, that is something that no one has ever tried to do—to start up a population of large feline predators where none currently exists. At first glance it might not seem all that difficult a task. Cats are adaptable beasts; put them where prey is plentiful and highways are few, and they should thrive.

It is not that simple. Nor did Belden expect it to be, when, in 1988, he began the next phase of his work with the Florida panther.

In North Florida, west of Jacksonville along the Georgia line, longleaf pine and slash pine cover the flat, coastal-plain landscape with a monotonous deep-green cloak. Gallberry, saw palmetto, and wax myrtle thrust up beneath the conifers. The swamps are choked with cypress, tupelo, laurel oak, fetterbush, and catbrier. John James Audubon wrote of the region in the winter of 1832: "All that is not mud, mud, mud, is sand, sand, sand." To the north, in Georgia, lies the great fastness of Okefenokee Swamp, protected as a national wildlife refuge. The Suwannee River winds south out of the swamp, moseying across Florida to the Gulf of

Mexico, past farms and towns and the extensive Osceola National Forest, the river more or less dividing Florida's panhandle from the peninsula proper. Unlike much of the Sunshine State, this part of Florida is not caught up in a growth boom. The largest community in the area is Lake City, population 9,300. Interstates 10 and 75 cross each other just west of Lake City. To the northeast of this intersection, paved roads are few, although sand roads vein the thousands of wooded acres. There, on lands owned by Gilman Paper Company (the same concern that owns White Oak Plantation), Chris Belden built wood-and-wire cages and in them placed five wild pumas that Roy McBride had caught in Texas.

Before importing the animals, Belden ran a thorough public-relations campaign. Since the cats would know no boundaries, the Florida Game Commission alerted the Georgia Department of Natural Resources. Belden contacted local officials, prominent landowners, cattle ranchers, and representatives of conservation groups and hunting clubs, inviting them to a press conference announcing the release. He had designed the experiment to see whether pumas, set loose in an unfamiliar terrain, would set up home ranges and adhere to them, or wander off in all directions. The unendangered Texas pumas would be surrogates for endangered Florida panthers: if the Texas cats could make it, someday Florida panthers might take their place. Belden reassured citizens that the pumas would not attack them. He explained to hunters that the pumas would not deprive them of game to shoot. He told ranchers it was unlikely that the cats would kill their stock. (The experiment so enthused one wood-products company that it volunteered to reimburse any rancher for losses up to ten thousand dollars.) The pumas had been surgically sterilized and fitted with radio collars; field biologists would fly daily to keep tabs on them, and if anything went awry, McBride and his hounds could effect a capture. Of forty-six key citizens contacted by Belden, thirty-nine said they supported the reintroduction project, six did not give a hoot about it, and only one, representing a hunters' organization, opposed it.

Belden put the pumas in "soft-release pens"—small enclosures with attached shelters like doghouses. He fed them deer that game wardens had confiscated from poachers. Working in the parking lot of a Game Commission building in Lake City, Belden would cut the frozen carcasses apart with a chainsaw, then haul the meat to the remote site where the pumas waited in their cages. One evening in June, three weeks after the cats had arrived from Texas, Belden went from cage to cage placing chunks of venison on the ground outside the wire. Then he retraced his steps, opening the door to each pen. He went back into the motor home where he was staying and watched through the window. One puma, a female, came to the door of her enclosure. She looked at the meat, went back inside, and lay down. Then she got up again, left the pen, ate the venison, and ambled away down a fire lane—"like she had all the time in the world," Belden recalls today.

Over the next few hours, the four other pumas ventured forth. One wonders what went through the cats' minds, going from the dry, rocky, nearly treeless mountains of West Texas to a place where moss drapes the trees, greenbrier throws its emerald tangles around the perimeters of swamps, mosquitoes cloud the air, and vistas are measured in yards rather than in miles.

The first thing the cats did was to head west. Home was fifteen hundred miles away, but they seemed to feel its tug. Then something—perhaps the abundance of game, or the breadth of the Suwannee River, or the drone of traffic on a highway—made them pause. The cats shuffled around. Gradually they settled into areas that suited them, more or less. They made brief jaunts out of those locales, possibly looking for something better, but generally they returned within a week. "After two or more excursions," Belden wrote in a report, "the lions [he used the name by which pumas are known in Texas] settled into what we classified as home ranges."

A month into the experiment, Belden flew one morning and was greeted by a mortality signal from the radio collar of one of the pumas. He traced it to the Suwannee River. The puma was floating in the river, dead. Although a necropsy revealed nothing suspicious, Belden suspected that the cat had met with foul play, cats being very unlikely to jump into rivers and drown themselves. (He never figured out who or what had killed the animal.) The experiment continued. The four remaining pumas behaved the way wild pumas are supposed to act. They avoided one another, although their home ranges partially overlapped. They traveled mainly at night. They hunted prey-rich thickets on the verges of swamps, just as panthers do in South Florida. When a cat stayed in one place for two or more days, Belden would walk in on it. Sometimes he would find a kill; sometimes he would smell rotting flesh but be unable to locate the carcass in the profoundly tangled undergrowth. Most of the kills were stashed in low tunnels, game trails that wound through the catbrier and fetterbush. The pumas killed hogs and deer; even the youngest of them, a year-old female, regularly hauled down deer. The cats generally avoided highways, although one was reportedly grazed by a car as he dashed across the intersection of Interstates 10 and 75.

Then the first crispness of autumn came to the air. The hunting season began. People took to the woods in pursuit of turkeys and hogs. They loosed their hounds after deer. They gunned their four-wheel-drive pickup trucks down the little-used woods roads. They tramped over land whose hunting rights they had leased from timber companies. They sat in tree stands on the edges of clearings, rifles in hand, waiting for deer to come and eat corn scattered at regular intervals by mechanized feeders. (Several of the cats, knowing a good thing when they saw one, had also been hanging around the feeders.)

The pumas scattered.

The next to die was a male, designated T-18 (T for Texas). One day in October Belden fished his collar out of a pond twenty miles from where he had been radio-located two days earlier. The collar had been cut with a knife. Tire tracks and boot prints on the banks of the pond matched tracks and prints at a deer-feeding station near where the cat had last been located.

On December 19 the mortality signal cut in for T-14, the year-old female. She had just returned to her home range after having made a big loop away from it. The necropsy showed that she had died from an infected wound to her left rear leg, caused by a bullet.

That left only two pumas in the woods. In November male T-16 departed his home range along the Suwannee River, where he had spent the last five months, and fled east to the outskirts of Jacksonville. There he killed some goats on a farm. Then he swam across the St. Johns River and reposed in the area of Waycross, Georgia, east of Okefenokee Swamp. A female, T-15, abandoned her home during the turkey season, shifted east some twenty miles, scaled an eight-foot fence surrounding a twelve-hundred-acre game farm, and feasted on black buck antelope from India. Belden caught her and took her back to her home area. Five days later, she was back on the farm, eating black buck. Belden caught her again and removed her from the study area.

In March—to replace the pumas that had been killed and the one that had succumbed to black-buck temptation—Belden brought in two new Texas cats, T-19 and T-21, and recaptured the male T-16, who was still hanging around in Georgia, because his range there did not border those of any other pumas and Belden did not expect him to stay put. The Florida Game Commission used the pumas' arrival at the release site as a media event. From a newspaper article: "The jittery cougars, angry at being crated before dawn Tuesday and trucked some 60 miles from the [Game Commission's] research labs near Gainesville, did not like their new digs. A 140-pound, tawny-colored male wanted nothing to do with TV lights, curious reporters and wildlife officers. He turned up his nose at venison and sulked behind a sleeping box in the cage."

After the reporters had gone to file their stories, Belden opened the pens. Instead of shifting toward the west, as his predecessors had done, T-21 made a beeline to the southeast, traveling sixty miles and ending up in a tree in a subdivision on the fringe of Jacksonville. "He was sleeping," reported the housewife whose yard he had chosen. "The only time he woke up was when a policeman came out with a shotgun and circled him." Belden raced to the scene and tranquillized the cat. Turned loose on the west side of the Suwannee, T-21 kept roving until Belden had to capture him.

With only two cats left in North Florida, Belden called it quits. He planned to repeat the experiment, using more surrogates: a minimum of ten. Even if several were killed, Belden hoped that the greater number of remaining animals might help keep a social structure intact. He hoped to put them out the day after hunting season ended, to give them as much time as possible to settle in. He reckoned that the area in which the five Texas cats had established their home ranges—about 1,250 square miles, within a much larger study area of 7,700 square miles—could support up to sixty cats, approximately the same number of panthers thought to be hanging on in South Florida. Sixty pumas, Belden estimated, would eat a maximum of 15 percent of the deer in the area, leaving plenty for human hunters.

"The cats can adapt," Belden told me, "though I'm not sure the people can. Cats are going to kill goats. They're going to walk downtown. They're going to get into trouble. But I think if we want to save the panther in the wild, it will have to be done by reintroducing it to new areas. The majority of the people in Florida want us to save the panther—but how many would want it in their own back yard? When you turn a large predator loose, there's always the chance that somebody's child will be killed. I think about that a lot."

It was springtime when Walt McCown took me into the woods in North Florida. McCown, a large, soft-spoken man, is nick-named The Bear. Sometimes he wears high L. L. Bean boots—the kind with the rubber bottoms and leather uppers—which rise to near his knees and make his legs, in combination with his barrel-shaped trunk, look spindly; and sometimes he wears rubber hip-boots and a sheathed machete at his belt. He has wavy brown hair and a small mustache. He hails from Columbus, Georgia, and has been a biologist for the Florida Game Commission for ten years. He likes to canoe down thundering whitewater streams in moun-tainous parts of the South, a form of recreation that he is denied in gradient-free Florida. One activity that he does not enjoy is flying around (and around, and around) in small airplanes, radio-locating panthers. He has flown hundreds of times, has never actually seen a cat from the air (although he usually finds the signals from their collars), and gets queasy every time he goes up, from being jolted and jerked around inside a noisy, smelly cockpit. He is allergic to flying, he has concluded. Also to deer hair and panther hair.

We drove in his pickup truck along a woods road. It was a cold, dismal morning in early March, so soupy aloft that Chris Belden had elected not to fly to check on the cats. We bumped along, occasionally skidding slightly in the mud. We passed through interminable stands of pines, tall and straight, with black burn marks on their reddish-brown trunks; the trees stood in close, regular ranks amid an understory of palmetto and rust-colored

grass, which McCown identified as broom sedge. Mile after mile
of pines, riven by the gray road with water standing in the ruts.
The only brightness in the woods came from a pileated woodpecker—a sudden semaphoring of black-and-white wings, a great
red-crested head—which looped across the road in front of us and
landed, as if magnetized, on a trunk. We came to a muddy clearing
where half a dozen machines—yellow and red beneath oil grime,
exhausting a bluish gas, with balloon tires and immense cutting
blades—labored at cropping and loading the pines. We were on
land owned by ITT-Rayonier Forest Products, McCown said. We
were still in Florida but were only a few miles south of Georgia.

Beyond the clearing, we came to a turnoff. McCown stopped
the truck and handed me a key. I got out and opened a padlock,
swung a gate; McCown drove through, and I shut the gate again
and padlocked it in place. (This opening and closing of gates is
about the only useful thing a writer can do when tagging along
with a biologist.) McCown explained that they had ten cats on
the ground, all of them from Texas. Six females, four males. Three
of the cats were eighteen-month-old youngsters whose mother,
pregnant when she was captured in Texas, had given birth to them
at White Oak Plantation; there, they had occupied a wooded fifteen-acre enclosure, into which live deer were periodically placed.
In Florida, they seemed to be getting along. By now the pumas
had been out for twenty-four days. A couple of them had crossed
the Suwannee River and come back. But no brushes with cars or
bullets, no slaying of goats, cattle, or black bucks, no napping in
suburban shade trees.

We passed through another locked gate. The release pens were
in the Osceola National Forest, near Pinhook Swamp, recently
bought by the Nature Conservancy and deeded over to the U.S.
Forest Service. The pens were ten by twenty feet each, stout cy-
clone fencing attached to wooden crates. Parts of deer (femurs,
backbones, a picked-over rib cage flecked with maroon flesh) lay
scattered about. "Most of the cats stayed near the pens for three
or four days after we released them," McCown said. "We fed
them for about a week." He assembled the antenna and held it
up. The receiver emitted a faint *chirp chirp chirp*, strongest when
the antenna pointed to the northwest. McCown changed frequencies. He swiveled the antenna: THUMP THUMP THUMP. Mc-

Cown's eyebrows went up and down, twice. "Whoa," he whispered, shooting me a glance. "D'you feel high balls on you?"

He led the way past the pens, on a sandy lane, one quiet step at a time. The sky was gray and lowering. Rain sprinkled. I could hear our feet compacting the sand. Mosquitoes tried for our faces and necks. The bundled pine needles hung silent and water-soaked.

"One of the young cats," McCown whispered. "Been hanging around in the area ever since we released 'em." We had not gone a hundred yards when McCown stopped and tapped with his toe. There, on the edge of the lane, lay a long olive-green curve of feces, loaded with short dark hair. "Good deal!" McCown whispered. "Somebody's killed him a hog." He lifted the antenna. The signal was faint when he pointed it away from the pens. But when he turned it back toward them, the sound came rasping out. I understood that we had walked past the puma, that he was between us and the pens. With a sideways nod McCown indicated that we should go into the brush. "Let's see if we can move him," he said. "Keep your eyes peeled."

We went side by side down two parallel rows between the planted pines. I walked on the tips of my toes. Dense palmetto, gallberry, catclaw vines. Look for a flattened spot—a bed. Keep the eyes open, for scat. Let the vision rove, slightly unfocused, to detect any movement, a tawny form slipping away through the brush. High balls? Yes.

We eased our way through the thicket until we came to another sand road. Again McCown blessed the terrain with his antenna. The cat had moved off ahead of us. Neither of us had heard or seen him. A fresh skid mark in the sandy bank angled down onto the road. Flat smudges, surrounded by tiny particles of fresh soil, led across the road into deep woods. The rain stepped up, falling on the tracks, smoothing out their edges.

En route to the next cat, McCown told me that the male Texas pumas had been surgically sterilized but the females had not. The Florida Game Commission claims that there are no wild panthers in North Florida; yet I remembered that John Lukas, at White Oak Plantation just a few miles down the road, had said that a puma or two were prowling around the countryside. "What are you going to do," I asked McCown, "if one of the females turns up pregnant?"

He shrugged and grinned.

"There you'd have it," I continued. "A Texas female impregnated by a Florida male. She'd be bringing in the outside genetic material, and from a neighboring subspecies. Wouldn't that be the best thing that could happen to the panther?"

McCown was noncommittal. Neither of us bothered mentioning that a pregnant female puma in North Florida would be separated by two hundred miles from the beleaguered, inbred population in South Florida. (You could take her offspring, though, and put them in the south.) The truck rattled on, rain streaking the windshield. There was a dull yellow cast to the palmetto fronds beneath the pines.

"Do we save the Florida panther," McCown mused, "or do we save panthers in Florida? According to the geneticists, the first option is no longer possible. I myself prefer the second option."

We passed a deer camp: rundown house, rusting trailers, a long row of empty dog pens; on the edge of the clearing, vultures hunched in trees. According to McCown, hunters lease thousands of acres from timber companies at five dollars an acre. Farther on, he stopped next to a small wood-and-wire crate, up on legs, at the road's edge. A hand-painted sign on the crate said LOST DOG BOX. If a person encounters a hound that has gotten separated from the pack while trailing deer, McCown explained, the neighborly thing is to crate it next to the road, where its owner can find it.

We broke out of the forest into mixed woods and farming country. Dogwoods flowered creamy-white along the edges of the woodlots. Spanish moss hung straight down from the oaks, a sodden, funereal green. We came to an intersection, with a convenience store. Pickup trucks that passed us had dog boxes in their beds.

The next cat was on private property. She had hung around in the same pocket of woods for eight days, near houses and farms. We turned off the highway and drove around the edge of a broad field, parked, and got out. The rumbling of trucks could be heard from Florida Route 2. We were in Baker County, Florida. The farm was a chicken farm. A tractor spread manure on an adjacent field. McCown tried with the antenna and did not pick up a signal.

We walked to a pit in the sandy soil, filled with bright green water in which dead white chickens floated. The stench plucked at the back of my throat. Tracks of raccoons and dogs pocked the soil. Around the pit grew burdock, pokeweed, blackberry. We slipped through a barbed-wire fence into a woods tangled with greenbrier and other inconvenient vines. The rain was coming down harder. We edged our way through the brush, scanning the ground.

"Maybe she's eating those chickens," McCown said. He sounded glum. "Or maybe she's picking off scavengers that come in for the chickens." We searched for a long time, and all we found were pieces of styrofoam and moldy soft-drink bottles.

I telephoned Belden and McCown when they were a year into the reintroduction experiment. Altogether, they had released thirteen Texas pumas in North Florida. There had been casualties. The day before I called, Belden had crawled down a game trail to retrieve the body of one of the unfortunates. The cat, a female, had run afoul of a snare that presumably had been set to catch coyotes. The device was made from a stainless-steel aircraft cable with a catch that allowed the cable to tighten but not to loosen. Finding the loop around her neck, the cat had surged against it, snapping the wire, but not before it cut to the bone, severing esophagus, larynx, and jugular vein. "She didn't last long," Belden said.

There had been a cat killed in Georgia. A man had been walking along an abandoned railroad grade with his dogs. He said he heard a ruckus, and out of the woods stepped a panther with one of his dogs in its mouth. He had his bow with him, so he put an arrow into the cat. "I'd guess that the dogs treed the lion," Belden said, "and the man went and shot it." Another puma met a similar reception but was luckier: an arrow in its back pierced the hide above the spine, shearing off the processes of two vertebrae. Belden and McCown sedated the cat, took it back into captivity, and, when its injury healed, freed it.

A cat got run over on U.S. Route 301. Another, in Levy County, Florida, seventy miles and dozens of roads and highways south of where it had been released, had been shot. The slug had

broken its spine. When found, the animal was paralyzed and had
to be destroyed. The shooting had taken place during the antlerless
deer season; Belden speculated that a hunter had blasted away at
a brown shape in the brush and might not even have known that
he hit a cat.

"We expected to lose some of them," Belden said. "That's
why we put out as many as we did." He spoke quietly and calmly,
without a hint of rancor or disappointment in his voice. "So far
it seems to me that things are going fairly well."

Four of the pumas were living along the Suwanee River north
of Lake City: a male whose home range overlapped, in classic
puma fashion, the territories of three females. The male, T-33,
was the one that McCown and I had flushed out of the woods
next to the release pens. It turned out that one of the females had
indeed become pregnant—not by an unknown suitor but apparently by the vasectomized T-33, who, it was believed, had for a
few weeks retained some viable sperm in his system. "He made
it count," McCown told me. The female had given birth to at
least one kitten, but unfortunately it had perished. "I guess you
could say it died of being captured," McCown said. "We darted
it in a tree, and it jumped out and ran. It was out of our sight for,
at the very most, forty-five seconds. The dart must have injected
directly into a vein, because the cat went down real quick. It went
unconscious, and its head slipped under water. It must have inhaled
some of the water. Four days later . . ." His voice trailed off. "I've
been in on way over a hundred captures, and this was the first
time a cat died."

Four pumas were in Georgia: one near Valdosta, one north of
Jacksonville, one northeast of Folkston, one on the Fort Stewart
Army Base near Savannah, almost up to South Carolina. Their
ranges, if they could be considered to be ranges, were anything
but contiguous. McCown and Belden could not guess whether
the pumas would stay where they were currently living. "One
interesting thing," McCown said, "is that these Texas cats—you
know they don't have much in the way of rivers and creeks out
there where Roy gets 'em, but they sure do recognize the advantages of the waterways in Florida and Georgia." The cats were
laying up in the hardwood hammocks. They were traveling and

hunting in the thick, undeveloped bottomlands following the wandering waters of rivers and creeks called Satilla, Suwannoochee, Withlacoochee, Altamaha, Canoochee.

I asked about public reaction to the project. "Mixed," Belden said. "We had to remove one cat who was hanging around a deer feeder on private land. It was a perfect place for the cat to be, but the owner just didn't want her there." In another case, responding to objections from a hunters' organization, the biologists picked up a cat before hunting season, held him in captivity during the season, and put him back after the season ended. In contrast, another hunters' club declared that they were glad to have a puma on their land. And a landowner east of Okefenokee Swamp was in the habit of phoning McCown in his office and happily reporting on deer carcasses left by one of the cats.

When asked about the possibility of putting real Florida panthers in the wild in northern Florida, Belden said it was too early to tell; the reintroduction experiment would not be over until late in 1995. I found myself thinking that indeed the time was ripe. There were those panthers languishing at White Oak Plantation, the nucleus of the captive breeding program that had never quite gotten rolling. Why not take those cats and free them in the company of fertile Texas pumas?

It was almost April, and the spring would be marching north through Florida. Talking to McCown over the phone, I described for him the scene out my office window: the woods full of snow that covered the huckleberry shrubs and reached high up against the gray-brown trunks of the oaks, not a leaf or a swollen bud anywhere in sight.

"I'm going canoeing next week," McCown told me. "It's real pretty down here now. The wild azaleas are blooming. My wife and boys and I are going to float down the Suwanee for three, four days. You get on that river, and even though you know there's a phosphate mine half a mile away on this side, and a town half a mile away on that side, and you can hear a highway in the distance—well, it's still a pretty wild place.

"Who knows?" he said. "We might even see a cat."

17

PANTHER IN THE STRAND

When I needed to remind myself that there was more to Florida than shopping malls, golfing communities, citrus groves, condominium-lined beaches, menageries, the Splendid China Theme Park (complete with Genghis Khan Mausoleum and a replica of the Great Wall), restaurants, bars, marinas, gasoline stations, truck stops with nude waitresses, and asphalt-paved rec-vehicle parks (full of Prowlers, Pace Arrows, Winnebagos, Frolics, Cobras, Chalets, Shastas, Leisurecraft, Southwinds, Sunlines, Trailseekers, Alumalites, Dutchmen, Coachmen, and Cabanas), I would go to Fakahatchee Strand.

I liked walking in the strand. Its vegetation was incredible. (John Muir would have been mightily impressed.) Also, I figured I stood a better chance of seeing a panther there than anywhere else. The swamp is striped with abandoned logging tramways that branch off to the east and west of Janes Scenic Drive, the gravel road halving the strand diagonally from southeast to northwest. Panthers and other creatures use the tramways as travel routes, and I reasoned that I might encounter the cats, or perhaps their droppings or tracks, on the built-up earthen paths. At least one female, who had been captured and collared, and possibly another uncollared one, had their territories in Fakahatchee Strand, and in the itinerant nature of panthers, males regularly visited there. It was in the Fakahatchee that Chris Belden had collared his first panther in 1981, and accidentally killed one two years later.

I was befriended by the resident biologist at Fakahatchee Strand State Preserve. Charles DuToit pronounces his last name in the

French manner. In his middle forties, bespectacled, with fair skin and brown hair, DuToit is married to an attractive, enthusiastic, red-haired woman named Mercedes McCallen. DuToit originally came to Florida from Boston, McCallen from Staten Island. When I got to know them, McCallen was working as an environmental planner for Collier County, whose boundaries encompass Faka-hatchee Strand and Big Cypress Swamp. Both she and her husband were fascinated by panthers, by the remote and secret aspect of the swamp, and by its botanical and biological profusion. Whenever I visited, they let me pitch my tent in front of their mobile home, a hundred yards or so from the preserve office. DuToit worked in the office—a small, unshaded, prefabricated building, mercifully air-conditioned—when he was not out on the preserve. In the field, his tasks included delineating areas to be burned (scorching off the old dead grass in the open, prairie-like portions of the Fakahatchee would bring on succulent new growth, boosting the deer population for the benefit of panthers); destroying exotic plants such as melaleuca; sampling water and sediments (Fakahatchee Strand was thought to have a mercury problem, but DuToit had discovered that the environment was, in fact, remarkably pure, although he doubted this situation would continue if citrus overspread the ranchlands to the north of the strand); picking up road-killed bobcats, deer, and bear (the Tamiami Trail cuts through the preserve, and Alligator Alley bounds it on the north); and conducting tours through the swamp for visiting school groups and nature enthusiasts.

I slept in the yard between the trailer and a large pond. The pulsing, pinging calls of toads lulled me to sleep. It was invigorating to rise in the night and urinate in the weeds, knowing that a six-foot alligator named Lena, who was blind in one eye, lived in the pond. (Once, McCallen had seen Lena rise in a swirl of water and seize an otter swimming past.) Roosters crowing at the small settlement of Copeland, a quarter mile down the road, woke me before first light. I emerged from the tent to the *swish-swish-swish* of egrets' wings as the birds pumped overhead in the misty dawn.

One day, DuToit and I drove down Janes Drive, parked on the edge of the gravel, and slipped past a metal gate. (The tram roads are gated to exclude vehicles but remain open to walkers.)

We hiked along the tram for a mile or so, then left it and waded into the swamp. The water reached to our knees. Bugs skated across the surface. Small bubbles ascended and popped. DuToit was wearing canvas gardening gloves. With one hand, he parted some tall green shoots. "Cutgrass," he said, turning his head so that the quiet words carried back over his shoulder. "I would avoid contacting it with my hands if I were you."

About twenty yards away I saw a long blackish-green object with angular bumps along its surface. For a moment I wondered what a spent truck tire casing—a snow tire, at that—was doing in Fakahatchee Strand. Then I realized it was a large, healthy member of the species *Alligator mississippiensis*. The reptile cast itself off the log where it had been sunning and hit the water with a loud splash. (DuToit had told me about a time, soon after he arrived at Fakahatchee, when he went exploring in the swamp by himself. Wading through a waist-deep pond, he was probing in front of his feet with a machete to test the bottom for gator holes. Alligators dig these pits as a means of concentrating water during the dry season. In the wet season, if you accidentally step into one, you can go in over your head. The blade of DuToit's machete entered the pond's muddy bottom, *zuck, zuck, zuck, zuck*. Then, *clunk*. He withdrew the machete. After a moment, up floated a snapping turtle. The turtle was dead. A semicircle of deep puncture wounds marked the top of its shell. The wounds described the broad radius of an alligator's jaw. It was apparent that DuToit had struck the turtle with his machete and dislodged it, either from the bottom of the pond or—and he considered this to be of equal likelihood—from the alligator's mouth.)

DuToit and I resumed wading along the perimeter of the pond; I tried not to tread on his heels. He stopped to examine a plant growing on a cypress trunk. "This is a leafless orchid," he said. "What it amounts to is a photosynthetic root." The "root" was less than a foot long, a quarter of an inch wide, and strongly flattened, so that it appeared to have been shrink-wrapped onto the cypress's bark. DuToit pointed to where a pale-green lichen the size of a bottle cap had grown over the ribbonlike orchid. "Even in Florida, lichens grow slowly," he said. "This orchid has been on this tree for a very long time." Around us in the jade swamp were dozens of orchids, small ones and large, some in brilliant flower, others that had gone to seed. DuToit tapped a dried-out pod, and thousands of dustlike seeds went floating through the air. Three botanists from the University of Florida once spent a morning wading in Fakahatchee Strand. They stopped for lunch in a natural chamber, an open area below six large trees. Standing in thigh-deep water, eating their sandwiches, they decided to estimate the number of air plants growing on the ceiling and the walls of their water-floored room. Each botanist made a spot count of a selected cube of space, then multiplied the number by figures which they thought approximated the total epiphyte-covered area in their immediate surroundings. Their totals ranged from one thousand to ten thousand orchids, and from ten thousand to one hundred thousand bromeliads—all growing in the space beneath six trees.

DuToit rested his hand on the rounded orangish summit of a cypress knee. All around, knees jutted above the water, reminders of the old growth that had once dominated the swamp. A stump four feet across still bore the notching marks of a logger's ax. The trunks of young cypress trees were a foot in diameter. The trees were snarled with poison ivy, catbrier, and grapevines. Stalks and leaves of turgid green plants poked up from the water. Boston ferns and leather ferns splayed out from the tops of knees and stumps; sword ferns arced fifteen feet through the air. DuToit pointed out a strangler fig; he explained how a fig will grow from a seed left by a bird in the high branches of a tree, sending down long ropy roots to the ground, which wrap around its host's trunk. By the time the host tree dies, its foliage shaded out by that of the fig, the strangler is sturdy enough to stand on its own.

We waded on. The water grew shallower. We clambered onto a hammock, our pant legs streaming. DuToit looked up, and I followed his gaze. High above the partial canopy formed by lesser plants, the crowns of palm trees spread their green starburst fronds. "I know it sounds corny," DuToit said, "but I call this place 'Paradise Island.'" These were royal palms, their long, feathery fronds rocking back and forth in a wind that was not present on the ground. The palms' ringed grayish-tan trunks resembled gargantuan stacks of dusty phonograph records.

We picked our way past Simpson's stopper (a twisted gnome of a tree), red bay, pigeon plum, bustic, torchwood, paradise tree, gumbo-limbo with its peeling reddish bark (Floridians call gumbo-limbo the "tourist tree," because its bark looks like sunburned skin), poisonwood, saw palmetto, cabbage palm, live oak, wild coffee, and orange and grapefruit trees dotted with fruit. "The citrus trees are exotics," DuToit said. "Most of them are concentrated along the old logging trams. Probably they came from the loggers chucking out seeds."

In a spot that seemed no different from any other, DuToit stopped. He took a military entrenching tool out of his daypack and unfolded it. He marked out an area about two feet square, went to one knee, and plunged the shovel into the ground, shearing through roots. Digging steadily, he piled the roots and humus off to one side. A mosquito landed on his chin; he scuffed it away with a grubby forearm. "You should try this place in the summer," he said, panting. "You literally suck mosquitoes in through all orifices."

He resumed his digging. "A typical Florida midden," he said, "is a pile of shells out on the coast." He set down the entrenching tool and began sifting the dark, rich-looking soil through his fingers. "This type of inland site is called a black midden. We may find some animal bones here, maybe even some pottery. I once found a conch-shell digging tool on one of these hammocks; I guess someone carried it in there eons ago."

I waved off the mosquitoes and peeled one of the tangerines I had brought. The sky was perfectly blue. Palm fronds waved and rustled in the gentle breeze. Insects stridulated. Birds called. The tangerine tasted tangy-sweet.

"Aha," DuToit said. "Bone chips." The fragments were stained dark brown and had broken, porous ends. "This looks like a tibia," DuToit said, "possibly of a deer. These are turtle-shell fragments. And this"—he held up a curved triangular chip an eighth of an inch thick—"is from a pot." The artifacts and bones had been left by Calusa Indians, a culture that was extinguished during the Spanish settlement of Florida in the 1600s and 1700s. In 1895, on Key Marco on the west coast, a man digging for garden muck in a mangrove swamp unearthed some ancient wooden artifacts. The noted anthropologist Frank Hamilton Cushing conducted an excavation that revealed a settlement eighty acres in extent, with numerous canals and mounds, including a burial mound fifty-eight feet high. In the burial mound, Cushing found a six-inch figurine, "a superbly carved and finished statuette," he wrote, "in dark-colored, close-grained wood, of a mountain-lion or panther god . . . Nothing thus far found in America so vividly calls to mind the best art of the ancient Egyptians or Assyrians, as does this little statuette of the Lion-God." Carved with a shark-tooth blade, the statuette was, Cushing deduced, "a fetish or god of war or the hunt."

DuToit put the bones and potsherds into a plastic bag, then picked up his shovel and filled the hole back in. He marked the location on a topographic map. The information would be kept in the preserve's archives, in case someone wanted to do a full-fledged archaeological dig someday. Before we left the site, DuToit asked me to inspect the ground where I had been sitting. He wanted to be sure I hadn't dropped any tangerine seeds.

Another day. I was alone in the Fakahatchee. A thin morning mist swirled among the trees; the sun, boring through the vapor, gave it a golden glow. I walked quietly along the tramway. Brush pinched in on either side, and beyond the dense vegetation lay the swamp. Every so often I had to stop and negotiate a dew-covered spiderweb that spanned the path. Some of the spiders had colorful bodies and legs spread as broad as beer coasters; they looked capable of subduing small birds. As I ducked and wormed my way past, they would sense my presence and instantly draw in their legs, making their webs quiver.

Lizards scooted off the path at the fringe of my vision. Birds searched for insects hidden in the crevices of air plants. Butterflies were everywhere, pumpkin-orange ones, ornate black-and-yellow zebra butterflies, browns, whites, yellows, blues, grays. I came to what had once been a dwelling built on pilings in the swamp. A tree had fallen onto the structure, crushing it. The doors were gone. Fragments of glass lay on the windowsills. Linoleum curled up from the floor. On the weathered bridge beams from the tram road to the building lay heaps of rust-colored dung: composed of fish scales, they looked to be otter scat. I wondered how many years it would take for nature to reduce this structure—probably a hunting camp—into an archaeological site like the Calusa camp that DuToit had shown me.

The path dipped into the swamp. My feet got muddy and then wet. Sweat plastered my shirt to my back, and biting flies kept landing there, trying for blood. A big tree had fallen across the trail, wedging itself between the trunks of two smaller trees. I sat down on the raised portion of the trunk, in the shade, and rested.

The evening before, DuToit, McCallen, and I had stayed up late talking about panthers. Panthers were part of what had drawn the couple to Fakahatchee Strand. DuToit had been a district biologist in the state park system, on the east coast of Florida, overseeing ten different parks there; when the position opened at Fakahatchee, he had jumped at it. Newly arrived at the preserve, he was invited to fly with a Florida Game Commission biologist monitoring cats in the area, to get an overview of southwestern Florida. He saw the vastness and the complexity of the swamp below him, and from within it came the steady electronic chirping of the transmitter worn by Florida panther number 9. Number 9 had been captured in 1985. In the fall of 1988 DuToit tagged along when a Game Commission team went in to change her collar. He watched them tranquillize her, recollar her, and take medical samples. It was the first and the last time that DuToit would see Number 9; he spent many days out on the preserve, but true to the wary nature of cats, neither 9 nor any other panther revealed itself to him.

DuToit and McCallen attended meetings of the Florida Panther Interagency Committee, the group composed of the leaders of the four governmental agencies. At the meetings Fakahatchee Strand was frequently discussed. Number 9, it seemed, had high levels of mercury in her body. DuToit questioned the prevailing opinion that Fakahatchee Strand was a mercury hotspot. He had found no significant levels of the element in his sampling of water and sediments there. His comments, he felt, were not welcomed by the powers of bureaucracy. He heard a rumor that the Florida Game Commission was planning to take Number 9 out of the Fakahatchee, put her into captivity, and feed her a prepared diet to "dry her out," get her mercury levels down.

Number 9 had come to fascinate both DuToit and McCallen.

McCallen had named the cat Freedom. Freedom symbolized the wide free expanse of Fakahatchee Strand, preserved against the destruction that humans were wreaking on the landscape of South Florida. Although he was not invited there, DuToit showed up at a meeting of the Interagency Committee in Tallahassee. He managed to gain the floor. Again he explained that he had found no evidence of mercury contamination in Fakahatchee Strand. He noted that Number 9 was a well-established breeding female. As a scientist, he strongly urged that she not be removed from the population, that she not be taken away from the Fakahatchee. Perhaps noticing the latent passion beneath DuToit's controlled words, the bureaucrats denied that they were planning to capture Number 9.

Late one evening in 1990, DuToit and a group of preserve employees were heading south on Janes Drive. They had spent a long day tending to a controlled burn that, whipped up by the wind, had kept threatening to get out of control. The men and women smelled like smoke, their eyes smarted, and soot blackened their clothing. They were exhausted. They had the trucks at the head and the tail of the column, the ATVs with their weaker headlights in between. Creeping along down the center of the road, they heard someone honking vociferously in the dark behind them. Tourists were not supposed to drive on the preserve at night, but here was one of them, obnoxiously making his presence known. After a long spate of honking, the column pulled over. What came past was a Florida Game Commission truck. The Game Commission biologists said they were homing in on a mortality signal from a collared panther in Fakahatchee Strand. DuToit and his colleagues took umbrage at being shunted aside by another agency on their own preserve. DuToit felt a little like a male panther smelling a scrape in his own home range left by another male panther. He thought about standing in front of the gate that blocked off the tramway down which the Game Commission biologists wanted to drive. In the interests of tranquillity, and of science, he suppressed this territorial urge. DuToit accompanied the Game Commission biologists. In the dark, they located the body of the dead cat, a juvenile male who had gotten himself crunched. The biologists raised their antennae and checked on other frequencies. Her signal showed that Number 9 was nearby.

The next day, McBride's dogs treed another male, an adult without a collar, whose wounds implied that he had abolished the young cat. He survived and became Florida panther number 37. DuToit was excited about the new male in Fakahatchee Strand. Number 37 possessed two testicles. Perhaps he had come over from Everglades National Park, where the males remained so equipped. Number 37 ranged widely. He was the first Florida panther to be videotaped, by a fixed camera, slinking through an underpass beneath Interstate 75. (He was identified by the fresh surgical sutures on his shoulder, left after he was processed by the veterinarians.) Unfortunately, 37 did not live long. Crossing Florida Route 29 one night, he was killed by a truck. He had, as it turned out, left something behind. Number 9 bore two kittens.

At the time, the push was on to establish a zoo population for captive breeding. Number 9 was considered a founder animal, whose genetic makeup needed to be preserved. Taking one kitten would theoretically safeguard 50 percent of her unique genetic material; taking a second kitten would gain another 25 percent. The restorers of the panther wanted both kittens. DuToit, ambivalent about captive breeding, was in no position to stop them.

The kittens were six months old. Their captors took them on separate days. DuToit and McCallen attended the second capture. It was a swift and inexorable event. The kitten—actually, by this time it was a young cat—was the healthiest-looking creature DuToit had ever seen. It was lithe and beautiful. It did not have a collar. It was run up a tree, darted, lowered down, and draped over a biologist's shoulder. The biologist waded out of the swamp, the kitten was stashed in a cage on the back of a truck, the truck started up, and DuToit and McCallen and the rest of the onlookers were left staring as it drove off down the road.

Walking on the tramway, I dared not go sloshing through the swamp, though I carried a compass in my pocket. I went west on the dim road, treading softly, heel to toe, one foot and then the other. They had had it right there, I reflected: the hybrid vigor that the panther so often is said to be lacking. The male, Number 37, if he came from the Everglades, carried outside genetic material; what DuToit jokingly had called "hot Latino blood." But he was dead, and his offspring were languishing at White Oak Plantation, where they *might* be used for captive breeding someday. By now, even the Florida Game Commission was admitting that outside genes needed to be brought in. At the time, the Fish and Wildlife Service was still mulling things over, listening to its dithering solicitors, who considered what might happen if the panther lost its subspecific classification, whether it might lose its endangered status also.

It would be best if the panther escaped its endangerment without losing its official Latin name—but if it came down to one or the other, was it not better for the subspecies to dissolve, for the panther to renew itself with outside blood, whether introduced accidentally or brought in formally by its human benefactors? Subspecies be damned, it was a panther. The Florida panther, like Florida, like the puma of which it is a small division, is today a creature in flux. It is still correct, and a panther, if it has South American genes. It is still correct, and a panther, if people save it with pumas brought from Texas.

The forest thinned; the swamp fell away. I looked at the map DuToit had given me: I had come to the Four Stakes Prairie. I started across the broad stretch of breeze-caressed grass. At a watery place, two snipe rose on whistling wings. Subtle yellow and pink flowers spangled the grass. Chitinous crayfish carcasses lay in the dirt. (Perhaps the prairie flooded in the wet season, letting the crustaceans arise from eggs, grow, reproduce—a slick swift cycle that would pause each year with more eggs and skeletal remains.) Puffy clouds came in from the Gulf and covered the sun. Greasy mud holes, raccoon tracks, the scattered skeleton of—I searched up the skull: needle-like canines, sharp carnassials—a bobcat. What had killed it? A panther could have.

Into more woods. I found another trail and followed it westward. I walked quietly and paused often, a rhythm of moving I had learned in the woods at home. How different, and yet how similar, was the Florida swampland. Wild, majestic country. I had not seen a soul all day. I remembered DuToit saying that Fakahatchee Strand is huge, far larger than its acreage. I wondered where Number 9 was. Freedom could have been fifty feet away, in the swamp. Freedom could have been miles removed. Freedom was entering old age. She had not born a litter since her two male kittens had been taken from her. I wondered whether Fakahatchee Strand would still be Fakahatchee Strand if a panther were not living in it.

Maples shaded the trail. The dense, mind-boggling vegetation stretched away into the swamp. I was getting up my nerve to actually go in there: take a compass coordinate, slosh along for an hour, then turn about and follow a reverse heading back to the path. Suddenly a tremendous rushing sound came from the grass. I froze—no, did not have time to freeze, or turn and run, or even raise a hand. All I managed to do was involuntarily suck in a breath. The alligator moved faster than I had imagined a reptile could go. Its body was poised on its four short blurring legs. Its big swaying belly looked yellow. It crashed across the path in front of me, its long tail lashing, and lunged into the swamp with a bellywhopper splash. The desultory conversation of birds abruptly ceased. I stood with my mouth open, my heart hammering. Sunlight shimmered in the swamp. Somewhere in the distance a barred owl called.

Through the diminishing glow of evening, I headed back. I had not found any panther scat. I had come across tracks of the approximate correct size, but since they showed claw marks in front of the pads, I figured they had been made by a dog.

Thoughts of home went through my mind. There, the woods were a safe place. No alligators (although it appeared I had little to fear from the reptiles, since they seemed even more frightened of me than I was of them). In Pennsylvania the last confirmed panthers were killed in the 1890s—yet people still continue to see them, or claim to see them, and apparently need to see them. A friend of mine, a biologist who heads Pennsylvania's non-game wildlife program, had chuckled when I mentioned pumas to him. "My biggest success," he said. "They don't cost the state a penny. People see mountain lions everywhere, and they never kill any deer, never eat any children, never get hit on the highway." Another biologist of my acquaintance had been led by an excited Pennsylvania outdoorsman to a rocky den where the man had seen two young pumas; he claimed they had leaped out and hissed at him. When the biologist crept forward, loud hissing issued from the den. The outdoorsman grabbed the biologist's sleeve and warned him against going any farther. The biologist persisted, and came upon two baby turkey vultures hissing and flapping their wings.

People in Pennsylvania report panthers more often than in any other Northeastern state. We do have a lot of wild, rugged territory. We have more deer than we need. D. J. Schubert had told me that if anyone could prove that the Eastern puma still existed, the Fund for Animals would sue the U.S. Fish and Wildlife Service to bring the subspecies back. (He characterized such a lawsuit as a "slam dunk," saying, "The service has filed a recovery plan for the Eastern puma. It has never been declared extinct, never been removed from the endangered species list, and yet they've never done a thing to restore it.")

My hike in the Fakahatchee was almost over; through the forest I could see the white glint of my rental car parked on the gravel road. The trees thinned out. It was that lovely time of day in South Florida, poised between light and dark, the sky pellucid, the breeze slipping through the boughs, the mingled perfumes of flowers in the air, a thunderhead murmuring on the horizon. I had seen no sign of panthers in the swamp, although in some strange way I had sensed their presence. I asked myself, Would I want to have pumas in my own back yard? Would I want to go hiking in the woods knowing that I might, just might, see a real long-tailed cat? Would I want my six-year-old son playing under the gaze of a wiry, killing predator? As always, when the situation became personal, the answers were no longer clear.

I hoped that a Florida panther—or an introduced Texas puma—would never kill a child. I had come to understand how costly it could be to keep the panther in Florida. But when I thought of the cat in its natural setting, when I considered the richness of its history, when I imagined the way it was holding the landscape together, my misgivings vanished.

The panther deserves to live: if not for its sake alone, then for ours. The panther belongs in Florida. The panther is Florida. In a manner of speaking, the panther is all that is left of Florida.

EPILOGUE

Melody Roelke, whose medical monitoring and genetic sleuthing revealed so much about the inner workings (and dysfunctions) of panthers, took a job with the Tanzania National Park Service. She is now studying lions in the Serengeti.

In 1994 Dave Maehr abruptly resigned from the Florida Game Commission. He told me, with great bitterness, that he had been pressured into quitting by his superiors in Tallahassee, who claimed they were acting on complaints about him lodged by the National Park Service. Maehr now works as a consultant to companies applying for permits to develop land in South Florida. He asserts that in his present position he can have "a much greater impact on the panther" than he could as a state biologist.

On April 7, 1995, Marjory Stoneman Douglas turned 105. She remains cogent but is in failing health and spends most of her time sleeping.

The oft-photographed Florida panther, Big Guy, was euthanized in his thirteenth year. He had gone blind, was barely able to move, and was afflicted with seizures.

Number 46, the young male panther whose capture I witnessed, fought with an older dominant male, killed him, and usurped his territory.

While I was working on *Swamp Screamer*, the Florida panther population maintained itself at around fifty adults and thirty juveniles. The human population in Florida grew from 13 million to 14 million.

ACKNOWLEDGMENTS

I would like to thank Leonard Rubinstein, Nancy Marie Brown, Ruth Fergus, and Upton Brady for reading a rough draft of *Swamp Screamer* and giving me clear and helpful criticism. I greatly enjoyed working with my editor, Paul Elie. Lynn Warshow's copy editing was thoughtful and deft. I offer special thanks to five people in Florida who sheltered this traveler and told him tales: Deborah Jansen, Ken Meyer, Frances Lane, Charles DuToit, and Mercedes McCallen.